Schools of Promise
for Multilingual Students

Schools of Promise
for Multilingual Students

Transforming Literacies, Learning, and Lives

EDITED BY

Althier M. Lazar
Patricia Ruggiano Schmidt

Foreword by Guofang Li

TEACHERS COLLEGE PRESS

TEACHERS COLLEGE | COLUMBIA UNIVERSITY

Published by Teachers College Press, 1234 Amsterdam Avenue, New York, NY 10027

Copyright © 2018 by Teachers College, Columbia University

Cover photo by Pattanaphong Khuankaew / iStock by Getty Images.

Library of Congress Cataloging-in-Publication Data

Names: Lazar, Althier M.
Title: Schools of promise for multilingual students : transforming
   literacies, learning, and lives / edited by Althier M. Lazar, Patricia
   Ruggiano Schmidt, Foreword by Guofang Li.
Description: New York, NY : Teachers College Press, [2018] | Includes
   bibliographical references and index.
Identifiers: LCCN 2018032874 | ISBN 9780807759479 (pbk.)
Subjects: LCSH: Multilingual education. | Multilingual persons—Education.
Classification: LCC LC3715 .S36 2018 | DDC 370.117—dc23
LC record available at https://lccn.loc.gov/2018032874
ISBN 978-0-8077-5947-9 (paper)
ISBN 978-0-8077-7730-5 (ebook)

Printed on acid-free paper
Manufactured in the United States of America

25   24   23   22   21   20   19   18   8   7   6   5   4   3   2   1

To those who believe in the power of schools to transform lives.

Contents

Foreword

On March 10, 2018, the American nation (and the world) was shocked to learn from CBS's *60 Minutes* interview that U.S. Secretary of Education Betsy DeVos had never intentionally set foot in any of the nation's disadvantaged schools, where millions of culturally, linguistically, racially, and socioeconomically diverse children work hard to achieve their potential every day. It is precisely such deliberate and persistent neglect from policymakers such as Ms. DeVos that has contributed to persistent achievement and opportunity gaps between these children and their more privileged counterparts, as documented by the annual report cards on students' educational achievement by the National Assessment of Educational Progress (NAEP).

Despite the fact that these underserved children typically need more linguistic and academic support, their schools and communities actually receive less local, state, and government funding; have less access to educational resources; and are provided with fewer state-of-the-art learning facilities than their more privileged peers. The recent educational reforms, such as the No Child Left Behind (NCLB) legislation and the Race to the Top initiative that lead to the adoption of the Common Core State Standards and the associated high-stakes assessments in 45 states, had proved to set an even higher percentage of the neediest children from poor, multilingual, and special education backgrounds to failure. These politicized, hegemonic educational policies and impositions on schools, coupled with recent changes in immigration policies and implementation of a travel ban on six Muslim-majority countries that had intensified racial and social conflicts in the United States, had dehumanized many multilingual, multiethnic schools (especially those in urban centers and rural areas) as unsafe and unwelcoming spaces for acquiring the knowledge and literacy skills needed for reaching one's potential. It is not surprising that many underserved students choose to disengage from learning in school, fail to find a sense of belonging, and eventually drop out.

In an educational system that is profoundly shaped by this spirit of "inhumaneness" from the top, how might teachers and school leaders on the ground work with diverse students, families, and communities to create safe, inviting sanctuaries of learning that allow a different social imaginary—one that respects personhood, values languages and cultures, and aims for social and academic success despite difficult circumstances and challenges surrounding students' lives? They must, as Paulo Freire suggested almost half a century ago, become an (and the only effective) instrument of rehumanizing the schools by taking up a revolutionary leadership that engages *every member* of the learning community in making intentional change; practicing pedagogies that affirm students' prior language, knowledge, and identities; and committing to taking action and seeing real changes in students' learning experiences. Therefore, this challenging task of "rehumanizing" the schools for diverse learners cannot be a piecemeal, individual, occasional occurrence, but rather must be a concerted, sustainable effort that is co-intentionally committed by like-minded, social justice–oriented teachers and school leaders and their allies and partners.

Althier Lazar and Patricia Ruggiano Schmidt's timely collection of teachers' and school leaders' extraordinary work to "rehumanize" their classrooms and schools in underserved communities in the United States, Canada, and other educational systems showcases how such critical, fruitful work from the ground up can be accomplished despite policy sanctions, funding shortages, and practical challenges in hard economic times. In this uplifting book, Lazar and Schmidt argue for "rehumanizing" the entire school ecological system from an ideology that governs school's positioning and promises for diverse students to a school climate that shapes the systems of care that school provides and to specific programs and practices that capitalize on students' multilingual repertoire to ensure success in academic language and content learning. They emphasize the importance of whole-school engagement and results from this holistic, co-intentional effort, and that both novice and seasoned teachers and leaders can successfully participate in and initiate this work. Finally, they take readers beyond U.S. systems to include work from Canada and other top-performing countries to offer lessons about how educators from these countries successfully "rehumanized" their education for the underserved students.

This book is a powerful resource for those in- and preservice teachers, educators, school leaders, researchers who are seeking to change the status quo in today's schools and is a must-read for those like Ms. DeVos who are unfamiliar with these schools and the innovative work that teachers and school leaders are doing. With a rich collection of powerful cases and best practices, this book offers hope and possibilities for everyone to reimagine different ways of doing school for the most disadvantaged. Indeed, change is possible, and we all can become agents of educational rehumanization.

—*Guofang Li*

Acknowledgments

This book would not have been written without the cooperation of a most dedicated group of educators. To the scholars who identified these extraordinary schools, we are so grateful for your willingness to join us in sharing your work. We know that much can be extracted from these chapters to produce schools that are grounded in the humanizing principles of multiculturalism, multilingualism, and a deep sense of caring. We are also thankful for the efforts of many teachers, administrators, staff, and caregivers who worked to create schools for multilingual learners. Without their tireless dedication to students, these schools would not exist.

We are especially indebted to Tolga Hayali, who opened his school to show what exemplary teaching and strong leadership can do to raise the learning outcomes of multilingual students in disenfranchised communities. His vision inspired us to look beyond Syracuse to see what other schools were doing to advance students' literacies and languages.

We are also grateful to Allyson Coughlin, a graduate assistant with an eye for detail, who helped us with editing and checking references.

Of course, we have to thank Mitch and Tom, our spouses, who graciously put up with our long hours on the phone and behind our computers.

Finally, we are grateful for being able to do this project together. A project of this type is an enormous undertaking. What helped us through the challenges was an enduring respect for each other's understandings and insights and the comfort of a decades-old friendship.

—*Althier M. Lazar*
Patricia Ruggiano Schmidt

PART I

WHERE WE ARE, WHERE WE'VE BEEN, AND WHERE WE NEED TO BE

Let us make our future now, and let us make our dreams tomorrow's reality.

—Malala Yousafzai

CHAPTER 1

Schools of Promise for Multilingual Students

Althier M. Lazar

Frances Willard Elementary School is situated in one of the most underserved communities in Philadelphia, yet its multilingual students made significant gains in literacy in 2016, and even larger gains in mathematics, on the state's standardized test. I spent time with Ron Reilly, Willard's principal, to find out why this public school is helping so many students achieve. With about 750 students, 53% identifying as Latinx and 35% identifying as Black, Willard is a large school with a boutique, small-school feel. Students smiled at us as we walked through the corridors. Teachers spoke respectfully to students. The few wayward students who walked the hallways were gently guided to where they should be.

We visited about a dozen classrooms where I saw engaged students and rigorous teaching. Ron praised Willard's teachers: "There are many spectacular teachers in this building, and others who will be once they get more experience." He noted that teachers met consistently in grade-level groups to discuss how to meet students' learning needs. There was a strong climate of teacher support at Willard, which included professional development through the Children's Literacy Initiative, a nonprofit organization with an excellent reputation for fostering literacy-rich learning environments in Philadelphia's classrooms. What I found at Willard was a committed school leader working with accomplished teachers to enlarge learning opportunities for all students.

Willard is not alone. Several other schools have supportive school leaders, outstanding teachers, accommodating structures and initiatives, and strong outreach programs to welcome caregivers' contributions to students' learning. They serve students from an array of language communities, with many who live in homes where languages other than English and variations of nonstandardized English are spoken. These schools provide a humanizing education that nurtures students' literacy and language development. The purpose of this book is to expose the inner workings of these schools so that readers—educator candidates, teachers, school leaders, teacher educators, policymakers, and anybody else who cares about the welfare of multilingual students—can work toward creating these kinds of schools for all learners.

MULTILINGUAL STUDENTS

Across almost all economically distressed U.S. cities, students who speak languages other than English, primarily Spanish, attend schools with students who identify as Black (Boschma & Brownstein, 2016). Many of these students are learning English, a group we call *emergent bilinguals* (Garcia & Kleifgen, 2010). They include recent immigrants who may not know English well but come to school with knowledge of many subjects, and those born in the United States who speak both English and their heritage language but may have difficulty using either language for academic purposes. And there are also those who are progressing in their use of academic English, but their ability to use their heritage language is declining. Though the chapters in this book focus on emergent bilinguals, these same schools also support their primarily English-speaking peers who affiliate as Black. Many use African American Language patterns, while others use more standardized forms of English, and still others use dialects and languages that reflect their heritage from many parts of the world (Charity Hudley & Mallinson, 2010). When identifying individuals or groups in this book, we use descriptors such as *Latinx* and *Black*, but these terms mask the infinite dimensions of people, including their positionalities, practices, choices, and perspectives (Mahiri, 2017). We focus on students' humanity by arguing that they are more likely to thrive in school when their languages, heritage, and communities are valued. Presently, several factors threaten students' linguistic rights and literacy potential.

FACTORS THAT WORK AGAINST MULTILINGUAL STUDENTS IN ECONOMICALLY STRESSED COMMUNITIES

Inequitable School Funding

Public schools in the United States have never afforded equal opportunities for students to achieve academically. It is not the *publicly funded* part of schools that undermines them; it is a problem of *uneven* funding. Children who live in affluent communities have better access to fully resourced classrooms, richer and more stimulating curricula, and more experienced teachers and school leaders than students in economically stressed communities. Most would agree that public schools are working well for the mostly White populations of students who live in middle-class or affluent communities. But this is not the case for the mostly Black and Latinx children who are disproportionately affected by poverty and underfunded schools (Boschma & Brownstein, 2016). In Philadelphia, where students of color and emergent bilinguals make up the largest percentage of the district's students, the per-pupil expenditure in 2015–2016 was $13,880, as compared to $28,495 for the predominantly White students living in the adjacent community of Lower Merion (National Center for Education Statistics, 2017).

School funding inequalities will persist unless fundamental changes take place in society to redirect resources to underserved schools and communities and to dismantle inequitable structures and institutions (Anyon, 2005). This solution, however, never seems to be considered. Reform efforts have largely focused on curriculum standardization, high-stakes testing, school choice and privatization, and the adoption of Common Core Standards, with the predictable result that too many students are still left behind.

Educational "Reforms"

Over the past 30 years, schooling in the United States has shifted from preparing students for their roles as citizens for the common good to preparing them for a global and competitive marketplace (Hursh, 2007). Neoliberal ideas about educating students for an increasingly competitive society have undergirded the No Child Left Behind law and Race to the Top grants program. These federal efforts focused on making schools accountable for student success, and almost overnight, school districts responded by standardizing their curricula and adopting high-stakes tests. Low-performing school districts were especially vulnerable to these machinations, which led to narrowing school curricula to those subjects tested—namely, reading, mathematics, and most recently, science. Many of these districts eliminated content areas that were not being tested; subjects such as art, music, and social studies disappeared from schools.

Most unfortunate are the alienating effects of high-stakes tests. Rarely do they communicate what students know and can do. Misidentifying students' capacities has meant that too many students get slotted into remedial programs and low-level academic tracks that limit their future possibilities (Kim, 2017). Serious ethical issues have been raised about having bilingual students take standardized tests in English (Garcia & Kleifgen, 2010). Not only do these tests confound students' content knowledge with their knowledge of English, but many of these tests are not normed on the populations of students who are being tested. Immigrant high school students who have been in the United States for less than 2 years are particularly vulnerable to these tests because they need to know enough English to be able to take and pass content-area courses to graduate from high school (Jiménez-Castellanos & García, 2017).

We have also seen a shift toward subtractive language practices in many U.S. schools that aim to eliminate students' home language and replace it with English (Menken & Solorza, 2012). English-only programs are not theoretically sound or supported by the empirical research (Garcia & Kleifgen, 2010). Research shows that students' use of and growth in their home language enhances their cognitive and literate development and their ability to learn English (Goldenberg, 2008; Krashen, Rolstad, & MacSwan, 2007). A major stumbling block to developing the literacies and languages of multilingual learners is that "few school leaders and not enough teachers are well-versed in issues surrounding bilingualism" (Garcia & Kleifgen, 2010, p. 84). Teaching and advocating for multilingual students requires special expertise and preparation (Lucas & Villegas, 2013), a goal that is still unrealized across all teacher education programs.

Racism and Segregation

Beyond unequal funding and market-driven policies that have made schooling less equitable for many students, sociopolitical factors, including systemic racism, have created hostile conditions for many students of color and their families. We see White supremacists with their Tiki torches parading the streets of Charlottesville, Virginia, spewing hate speech. We hear President Trump's racist remarks about Mexicans "being rapists" and we read about his view that the U.S. should welcome more people from Norway instead of from Haiti or "shithole" countries in Africa. We also witness the state of immigration limbo imposed on 1.8 million undocumented "Dreamers" who were brought to the United States as children and have lived in the only country they have ever known. These events are a major assault on the racial, ethnic, and religious mosaic that defines America.

One of the entrenched problems in America is that high percentages of students attend racially segregated schools, as a consequence of living in racially segregated communities. Racial segregation remains at high levels across America, with Black communities being the most segregated (Bonilla-Silva, 2017). More than 50 years after the desegregation landmark case *Brown v. Board of Education*, schools are more segregated and unequal than ever (Gamoran & Long, 2006). Kozol (2005) calls these "apartheid" schools because they serve almost exclusively African American and Latinx students. He describes these schools as having culturally barren instruction, punitive high-stakes testing, and proto-military forms of discipline. These schools systematically disadvantage students of color and bilingual learners along dimensions of teacher quality, curriculum, and student resources, and these disadvantages directly undermine literacy achievement.

THE IMPACT ON ACHIEVEMENT

All of these factors converge to compromise the literacy and language development of students of color, including emergent bilinguals living in underserved communities. Far too many are achieving at staggeringly low levels and many fail to graduate from high school. Among the nation's 4th-graders, only 18% of Black students and 21% of Latinx students scored at or above the basic level on NAEP's reading achievement test (www.nationsreportcard.gov). Emergent bilinguals lag behind non-ELLs in reading by an average of 37 points for 4th-graders and 45 points for 8th-graders, revealing a widening achievement gap as students progress through school (www.nationsreportcard.gov). Also, although Latinx students are receiving more high school diplomas than ever, about 65% do not graduate from high school, a higher dropout rate than for either White or Black students (National Center for Education Statistics, 2017). This is happening at a time when we know so much about how to develop students' literacy and language abilities.

To protect students against these elements, we need schools that provide supportive conditions for acquiring English proficiency while preserving and growing the cultural and linguistic knowledge they bring to school. These schools offer a humanizing pedagogy where educators honor students' lives, languages, and experiences and attend to their well-being (Salazar, 2013). They preserve students' basic rights, including the linguistic right to identify with one's own language and use it in and out of school, and the right to learn the official language of the state (Skutnabb-Kangas & Phillipson, 1994). Next, I will describe the qualities of these schools, beginning with schools that were established specifically for multilingual students.

SCHOOLS MAKING A DIFFERENCE

The Small Schools Movement

The "critical small schools movement" of the 1980s and 1990s centered on creating schools with equitable teaching and learning practices, shared decision-making, inquiry-based and culturally informed teaching practices, and caregiver/community outreach (Fine, 2012). One example is the El Puente Academy for Peace and Justice in Brooklyn, New York. This school was founded in the late 1970s by community activists who sought to affirm the "language, culture, and identities of Latino students and link the individual development of students to a broader vision of community development" (De Jesús, 2012, p. 66). The El Puente community is guided by 12 principles of peace and justice and grounded by notions of authentic caring (Noddings, 1984; Valenzuela, 1999), an ethic of caring or *confianza* (Rauner, 2000), and culturally relevant instruction (Ladson-Billings, 1994). The school uses a strengths-based approach to behavior and counseling called the Holistic Individualized Process (HIP). The goal of HIP is to understand students' needs and histories, resolve conflicts, and develop goals and individual action plans through weekly seminars that emphasize well-being of mind, body, and spirit. With these structures in place, "students consistently reported that they were significantly engaged in the learning process through high quality interpersonal relationships with adult facilitators and that these relationships were characterized by high academic expectations of the students by staff" (De Jesús, 2012, p. 75).

Another example is Gregorio Luperón High School for Science and Mathematics in Washington Heights, a community in Upper Manhattan (Bartlett & Koyama, 2012). Luperón offers a bilingual program that includes both English and Spanish instruction in content courses for the first 2 years. Teaching at Luperón centers on "language acquisition as a social process that involves an entire speech community while attending to sociocultural and sociopolitical contexts, including the ways in which practices, identity and power interact to provide a context for learning English" (p. 87). Language teaching is based on *dynamic bilingualism*, which emphasizes a flexible, context-based use of different language practices depending on students' goals and purposes, and *translanguaging*, the practice of using different language systems to learn (Garcia & Kleifgen, 2010). Examples of translanguaging include writing notes in Spanish while listening to and participating in discussions in English, or translating scientific terms in both English and Spanish. Bartlett and Koyama (2012) report that Luperón's 4-year graduation rate for immigrant newcomers was 83% in 2008, vastly outperforming its counterpart schools.

Schools That Continue to Foster Achievement

Schools like El Puente and Luperón, established by local community and educator organizations, are not typical of most available to multilingual learners in large cities today. Neoliberal ideas that resulted in the deprofessionalization of teachers and the widespread uptake of standardized testing and teaching have eroded some of what the small schools movement stood for (Fine, 2012). Yet some components of the small schools movement live on in schools that are succeeding with multilingual learners. These schools provide culturally welcoming settings that focus on students' academic achievement and honor students' heritage languages (Bartlett & Koyama, 2012; Jesse, Davis, & Pokorny, 2004; Tung, Uriarte, Diez, Gagnon, & Stazesky, 2011). Studies indicate that emergent bilingual students educated in dual-language programs make significant achievement gains over those in English-only programs (Collier & Thomas, 2017; De Jesús, 2008; Krashen, Rolstad, & MacSwan, 2007). Some schools deemed highly successful with multilingual populations do not include dual-language programs, although they are described as culturally welcoming, through either the composition of faculty and staff that share students' cultural backgrounds or a commitment to honoring students' culture through strong leadership and teacher education (Jesse et al., 2004; Tung et al., 2011).

One study looked at several components of four high-achieving Boston-based schools, including three elementary schools, Josiah Quincy, Sarah Greenwood, and David Ellis, and one high school, Excel (Tung et al., 2011). Tung et al. identified four broad components common to all of these schools: (1) school leaders who shared their students' cultural backgrounds and communicated a vision for their students' success; (2) an organizational structure that included clear procedures for identifying and educating English language learners and educator teams responsible for coordinating and enhancing students' learning opportunities; (3) a culturally familiar climate that welcomed family involvement and collaboration and provided an atmosphere of safety and belonging; and (4) standards-based instruction that included explicit English teaching, the use of students' languages as scaffolds, and high levels of linguistic engagement through workshop approaches to literacy learning informed by multiple forms of assessment. A significant number of the staff at two of the schools, Quincy and Sarah Greenwood, shared their students' ethnic heritage. Staff at the other two schools, Ellis and Excel, were less representative of their students' backgrounds, but these schools' professional development programs focused on understanding and appreciating students' culture and language. Also, these schools had structures and staff in place to support students' language development, including Language Acquisition Team facilitators (LATs) who were responsible for assisting teachers and overseeing the "identification, placement, services, scheduling, assessment, and reclassification of all ELL students" (Tung et al., 2011, p. 17).

One of the schools described in the Tung et al. (2011) study, Sarah Greenwood, served African American and Latinx students; about half of this latter group were native Spanish speakers. The school had established a two-way dual-language program in order to create a community where all students were language learners. The school's principal indicated, "We wanted children to be able to talk in whatever language they were comfortable. It was important that everybody felt that they were going to be part of that community too—that everybody could become bilingual in the school. So that's how the Two-Way Bilingual program started" (p. 10). Researchers concluded that "the emphasis on teaching English and Spanish equally in the early elementary grades created conditions for collaboration and equal exchanges among all students who were learning a new language" (p. 10). Further, the researchers linked dual-language learning to positive identity formation among both Latinx and African American students.

The other three schools in the study, Josiah Quincy, David Ellis, and Excel High School, did not include dual-language programs, but structures and routines were in place to make them culturally welcoming. These schools used Sheltered English Immersion (SEI) programs based on students' specific language backgrounds. In the elementary schools, licensed English as Second Language (ESL) specialists delivered scaffolded instruction that matched students' English proficiency levels. Also, at Quincy, where a high proportion of staff lived in the school's Chinatown neighborhood and spoke the same Chinese dialects as students, all of the students studied Mandarin at least once per week. The staff at Ellis was additionally supported through an external, grant-funded team that used a Scaffolded Apprenticeship Model (SAM), to analyze students' development as they progressed through school. At Excel High School, ESL support was provided in English classrooms. The principal "led a process of prioritizing the cultural competence of teachers whose cultural backgrounds were different from those of ELL students and other minority students at the school" (Tung et al., 2011, p. 9).

The Tung et al. (2011) study highlights how strong leadership, the cultural competence of educators, and supportive structures matter in the education of multilingual students. It also communicates the uniqueness of schools in the cultural backgrounds of their staffs, their language programs, and their specific efforts to make these places culturally welcoming. These findings match an earlier study of nine Texas schools that served primarily Latinx students from low-income families (Jesse et al., 2004). These schools employed school leaders and teachers who maintained positive, caring relationships with their students while also establishing high academic expectations for them. The majority of the principals (six of nine) and teachers (68%) identified as Latinx and spoke Spanish. Although Spanish was frequently used in the hallways and playgrounds, instruction was primarily in English. However, the bilingualism of many of the staff allowed for easy and frequent communication with caregivers. Also, most of the teachers in these schools had participated in special professional development sessions that focused on working with English language learners. Researchers also found these schools to be cohesive in their focus on student achievement, a goal that was communicated frequently by principals, teachers, parents, and students.

Attributes of caring, cultural affirmation, acceptance of students' home languages, a unified and research-based vision for teaching and learning, and supportive structures surface across the studies described here. Also, nearly all discuss the positive impact of knowledgeable, reflective, and dedicated teachers and school leaders—key participants in making successful schools work for multilingual learners.

THE SIGNIFICANCE OF TEACHERS AND SCHOOL LEADERS

Caring and Culturally Informed

Several students at the El Puente Academy for Peace and Justice expressed that teachers and school leaders cared for them (De Jesús, 2012). These teachers exhibited what Nell Noddings (1984) called *authentic caring*, or the ability to form respectful and genuine relationships with students. Authentic caring is different from *critical caring*, which is manifested by advocating for students and challenging oppressive schooling policies and practices that get in the way of their learning (Rolón-Dow, 2005; Valenzuela, 1999). An example of critical caring would be the efforts of the Latinx community to establish El Puente to address unequal schooling for Latino students. Critical caring is based on understanding the systemic disadvantages that students face as members of culturally nondominant communities. Teachers who care critically strive to offset these inequities through their teaching and advocacy efforts. To care critically, teachers need to understand the complex sociopolitical and sociohistorical ecology that shapes students' opportunities to learn.

Critical caring is tied to culturally relevant teaching and exemplified by a focus on students' academic excellence, cultural competence, and their ability to challenge the social inequities that schools and other institutions perpetuate (Ladson-Billings, 1994). Teachers and school leaders who are committed to preserving students' culture and linguistic assets are not only engaged in culturally relevant practice but work to "perpetuate and foster—to sustain—linguistic, literate, and cultural pluralism as part of the democratic project of schooling" (Paris, 2012, p. 95). Culturally sustaining teaching is informed by students' *funds of knowledge*, the "historically accumulated and culturally developed bodies of knowledge and skills essential for household functioning and well-being" (Moll, Amanti, Neff, & González, 1992, p. 133). Instruction that infuses students' household knowledge, heritage, day-to-day experiences, and popular culture is empowering and it contributes to students' identification with school.

Culturally informed literacy instruction is based on knowledge of the literacy and language practices of particular cultural groups (Au, 1980; Heath, 1983). Teachers and school leaders who embrace an expansive view of literacy tend to think of literacy as *literacies*. They know that literacy is not limited to school-valued ways of using print and language, such as reading books and writing essays. Instead, they recognize the many literacies that are used across different contexts, including homes and communities. Posting on Facebook, reading a train schedule, memorizing a song, or telling a story at the dinner table—these ways of using print and language are shaped by people's beliefs, values, and practices (Heath, 1983). Teachers who understand the culturally situated and expansive nature of literacy invite a wide variety of literacy engagements in the classroom, including those that involve alternative and digital texts. They also see oral communication and storytelling as an integral part of literacy learning and one that students associate with pleasure, peers, and play (Souto-Manning & Martell, 2016).

Successful second-language teachers and school administrators know that knowledge and abilities acquired in one language can be used to learn another (Cummins, 1981). Instead of seeing students' first language as an impediment to second-language learning, they view it as an asset and encourage students to draw from their knowledge of the first language to learn the second—a task that is easiest if the languages share many linguistic features, as Spanish and English do. At Gregorio Luperón High School for Science and Mathematics, teachers endorsed the practice of translanguaging so students could use both English and Spanish flexibly to construct knowledge. They not only employed students' home language to develop English, but also understood the importance of developing students' bilingualism. These teachers understood that language and identity are entwined and that students need nonthreatening opportunities to use language flexibly. Successful teachers of emergent bilinguals understand that their teaching must not only be culturally sustaining, but also challenging, creative, and academic (Garcia & Kleifgen, 2010). They know to scaffold instruction for emergent bilinguals so they can meet the same high standards as their English-speaking counterparts.

Supportive School Leaders

For teachers to be successful, they must be supported. In many underserved communities, too many students do not have continual access to high-quality teachers from one year to the next. Teachers leave low-resourced schools for a number of reasons, including salary, but they are primarily driven out by poor working conditions and a lack of support (Simon & Johnson, 2015). They tend to stay, however, if they have strong and supportive administrators and positive collegial relationships and feel that their opinions and decisions are valued. The Tung et al. (2011) study identified school leaders who articulated their visions for students' success, which were shaped by their own shared experiences as English language learners and as former bilingual teachers. They also made organizational decisions that positively affected the delivery of services to bilingual learners, such as coordinating Instructional Leadership Teams and Language Acquisition Team (LAT) facilitators. Researchers of the Texas-based study of high-performing schools for emergent bilinguals (Jesse et al., 2004) found that school leaders made organizational decisions to improve the delivery of learning support to students, while simultaneously providing teacher support. Effective school leaders communicate with teachers in ways that prompt self-reflection and professional growth; they provide suggestions and feedback, model practices, encourage classroom inquiry, and solicit teachers' advice and opinions (Blase & Blase, 2000).

Willard principal Ron Reilly, introduced at the beginning of this chapter, exemplifies these leadership qualities by supporting meaning-based literacy instruction, recognizing teachers' expertise, organizing schedules that allow teachers to co-plan, and establishing a safe and culturally welcoming school climate where teachers can focus on instruction. Willard is an example of a humanizing school. The goal of this book is to showcase these types of schools and describe how they are making a difference with multilingual learners.

ORGANIZATION OF THE BOOK

Part I continues with descriptions of two schools that offer very different humanizing climates. In Chapter 2, Nadia Granados and Norma González offer a retrospective look at a K–5 dual language immersion school that provided a linguistically rich and academically supportive context for emergent bilinguals. Graduates, now in their 20s, attributed their academic success to this school. The authors identify six principles of humanizing and culturally sustaining pedagogy that guided the school's literacy and language learning. In Chapter 3, authors Lee Gunderson and Reginald D'Silva describe a high school that provides a safe and supportive climate for immigrant students, one that allows them to build strong and respectful relationships with others as a foundation for learning.

Part II illustrates how schools are transformed through educator, caregiver, and community collaborations. In Chapter 4, Patricia Ruggiano Schmidt shares her work as a consultant to the Syracuse Academy of Science Charter School system to bring teachers and caregivers of several language communities together to provide classrooms where students' cultural heritage and language is used to create meaningful and intellectually rigorous literacy lessons. In Chapter 5, Steven Z. Athanases and Marnie W. Curry discuss five elements of schooling for multilingual, low SES youth that include: a sustained vision of a community-engaged school; leadership distributed among faculty, staff, and community partners; a purposeful vision of literacy; support for multilingualism across school spaces; and academic extension activities beyond school hours to foster language-rich work related to social issues and social justice. In Chapter 6, Melissa Pérez Rhym writes about her experiences as a Latinx teacher in Georgia who initiated a schoolwide campaign to make her school more welcoming for Latinx families, based on information provided by students' caregivers.

Part III shows schools that embrace culturally responsive and sustaining climates for literacy and language learning. In Chapter 7, Suniti Sharma and Usha Gurumurthy describe the components of a border school in South Texas that contributes to bilingual students' literacy engagement. Using Freire's notion of school transformation, these researchers examine a number of humanizing school components, including school leadership, a close-knit school ethos of caring, and a schoolwide commitment to the historical, geographical, and cultural context of students' experiences. In Chapter 8, Ivana Espinet, Brian Collins, and Ann Ebe describe a school in the Bronx that supports emergent bilingual learners by adopting translanguaging practices. The authors also explore how students contributed to designing new initiatives that benefited emergent bilinguals and their families, such as a home language-mentoring program in which students provide classroom support and after-school mentoring for newcomers. In Chapter 9, Douglas Fisher and Nancy Frey discuss an 11-year effort to help students develop academic literacies through embedded language learning that involves teacher modeling, collaborative conversations, and sophisticated response-to-intervention procedures. In Chapter 10, Shelley Hong Xu and Jamie Schnablegger detail Jamie's experience of teaching literacy in an award-winning school that serves a high percentage of Latinx students, and how she was able to work with her mentors to create stimulating and culturally relevant lessons.

Finally, Mark Conley will extract from the chapters to highlight the schooling components that advance learning in these predominantly U.S. schools. He discusses these schools within a broader context of schoolwide initiatives around the world and examines how top-performing countries serve their economically disadvantaged students. By detailing how the top-performing nations act on their commitment to move all children forward to success, Conley sets an agenda for creating schools where all students can thrive.

CONCLUSION

This book profiles schools that are succeeding with multilingual students in underserved communities. We are losing too many of these students to inadequately resourced schools, unsound educational polices, and inappropriate instructional practices. Understanding how some schools are making progress with multilingual students must be a research priority. The chapters ahead will uncover how some schools have helped many students realize their learning capacities. It is our hope that the book brings us one step closer to creating these schools for all students.

REFERENCES

Anyon, J. (2005). *Radical possibilities: Public policy, urban education, and a new social movement.* New York, NY: Routledge.

Au, K. H. (1980). Participation structures in a reading lesson with Hawaiian children. Analysis of a culturally appropriate instructional event. *Anthropology and Education Quarterly, 11*(2), 91–115.

Bartlett, L., & Koyama, J. P. (2012). Additive schooling: A critical small school for Latino immigrant youth. In M. Hantzopoulos & A. Tyner-Mullings (Eds.), *Critical small schools: Beyond privatization in New York city urban educational reform* (pp. 79–102). Charlotte, NC: Information Age Publishing.

Blase, J., & Blase, J. (2000). Effective instructional leadership: Teachers' perspectives on how principals promote teaching and learning in schools. *Journal of Education Administration, 38*(2), 130–141.

Bonilla-Silva, E. (2017). What we were, what we are, and what we should be: The racial problem of American sociology. *Social Problems, 64*(2), 179–187.

Boschma, J., & Brownstein, R. (2016, February 29). The concentration of poverty in American schools. *The Atlantic.* Retrieved from www.theatlantic.com/education/archive/2016/02/concentration-poverty-american-schools/471414/

Charity Hudley, A. H., & Mallinson, C. (2010). *Understanding English language variation in U.S. schools.* New York, NY: Teachers College Press.

Collier, V. P., & Thomas, W. P. (2017). Validating the power of bilingual schooling: Thirty-two years of large-scale, longitudinal research. *Annual Review of Applied Linguistics, 37*, 1–15.

Cummins, J. (1981). The role of primary language development in promoting educational success for language minority students. In California State Department of Education (Ed.), *Schooling and language minority students: A theoretical framework* (pp. 3–49). Los Angeles, CA: Evaluation, Dissemination and Assessment Center, California State University.

De Jesús, A. (2012). Authentic caring and community driven school reform: The case of El Puente Academy for Peace and Justice. In M. Hantzopoulos & A. Tyner-Mullings (Eds.), *Critical small schools: Beyond privatization in New York City urban educational reform* (pp. 63–78). Charlotte, NC: Information Age Publishing.

De Jesús, S. C. (2008). An astounding treasure: Dual language education in a public school setting. *Centro Journal, 20*(2), 192–217.

Fine, M. (2012). Critical small schools—windows on educational justice in a neoliberal blizzard. In M. Hantzopoulos & A. Tyner-Mullings (Eds.), *Critical small schools: Beyond privatization in New York City urban educational reform* (pp. ix–xvii). Charlotte, NC: Information Age Publishing.

Gamoran, A., & Long, D. (2006, August). School effects in comparative perspective: New evidence from a threshold model. In *Presentation of The Annual Meeting of the American Sociological Association*, Montreal Convention Center, Montreal, Quebec, Canada.

Garcia, O., & Kleifgen, J. A. (2010). *Emergent bilinguals: Policies, programs, and practices for English language learners.* New York, NY: Teachers College Press.

Goldenberg, C. N. (2008, Summer). Teaching English language learners: What the research does—and does not—say. *American Educator*, 8–44.

Heath, S. B. (1983). *Ways with words: Language, life and work in communities and classrooms.* New York, NY: Cambridge University Press.

Hursh, D. (2007). Assessing No Child Left Behind and the rise of neoliberal education policies. *American Educational Research Journal, 44*(3), 493–518.

Jesse, D., Davis, A., & Pokorny, N. (2004). High-achieving middle schools for Latino students in poverty. *Journal of Education for Students Placed at Risk, 9*(1), 23–45.

Jiménez-Castellanos, O., & Garcia, E. (2017). Intersection of language, class, ethnicity and policy: Toward disrupting inequality for English language learners. *Review of Research in Education, 41*(1), 428–452

Kim, W. (2017). Long-term English language learners' educational experiences in the context of high-stakes accountability. *Teachers College Record, 119*(9), 1–32.

Kozol, J. (2005). *The shame of the nation: The restoration of apartheid schooling in America.* New York, NY: Crown Publishing.

Krashen, S., Rolstad, K., & MacSwan, J. (2007). Review of "Research summary and bibliography for structured English immersion programs" of the Arizona English language learners task force. Institute for Language Education and Policy. Retrieved from www.elladvocates.org/documents/AZ/Krashen_Rolstad_MacSwan_review.pdf

Ladson-Billings, G. (1994). *The dreamkeepers: Successful teachers of African American children.* San Francisco, CA: Jossey-Bass Publishers.

Lucas, T., & Villegas, A. M. (2013). Preparing linguistically responsive teachers: Laying the foundation in preservice teacher education. *Theory into Practice, 52*(2), 98-109.

Mahiri, J. (2017). *Deconstructing race: Education beyond the color-bind.* New York, NY: Teachers College Press.

Menken, K., & Solorza, C. (2012). No child left bilingual: Accountability and the elimination of bilingual education programs in New York City schools. *Educational Policy, 28*(1), 96-125.

Moll, L. C., Amanti, C., Neff, D., & Gonzalez, N. (1992). Funds of knowledge for teaching: Using a qualitative approach to connect homes and classrooms. *Theory into Practice, 31*(2), 132-141.

National Center for Education Statistics. (2017). Philadelphia district directory information (2016–2017). *National Center for Educational Statistics.* Retrieved from nces.ed.gov/ccd/districtsearch/district_detail.asp?Search=2&ID2=4218990

Noddings, N. (1984). *Caring: A feminine approach to ethics and moral education.* Berkeley, CA: University of California Press.

Paris, D. (2012). Culturally sustaining pedagogy: A needed change in stance, terminology, and practice. *Educational Researcher, 41*(33), 93-97.

Rauner, D. M. (2000). *They still pick me up when I fall: The role of caring in youth development and community life.* New York, NY: Columbia University Press.

Rolón-Dow, R. (2005). Critical care: A color (full) analysis of care narratives in the schooling experiences of Puerto Rican girls. *American Educational Research Journal, 42*(1), 77-111.

Salazar, M. D. (2013). A humanizing pedagogy: Reinventing the principles and practice of education as a journey toward liberation. *Review of Research in Education, 37,* 121-148.

Simon, N. S., & Johnson, S. M. (2015). Teacher turnover in high-poverty schools: What we know and can do. *Teachers College Record, 117*(3), 1-36.

Skutnabb-Kangas, T., & Phillipson, R. (Eds.). (1994). *Linguistic human rights, past and present.* New York, NY: Mouton de Gruyter.

Souto-Manning, M., & Martell, J. (2016). *Reading, writing, and talk: Inclusive teaching strategies for diverse learners, K–2.* New York, NY: Teachers College Press.

Tung, R., Diez, V., Gagnon, L., Uriarte, M., & Stazesky, P., de los Reyes, E., & Balomey, A. (2011). Learning from consistently high performing and improving schools for English language learners in Boston public schools. *Center for Collaborative Education and the Mauricio Gaston Institute for Latino Community Development and Public Policy.* Retrieved from scholarworks.umb.edu/gaston_pubs/155/

Valenzuela, A. (1999). *Subtractive schooling: U.S.-Mexican youth and the politics of caring.* Albany, NY: State University of New York Press.

CHAPTER 2

Nurturing Lifelong and Life-Wide Literacies Through Humanizing Pedagogies

Nadia Granados and Norma González

> Dalton (pseudonym) was and will always remain the foundation of why I have the level of success in my personal, private, and my professional career. It gave me so many of the tools and it brought me to so many of the teachers. And I think because Dalton was a bilingual institution, it brought really dynamic teachers and educators who cultivated this culture and environment of bilingualism, multiculturalism, and acceptance, and infused it with learning. We made so many connections because were able to be ourselves in this kind of environment. . . . I think I learned more in elementary school than I learned anywhere else in terms of like the fundamental things that I carried through the rest of my life.
>
> —Jaime (adult graduate of Dalton Elementary)

This chapter is a retrospective look at a previously studied public dual-language (DL) school, Dalton Elementary (pseudonym), through the eyes of its graduates. Although retrospective constructions may be idealized and romanticized, graduates of this school, now adults, voice the powerful and enduring impact of their schooling experiences on their lifelong cycles of bilingualism, literacy, and biliteracy, as well as their critical consciousness. This dual-language school allows us a glimpse into the makings of a "sanctuary school" that allowed for a deliberate and affirming embrace of students' families, communities and languages, nonscripted and expansive learning opportunities, and enhanced after-school programs that afforded literacy-rich learning spaces. This chapter describes one notable DL school and the constellation of variables that coalesced to enable the fluorescence of a linguistically rich and academically supportive context for dual-language learners. Because this K–5 dual-language immersion school has been the subject of numerous studies (e.g., González & Arnot-Hopffer, 2003; Moll & Arnot-Hopffer, 2005; Smith, 2001, 2002; Smith & Arnot-Hopffer, 1998) there are abundant data that document the contours of curriculum, ideologies, and practices as the school implemented its dual-language program in the 1990s. The description of the language and literacy practices of this school site are drawn from this corpus of literature. Recent data collected on graduates of this program, now adults in their 20s, illustrate graduates' academic and professional success as well as their overwhelmingly affirmative reflections of their early language-learning experiences during their elementary school years (Granados, 2017). We also draw on our positionalities within this research site, as González participated as both a researcher and a parent during the time frame and Granados as a student at the school during her elementary years. Graduates' continued uptake of multiple literacies and global awareness perspectives begs the question: What did this school get right? By carefully theorizing the practices that led to the long-term success of graduates, a nuanced picture emerges of how schooling that allows teacher autonomy, forges strong linkages to the community, and encourages the multicompetencies of students through a humanizing pedagogy can go beyond the current narrowing of the curriculum and the muting of teacher voices.

We couch this chapter within two frameworks that are conceptually aligned and theoretically congruent: Salazar (2013) on humanizing pedagogy and Paris and Alim (2017) on culturally sustaining pedagogies. Both draw on the principles of repositioning community knowledges as "asset pedagogies," validating and honoring these as pedagogical strengths. Culturally sustaining pedagogies extend concepts of asset pedagogies by reimagining schools as places where community practices are not only valued but *sustained*. Because the principles enacted at Dalton were documented over 20 years ago, the notion of "sustaining" becomes relevant. These abiding principles are enduring in the sense that even within current multimodal and digital literate practices, the sustaining of humanizing pedagogies demands a rethinking of how local affordances can be curricularized within specific local settings. These humanizing approaches to schooling are detailed within a unique and perhaps exceptional set of circumstances that produced measurable success for students.

DUAL-LANGUAGE SCHOOLING

Typically and ideally, DL programs incorporate equal numbers of speakers of the majority language with speakers of a second language. The "astounding effectiveness" (Collier & Thomas, 2004) of DL schooling has been examined from critical perspectives that focus on inequities within asymmetries in language and literacy policies (López and Fránquiz, 2009), placement practices (Palmer & Henderson, 2016), race and power (Palmer, 2010), as well as the larger neoliberal discourses that privilege economic benefits for future multilingual workers within a globalized marketplace (Delavan, Valdez, & Freire, 2017). In a critical and comprehensive review of the literature on DL programs (Cervantes-Soon, Dorner, Palmer, Heiman, Schwerdtfeger, & Choi, 2017), it is argued that the stated goals of DL programs may privilege White, English-speaking students in ways that produce inequities for emergent bilinguals and transnational students. In this chapter, we acknowledge and recognize the potential for the inequitable allocation of resources and opportunities (Williams, 2017), yet the laudable goals of DL schooling can have long-term and perhaps unexpected results within a longitudinal framework that incorporates the perspectives and voices of DL students themselves as they reflect back on their schooling.

SCHOOL COMMUNITY CONTEXT

Although it is tempting to argue for generalizable principles for successful schools, we must always acknowledge the sociohistorical context within which local schools operate. We describe here a school and community context that is multilayered and is perhaps not typical, nor effortlessly re-created.

Dalton Elementary School is one of the oldest schools in a southwestern city in Arizona, located 90 miles from the U.S. border with Mexico. Established in 1902, it is located within one of the oldest Mexican *barrios* of the city and historically most of the families have been speakers of minoritized languages, primarily Spanish, but also Chinese, Tohono O'odham, and Yoeme (Yaqui) (Smith et al., 2002). The *barrio* was characterized as economically stressed and according to 1990 census data, the median family income in 1990 was $9,468, with the percentage of "families in poverty" at 64.8% (Smith, 2000).

A monolingual school that initially served the families and children from the *barrio*, it had a high dropout rate and low academic achievement compared to wealthier schools in the city (Smith et al., 2002). In 1981, its monolingual status changed and it became the school district's first bilingual magnet school. However, the path to becoming a magnet school was fraught with divisions and controversy, as magnet status was the result of a federal desegregation order filed against the school district in 1978 (see Smith, 2000). The federal desegregation order has had a profound impact on the student population at Dalton and the contours of its language and literacy programmatic decisions. Because the court order was based on a desegregation design, foregrounding ethnicity as the basis for attendance by magnet students rather than language dominance, language and literacy policies at the school had to adjust to provide a linguistically rich environment. The school would receive, as part of the court settlement, full-time instructional aides for each classroom, as well as certified specialists in art, music, and physical education. Significantly, the settlement also provided for creation of an extended-day program to include instruction and supervision before and after school, as well as providing the stipulation that the large majority of the staff should be bilingual. Because of increased resources, the learning environment was reconfigured to serve the children from the local *barrio* and to attract sufficient numbers of White students from the larger community. Although the number of *barrio* students has statistically been smaller than the number of magnet students, according to Conrado Gómez, founding principal of the school after the court order, "You have to remember—and this is something that a lot of people forget—these programs were designed to put the neighborhood kids foremost. The plans could be good for all kids, but the educational needs of the Barrio kids will be foremost" (Smith, 2000, p. 251).

The school began a maintenance bilingual education model where teachers were expected to use Spanish as a vehicle for instruction 50% of the time and English 50% of the time. However, after several years of this model, the teachers noted that students who entered the program dominant in Spanish exited 5th grade as bilingual and biliterate, but those who entered the program dominant in English did not exhibit the same success. This conscious questioning by the faculty and the autonomy that was afforded to them by the supportive principal, *Doctora* R., allowed the teachers to pursue avenues to address how fuller bilingualism and biliteracy could be achieved. The teachers began to identify and study successful bilingual education programs, especially dual-language programs, in Canada and in the United States. Their enthusiasm for DL models was tempered by the recognition that the desegregation settlement did not allow for the even distribution of majority- and minority-language-speaking children, one of the guiding principles of most DL programs. In an exceptionally incisive decision, the teacher's study group proposed that teachers would use a much higher percentage of Spanish for instruction and in this way promote the use of Spanish in the classroom. Consequently, during the 1993–1994 school year, the "Spanish Enrichment" model, later formally known as *El Programa de Inmersion en Dos Idiomas*, had its genesis.

Within the model implemented by the teachers, which is unique in the literature, all students in this schoolwide program, regardless of language background, received all instruction in Spanish during the first 2 years (K–grade 1). This is significant because it meant that all early reading experiences would begin in Spanish. In grade 2, instruction was 85% in Spanish and 15% in English, and in grades 3, 4 and 5, it was 70% in Spanish and 30% in English, weighting the amount of Spanish throughout the students' elementary schooling experience. Language of instruction, however, was not equivalent to language spoken by students in peer interactions or other communicative purposes outside of the classroom instruction, which was usually English (Smith, 2001).

During this time period, *barrio* students made up 35% of the student population and the remaining 65% was composed of magnet students. Most magnet students were from middle-class households, and most *barrio* students were from low-SES households. In the 1990s, the student body was approximately 250 students: 66% Latinx, 23% Anglo, and African American, Native American, and Asian American composing the remaining 11% (Smith, 2000). The Latinx population was largely second-, third-, or fourth-generation Latinx, and most students entered the school as English-dominant speakers. Many families cited a desire for their children to recapture Spanish, often erased by English-only instruction in their parents' and grandparents' schooling. Approximately 50% of students qualified for free or reduced-price lunch (Smith & Arnot-Hopffer, 1998). In alignment with the court settlement, the majority of teachers and staff were Latinx, and all were bilingual Spanish-English speakers. Over 90% of Dalton students stayed after school for the extended-day program, which consisted of 2 hours of after-school activities of the students' choice, including mariachi music and *folklórico*, as well as athletics, cooking, crochet, and homework help.

THE STUDY

This research draws from and cites (1) data from a doctoral dissertation (see Granados, 2015a, 2015b, 2017); (2) data described in previously published literature from studies at the school site; and (3) researcher notes, experiences, and reflections. The dissertation study used qualitative methodology to highlight the bilingual and biliterate trajectories of graduates of Dalton who are now young adults. Participants were graduates of Dalton's dual-language program who completed their 5th-grade year between the years of 1997 and 2003. These Dalton graduates have now grown into adulthood, and, at the time the study was conducted, were between the ages of 22 and 28 years old. As part of a larger study, a total of 52 graduates contributed to an online discussion board via a Facebook group. Ten of these also participated in two separate focus-group discussions. Three case study participants were also selected as part of the study and each was interviewed three times using a modified version of Seidman's (2006) three-interview series.

Though all 52 participants are included in the outcomes section of this chapter, we focus primarily on interview and focus-group data from two focal participants: Jaime and Mariana. Jaime's data derive from three interviews conducted with him as a case study participant, while Mariana was a focus-group participant and her data are from one focus-group discussion. Both Jaime and Mariana are from the *barrio* and lower-socioeconomic households. Jaime is a Mexican American from a Spanish-dominant, bilingual household. He, however, entered Dalton as an English-dominant speaker. He was raised primarily by his bilingual mother and Spanish-dominant grandmother. He is now a successful professional who was recently named Pacific regional director of an animal shelter. Mariana was raised by her mother and father, both of whom were recent immigrants from Mexico and monolingual Spanish speakers. Mariana entered Dalton as a Spanish speaker. She has now earned her master's degree in public health at the local university and works as a disability examiner.

In addition to data from the dissertation study, we also draw from examples that have been described in previously published research literature at the school site to underscore our suggestions for guiding principles. We have also been personally involved with the school site, its students, and faculty. González was a parent of two attending students as well as a researcher at the school during that time, and Granados was a student during elementary school and later a researcher of the program and its graduates. Using these three varieties of data, we theorize six guiding principles for humanizing and culturally sustaining pedagogies.

ADVANCING LITERACY AND LANGUAGE LEARNING: SIX GUIDING PRINCIPLES

Schools are built environments, socially constructed within sociocultural matrices. We have focused on this school as a microcosm of principles that brought together an array of foundational premises that succeeded, in the eyes of its graduates, in laying the foundation for their success in later life. Although not all-encompassing, these principles can guide our deeper understandings of successful schools and how lessons from the past can be drawn upon to impact our future theorizing.

1. Whole School Investment in Language and Literacy in Two Languages

Many of the critiques of inequities within DL schooling concern programs that incorporate only a strand of DL within the larger school. Depending on the larger demographic profile of the school community, as well as the school district policy on placement in these strands, imbalances can result in the disadvantaging of emergent bilinguals. Similarly, the strand model can result in divisions within the larger student body regarding those enrolled in the DL strand and those who are not enrolled (Dorner, 2011). In contrast, Dalton elementary was consciously and proudly a fully bilingual whole-school program. Environmental print and displays of student work, as well as daily intercom announcements, foregrounded the whole-school investment in language and literacy in two languages. Parents were informed before registering their child that all students would be immersed in 100% Spanish instruction in kindergarten and 1st grade, although there was an initial 2-week transition where both languages were spoken. Whole-school commitment requires a leap of faith for some parents, as high-stakes testing is (and was) only in English. Although parents could enthusiastically embrace the stated goals of a whole-school DL program, circulating discourses concerning measures of academic achievement were often fielded by teachers and the principal.

2. Schoolwide Ideological Clarity

A vital component of the whole-school commitment to language and literacy learning in two languages is a clear vision regarding the purposes and assumptions of DL schooling. Moll and Arnot-Hopffer (2005) identify "ideological clarity" as one component of the ecology of Dalton and claim that through this clarity, "teachers become well aware of how much teaching is a political activity. . . ." (p. 242). The political nature of schooling became abundantly clear in the years 1999–2001 leading up to the passage of Arizona's Proposition 203, the ballot initiative also called "English for the Children" that attempted to dismantle bilingual education programs. The controversy surrounding this proposition had a major impact on the school: "It would be accurate to state that the administrators and teachers are constantly vigilant of any attempts to either alter the dual-language agenda of the school or impose an English-only curriculum and do not hesitate to activate the school's social network of parents and other allies to defend the school" (Moll & Arnot Hopffer, 2005, pp. 242–243).

3. Faculty *Compromiso* (Commitment) and Faculty Autonomy

As all of the elements we describe here are intricately connected with one another, the commitment of the faculty, an exceptional group of educators who were invested in their students and in DL education, was pivotal. As a whole, they were highly educated and experienced; 71% of Dalton faculty had earned a master's degree or higher, had taken academic courses in Spanish, and had taught for at least 5 years at the school (Smith et al., 2002). There was low faculty turnover at the school and there were close ties between faculty members, the instructional aides, noninstructional staff, the principal, and the surrounding community. Many of the teachers had received their education at the local university through the "bilingual block" where they received methods courses in both Spanish and English that shaped their bilingual competencies. This underscores the importance of the formation of teachers within a framework for advocacy for local communities, as teacher education programs can be transformative vehicles for nurturing in their teacher candidates their long-term commitment to equity in teaching.

In reflecting back on their experiences, graduates of the program have vivid memories of the unwavering and constant support as learners that they experienced at Dalton. Jaime, for example, recalls:

> Whether it was cognizant or not it was strategy to put the right people in the right places. . . . I think it all starts with the right principal that is going to pick the right teachers that are going to create the right environment. And . . . making sure we have the right diverse group of people that are going to enrich the environment. I don't think that anything was a coincidence.

Faculty solidarity, however, must be nurtured and maintained. Their teacher study group grew into a weekly meeting entitled "*reflexiones*," which revisited and reflected on their instructional practice and considered how it might evolve. Unhappy with formulaic assessments of students that measured bilinguals as two monolinguals, teachers designed their own formative assessments, taking into account bilingual competencies holistically. Although the teachers were often distrustful about the results of standardized tests, students during this time frame achieved at high levels, scoring at or above district and national averages on the Stanford 9 test. The state measurement criteria were also encouraging, as 100% of 3rd-graders in the spring of 2000 met or exceeded the state standard in English reading. This was particularly noteworthy because students had received at least 70% of their schooling in Spanish (Smith et al., 2002).

In another instance, faculty transformed a districtwide mandate for a "balanced literacy" emphasis and adapted elements that were particular to their school population. Responding to the particularities of their school context, teachers decided to create a schoolwide multiage nonscripted Spanish language arts program to better meet the needs of students at all levels of Spanish literacy development, incorporating selected components of the district "balanced literacy" program. This was designed as a schoolwide program for all students from 1st through 5th grade, and the result was a program entitled Éxito Bilingüe. These humanizing pedagogies move away from restrictive policies and practices and standardized one-size-fits-all approaches (Salazar, 2013), and produce successful measurable outcomes. At Dalton, teachers found ways to agentically move between systemic constraints and the immediate and perceived values of the school.

4. Humanizing Pedagogies: Teachers as Caring, Compassionate, and Humane

Salazar (2013) affirms that humanizing pedagogies are founded, among other tenets, on trusting and caring relationships that advance the pursuit of humanization. As graduates of Dalton recall their schooling experiences, their most salient, and often most cherished, memories are those that recognized their worth and latent abilities.

Jaime is now a respected professional who works with animal welfare. His narrative evocatively relates how his teacher, *Señora* M., tapped into his interest in animals while he was in her class:

> She taught you about life; she tapped into your interests, mine being animals. . . . I remember the snake "Cuca"; we had the funeral and everything. And I think about how she was so gifted in tapping into what was special and different in all of us. She probably made each of us feel like we were all special which to me is the true test of a true educator. . . . But she, through her teaching, really cultivated a love of animals and I built on that ever since from there. . . .

He also recollects how his teacher and his principal leveraged his innate interests in spite of his own (never the school's) perceived categorization of himself as a "struggling reader":

> It was interesting, because *Doctora* R. (the principal) noticed that [I did not like reading]. . . . I was like *not* interested . . . (and) she went out and bought me an Encyclopedia A–Z on animals. And I mean, I think about it now, these are expensive books. And then *Señora* M., subscribed me to get these zoo books, so every month I would get something delivered to my house and

so those growing up were the only things I read. . . . They found content that naturally interested me. I mean, there was no way we could have afforded that in my family.

Jaime intuitively identifies principles of humanizing pedagogy, especially in connecting to his life and experiences. Similarly, Mariana reminisced about Dalton and incisively wondered about the convergence of caring educators:

> I wonder if Dalton had a higher standard [for hiring]. I feel like they might have handpicked their teachers. . . . I think all the teachers were very encouraging of what you wanted to do or wanted to learn.

A humanizing pedagogy must go beyond "caring." Moll and Arnot-Hopffer (2005) identify a "culture of caring" related to the concept of *confianza*, or mutual trust, that "helped the teachers define themselves as a particular type of professional, and as a particular type of person, with the necessary funds of knowledge to make curricular decisions that help define the nature of the educational relationships in the school" (p. 242). In this way, caring and *confianza* were intimately connected, in much the way that Cammarota and Romero (2006) define their concept of "critically compassionate intellectualism." Within their framework, a trilogy of educational practice combines characteristics of critical pedagogy, compassionate student–teacher relationships, and social justice content, all elements that were observable at Dalton.

5. Critical Consciousness and Global Awareness

Humanizing pedagogies are not a one-way street. Although teachers and administrators may ostensibly be the transmitters of a critical consciousness within a humanizing pedagogy, children's voices are not absent in their own constructions of counterdiscourses. One classroom example, considered in González (2005), describes the following interaction:

> Students in one classroom are discussing the concept of opposites. The teacher asks for a word in Spanish that means the opposite of the word they are given, and students go around in a circle. When the teacher says "Bilingüe" (bilingual), there's a moment's hesitation before the student blurts out "Tonto" (stupid, foolish), clearly refuting stereotype that bilinguals are in need of remedial or compensatory programs. This child inverts the deficit discourse of bilingual education and recasts those who do not have skills in more than one language as lacking academic achievement. Through the activity of articulation, this child can subvert the rationale of hegemonic discourse and relocate an imposed negative identity. (p. 169)

For children at this school, bilingualism is an unquestioned asset, one that they deploy in a variety of contexts. During the contentious campaign leading up to the passage of Proposition 203 in Arizona, the antibilingual initiative, students were active agents in drawing up signs in English and Spanish, writing incisive and penetrating letters to the local newspaper, and speaking on radio shows. They marshaled their full linguistic and literate skill sets in advocating for the type of education they were receiving (González & Arnot-Hopffer, 2003).

In keeping with the school ideal of "respect," students were given voice as "critical theorists" (González, 2005) and were listened to when they had concerns about school issues, from the mundane to aspects of pedagogy. Second-graders lobbied for cleaner bathrooms and better care of utensils (Smith et al., 2002). They also challenged the concept of Éxito Bilingüe, claiming that it was not bilingual, but in actuality, it was only Spanish immersion.

Within a framework of critical consciousness, teachers were proactive in framing a multicultural world for students through a variety of assembled materials and sources, inviting, for example, Rigoberta Menchú, the Guatemalan human rights activist, who was in town visiting the university, as well as international graduate students. Awareness of global issues conveyed the sustaining of multiculturalism or "multiculturally sustaining pedagogies" (Granados, 2015b, p. 62) as Jaime retrospectively appreciates:

> [Dalton] introduced me to Spanish in a new way. It wasn't just about the language, it was about the culture. . . . Like the 16th of September, there was always some kind of fiesta. We were always learning about all these important Mexican figures really early on and I think that was a conscious effort. When people were learning about Gandhi, we were learning about Hidalgo. . . . But in regard to Spanish, it taught me a lot. . . . You think you're Mexican and you think that [being Brown] that's the only type of color . . . then you learn that Guatemala is not the same thing (laughs). What it means to be Latin; it expanded my views of who we were.

Children were well aware that there were many pathways to knowledge, and literacy in more than one language could be a key to unlock knowledge. Jaime reflects on his growing consciousness of internal cultural diversity and connects his critical consciousness to lifelong and life-wide issues, reading the world within an insightful and discerning stance:

> The thing about Dalton was that it was so much more than a school; it was a community, which is what schools should be . . . it's just really interesting how that place really was this little melting pot of all these different people. . . . I think one of the things when you grow up without things and you're hyperaware of what you have and what you don't have. . . . I remember being in 4th grade and Richard was my best friend . . . and going to his house . . . and thinking "my house doesn't look like this." So I thought all Mexican people were like me. . . . So, you realize that within our sector there's all these subsectors in it and I had no idea 'cause everyone in [the *barrio*] we're in the same circumstances and just brought up very similar. So yeah, I definitely learned that within each other we are very different.

Mariana echoes his themes, while underscoring her growing awareness of her own social networks:

I'm thankful I had the good experience to mingle among other kids who were children of professionals, which kind of like upped the bar and made you want to do better. . . . So I think it's an advantage for me that I came from the *barrio*.

6. Community as Resource and Creating Community

Throughout the literature on Dalton, the notion of "being in community" is well documented. As Mariana astutely declares: "'It takes a village to raise a child.' I definitely think that concept was implemented at Dalton. It just had all those elements but the [most important] was the community."

Smith (2000, 2001) details the many ways in which students interacted with Spanish-speaking members of the surrounding community through school-initiated activities. Students were known to go on walking fieldtrips to different points of interest nearby in the neighborhood, such as a local *tortillería*, or a fieldtrip to a family farm in the *barrio* (Smith, 2001), or as one graduate recalls, walking to a nearby repurposed bicycle shop and touring some of the original adobe homes in the neighborhood. Dalton also began a community garden that involved students, parents, and community members. Aside from the physical spaces of being in the community, Dalton also had many ways of creating a closely knit school community. The school adopted the notion of parents as co-constructors within the curriculum by inviting parents and family members into the classroom (Smith, 2000, 2001). Mariana recalls this vividly: "It was like an open-door policy. 'Come and talk to me and we will help you out.'"

Furthermore, Dalton hosted *Escuela Nocturna* (School After Dark) two evenings a week, which featured classes in Spanish and English as a Second Language for parents and community members, in addition to computers, child care, tutoring, and other classes for adults and children. In this program, parents were also engaged as second-language learners. They were able to identify with their children who were learning English or Spanish, as they took on the role of the learner. Two English-speaking parents, one African American and one Latinx raised as an English monolingual, explained their involvement in *Escuela Nocturna*.

The African American father explained: "In the area that I live in, there are a large number of Hispanic people. I have two kids, and we have them at a bilingual school, and it's to my advantage to learn because I don't want my kids standing in front of me saying things that I don't understand." Similarly, the English monolingual Latina recounts: "It was my daughter's first year in a bilingual school . . . so when they offered the after-school program for us, we thought it was only fair. If she had to learn, so did we" (Smith et al., 2002, p. 109).

These relationships among students, teachers, and parents were further developed because of the after-school extended-day program, again underscoring that well-resourced programs can have lasting effects. Because many of the children were involved with the mariachi program, families would commonly interact after school hours at regular mariachi "*tocadas*" (performances). Mariachi and music became a lifelong endeavor for many of the graduates (Granados, 2015a) as many continued to play in local mariachi ensembles and developed deep and abiding relationships to the music, the culture, and the historical legacy of mariachi music.

The process of actually creating community seems increasingly difficult. Dalton provided one example of a multipronged approach involving building on community resources and students' funds of knowledge; parents and families as co-constructors; opportunities to build social relationships outside of school; and students physically venturing into the local neighborhood. All of this combined created a lasting impression on students, as the word *community* became the most robust open code in Granados's (2015b) original analysis of graduates' data years later.

OUTCOMES: A GLIMPSE AT DALTON GRADUATES NOW

Graduates report that they have continued to use their bilingual and biliterate practices across time and in multiple and varied communities of practice (Granados, 2015a). Approximately 70% of graduates believe they have increased proficiency in Spanish at least orally since Dalton. Approximately 60% of graduates continued to play in mariachi groups after Dalton; others have participated in study abroad or volunteer programs in Spanish-speaking countries; still others report obtaining employment because of their bilingual and biliterate proficiencies, and many report that their bilingual proficiencies have played an important part in developing relationships with others.

All 52 of the dissertation study participants earned a high school diploma. What is even more impressive is that 96% of graduates have attended some college. At the time the data were collected on graduates in 2015, 90.4% of graduates had earned at least an associate's degree, and many had earned or were working toward undergraduate and graduate degrees. This number is likely even higher today, as many graduates were attending college and may have earned more degrees since then. Interestingly, there were no significant differences in college attendance between magnet students, who were primarily from middle-class households, and *barrio* students, who grew up in economically stressed households. Furthermore, there were no significant differences in types of employment among graduates. Examples of employment for *barrio* students included hotel manager, sales representative, and community outreach program coordinator. Examples of employment of magnet students included teacher, university staff, customer service representative, and bank teller. The DL program appears to have had an "equalizing effect" for college attendance magnet and *barrio* students (Granados, 2017).

Further, the graduates' global awareness and investment in social issues appear to be a durable and persistent lifelong endeavor:

As both groups [magnet and *barrio*] indicate involvement with the nonprofit sector, community outreach, and volunteer work, the data suggest graduates are more concerned about issues of community and collective value as opposed to individual endeavors. This can be considered a form of humanistic capital, one that benefits society as a whole through investment in long-term social missions and the common good. The dual language foundation fostered global awareness that is evident in graduates' present-day attention to and investment in broader social issues. (Granados, 2017, p. 234)

The numbers speak for themselves. This is a remarkably successful group of graduates. Although it is difficult to directly correlate their current education and employment to their early experiences in a dual-language setting, many graduates do, in fact, believe that Dalton played an important role in their later trajectories, like Jaime who states:

I look at a lot of us [graduates], and there's such a dynamic group of people doing incredible things, and we still have so much more to accomplish, and the one thing that we all share is Dalton, which is a bilingual institution and I don't think there's a coincidence. I think there's a correlation between that school setting as a foundation for setting us up for personal and professional success.

DISCUSSION AND CONCLUSIONS

As we have looked back in time, Janus-like, to move forward with potential future practices, there are some lessons learned as well as missed opportunities. This backward glance allows us to examine critically the current legitimized tools of accountability in the form of standardized assessments, and the concomitant pressuring of teachers to narrow the scope of instructional time without allowing opportunities for individualized and humanizing moments of deep teaching and learning. Teachers at this school were allowed extraordinary autonomy, noteworthy within any context. They were recognized as intellectuals whose own repositories of knowledge of bilingualism, biliteracy, and pedagogy were acknowledged to be as valid as published research on the topic. As teachers now are constrained in their opportunities to connect meaningfully with their students, this school offers a vision of possibilities of what has been and could be again.

Students were also allowed to become critical theorists in their own right as they "talked back" to their perceptions of unfair forces that surrounded them. Although there were economic and market advantages for these students regarding their bilingual abilities, the neoliberal argument for a globalized multilingual workforce falls flat as these students identify their greatest "take-away" as being their increased global awareness, their critical consciousness, and their abilities to be nimble and collaborative in the construction of knowledge. As we now engage public discourses that continue to devalue linguistic pluralism and that combine with anti-immigrant rhetoric, the examination of the context and pedagogy of this particular school site reveals that a humanizing, culturally sustaining pedagogy can have long-term and unexpected outcomes.

The enactment of *confianza* or mutual trust at multiple levels and how this evolved is also central to the success of this school. It is difficult to overstate the importance of the principal at this school, and the deep relationships of *confianza* that she was able to bring about through her long-term relationships with the teachers. As noted, she had deep and abiding roots in the bilingual education movement and had been an instructor in the bilingual block at the local university, where many of the teachers at Dalton had been her students. She then worked as the curriculum specialist at Dalton for many years before taking on the principalship, and so her involvement with the school was enduring and consistent. The *confianza* between the school and the community was also longstanding. An inescapable factor contributing to the establishment of relationships of *confianza* is the school's small size, which enabled close relationships between teachers and parents.

Similarly engaging the community, the school tapped into proximal linguistic resources, inviting community elders to narrate their story in their own words (Smith, 2000). More important, it brought the community linguistic funds of knowledge into the classroom and encouraged closer relationships with community members. Community members took notice, and many saw the school as a local resource for a variety of issues. One *barrio* "*abuela*" jokingly remarked that "*La Dalton es mi 911*" (Dalton is my 911), indicating that it was her source of emergency information.

Even within this abundantly and richly textured linguistic environment, we missed opportunities to theorize bilingualism and literacy as a social practice. The school, especially in Éxito Bilingüe, did not always encourage the full array of linguistic resources through the academic use of translanguaging, a practice that is recognized as a viable and commonsense approach to classroom practices. Although students could choose to respond in the language of their choice, teachers were operating by their school-adopted allocation of Spanish and English. During the time that was designated as "Spanish," teachers went to great lengths to convey meaning only in Spanish. However, since these students were exposed to an assortment of linguistic competencies in both Spanish and English, the openings for building on the complexity of their emergent bilingualism could have afforded a recognition of languages as not bounded, discrete, or unified. The permeable boundaries of languages are vividly evident as we engage with the more recent epistemologies of languages that promote translanguaging (García, 2009). Because of language separation policies, the currently recognized theoretical basis for translanguaging was not fully appreciated during this time frame. Although the language practices of the students outside of the school regularly leveraged their translanguaging skills, the school itself adopted a monoglossic separation-of-languages policy.

This backward look reveals two interrelated and overarching factors that have impacted the school since the implementation of the dual-language program and continue to impact schooling in general for all multilingual populations. The first was the passage of Proposition 203 in Arizona, the ballot referendum undercutting bilingual education. Despite the dedicated efforts of the schools' students, teachers, parents, and community members, the proposition passed in 2000. Because of its status as a bilingual magnet school, the school was able to maintain a certain amount of autonomy. One unfortunate effect of the passage was the gradual disinvestment in bilingual education by potential teacher candidates. The bilingual block at the local university, which had produced most of the bilingual teachers at this school, began to experience a precipitous drop in enrollment, which continues to this day. If these programs are to be implemented in the future, a robust and sustained effort to produce high-quality bilingual teachers is an indispensable and critical component.

The second disheartening movement has been the intensification and hardening of anti-immigrant discourses and the subsequent legislative enactments that have also had a chilling effect on the communities of many schools. With a nationwide climate of fear and distrust, gaining the trust of families and communities becomes increasingly problematic. Open and honest communication might potentially identify families or family members at risk for deportation. The fear of state institutions, even schools, has become regrettably widespread.

Schools can be places where students can be sheltered from the ongoing disparagement of their languages and communities. The principles that we have identified at Dalton are one pathway, certainly not the only one, and certainly not a flawless one. However, this portrait of a school that continues to resonate in those children who experienced it fully reveals that schools can be additive, humanizing, and linguistically rich while promoting a rigorous and enriching learning experience that allows students to thrive as learners. Public education should be more than individual attainment but should take into account the public good. The demonstrated outcomes of this school, through the voices of its graduates, is evidence that we can extend Culturally Sustaining Pedagogy (CSP) to consider a "multiculturally sustaining pedagogy" (Granados, 2015b, p. 62) that builds on pluralism and respect for that pluralism, as we continue to refuse to give up on public education.

REFERENCES

Cammarota, J., & Romero, A. (2006). A critically compassionate intellectualism for Latina/o students: Raising voices above the silencing in our schools. *Multicultural Education, 14*(2), 16.

Cervantes-Soon, C., Dorner, L., Palmer, D., Heiman, D., Schwerdtfeger, R., & Choi, J. (2017). Combating inequalities in two-way language immersion programs: Toward critical consciousness in bilingual education spaces. *Review of Research in Education, 27*(41), 403–427.

Collier, V. P., & Thomas, W. P. (2004). The astounding effectiveness of dual language education for all. *NABE Journal of Research and Practice, 2*(1), 1–20.

Delavan, M. G., Valdez, V. E., & Freire, J. A. (2017). Language as whose resource? When global economics usurp the local equity potentials of dual language education. *International Multilingual Research Journal, 11*(2), 86–100.

Dorner, L. M. (2011). US immigrants and two-way immersion policies: The mismatch between district designs and family experiences. In T. W. Fortune, D. Christian, & D. J. Tedick (Eds.), *Immersion education: Practices, policies, possibilities* (pp. 231–250). Clevedon, England: Multilingual Matters.

García, O. (2009). *Bilingual education in the 21st century.* Oxford, England: Wiley-Blackwell.

González, N. (2005). Children in the eye of the storm: Language ideologies in a dual language school. In A. C. Zentella (Ed.), *Building on strength: Language and literacy in Latino families and communities* (pp. 162–174). New York, NY: Teachers College Press.

González, N., & Arnot-Hopffer, E. (2003). Voices of the children: Language and literacy ideologies in a dual language program. In S. Wortham & B. Rymes (Eds.), *Linguistic Anthropology of Education* (pp. 213–243). Westport, CT: Praeger.

Granados, N. R. (2015a). Dual language graduates' participation in bilingual and biliterate communities of practice across time and space. *Bilingual Research Journal, 38*(1), 45–64.

Granados, N. R. (2015b). *Mapping mobilities as transformative practices: Dual language graduates' bilingualism and biliteracy across spatiotemporal dimension* (Unpublished doctoral dissertation). University of Arizona, Tucson, AZ.

Granados, N. R. (2017). Mobilities of language and literacy ideologies: Dual language graduates' bilingualism and biliteracy. *Journal of Literacy Research, 49*(2), 210–239.

López, M. M., & Fránquiz, M. E. (2009). "We teach reading this way because it is the model we've adopted": Asymmetries in language and literacy policies in a Two-Way Immersion programme. *Research Papers in Education, 24*(2), 175–200.

Moll, L. C., & Arnot-Hopffer, E. (2005). Sociocultural competence in teacher education. *Journal of teacher education, 56*(3), 242–247.

Palmer, D. (2010). Race, power, and equity in a multiethnic urban elementary school with a dual-language "strand" program. *Anthropology & Education Quarterly, 41*(1), 94–114.

Palmer, D. K., & Henderson, K. I. (2016). Dual language bilingual education placement practices: Educator discourses about emergent bilingual students in two program types. *International Multilingual Research Journal, 10*(1), 17–30.

Paris, D., & Alim, H. S. (Eds.). (2017). *Culturally sustaining pedagogies: Teaching and learning for justice in a changing world.* New York, NY: Teachers College Press.

Salazar, M. (2013). A humanizing pedagogy: Reinventing the principles and practice of education as a journey toward liberation. *Review of Research in Education, 37*(1), 121–148.

Seidman, I. (2006). *Interviewing as qualitative research: A guide for researchers in education and the social sciences* (3rd ed.). New York, NY: Teachers College Press.

Smith, P. H. (2000). *Community as resource for minority language learning: A case study of Spanish-English dual language schooling* (Unpublished doctoral dissertation). University of Arizona, Tucson, AZ.

Smith, P. H. (2001). Community language resources in dual language schooling. *Bilingual Research Journal, 25,* 375–404.

Smith, P. H. (2002). Ni a pocha va a llegar: Minority language loss and dual language schooling in the US–Mexico borderlands. *Southwest Journal of Linguistics, 21*(1), 165–184.

Smith, P. H., & Arnot-Hopffer, E. (1998). Éxito Bilingüe: Promoting Spanish literacy in a dual language immersion program. *Bilingual Research Journal, 22*(2–4), 261–277.

Smith, P. H., Arnot-Hopffer, E., Carmichael, C. M., Murphy, E., Valle, A., González, N., & Poveda, A. (2002). Raise a child, not a test score: Perspectives on bilingual education at Davis Bilingual Magnet School. *Bilingual Research Journal, 26*(1), 103–121.

Williams, C. (2017, December 28). The intrusion of White families into bilingual schools. *The Atlantic.* Retrieved from www.theatlantic.com/education/archive/2017/12/the-middle-class-takeover-of-bilingual-schools/549278/

CHAPTER 3

A School That ROARS

Lee Gunderson and Reginald D'Silva

Culture is the root of our lives, and love is the most powerful force.

—Mao Jomar Lanot (Vancouver School Board, n.d.-d)

Teenage immigrant students experience life as members of multiple, evolving cultures within an environment that is foreign, and often without the support of others who speak their first language (L1) or are members of their first cultures. Socioeconomic status often defines the parameters within which immigrants can expect success in their new countries. One unfortunate outcome is that, often, they do not succeed (Gunderson, 2008; Gunderson, D'Silva, & Odo, 2012; Odo, D'Silva, & Gunderson, 2012). Our purpose in this chapter is to describe an exceptional school and its programs designed to address diversity and inclusion issues.

IDENTIFYING AN EXCEPTIONAL SCHOOL

We consulted with a local group of experts, the British Columbia ESL Assessment Consortium, on issues related to the identification of exceptional classrooms or schools (see http://eslassess.ca). They viewed issues such as recognition and acceptance of students' first cultures, self-acceptance, development of positive self-image, mutual respect (for everyone), acceptance of exceptionality, including ESL(ELL)/EAL learners, as cornerstones of exceptional school programs. (The accepted term in British Columbia since the 1960s has been *English as an Additional Language* [EAL], although ESL and ELL are often used by individuals in different jurisdictions.) No one mentioned success as measured by achievement tests. Members' views align with a growing consensus that the mission of schools should extend beyond academic achievement in aspiring to prepare students for life, their communities, and to be global citizens (Staff Writer, 2017; Westheimer & Kahne, 2004). "The focus of any curriculum should not simply be on attainment and 're-silience'—the current buzzword—but on producing confident, well-rounded citizens who feel as though they belong and have value in society" (Cosslett, 2017). Based on members' suggestions, we selected a secondary school on the basis of its reported exceptional contributions to diversity and inclusion.

COMMUNITY AND SCHOOL CONTEXT

Sir Charles Tupper Secondary School is located in Vancouver, British Columbia, Canada. "The Vancouver School Board has 18 secondary and 91 elementary schools" (Vancouver School Board, n.d.). It is noted online, "The Vancouver School District is among the most diverse public school systems in Canada with an annual enrolment of approximately 54,000 students in Kindergarten to grade 12" (Vancouver School Board, n.d.-b). In addition, "25% of K-Grade to 12 students, are designated ESL, 60% speak a language other than English at home, 126 languages have been identified in our schools, (and) 7% of elementary and secondary students are special education learners. . . ." While 60% speak a language other than English at home, only 25% are designated as needing ESL services. According to Provincial Ministry of Education policy, students who are deemed to be in need of ESL services can be funded for a period of 5 years, after which they are no longer eligible for funding, and are not designated as ESL (ELL).

Tupper is in a neighborhood called Mount Pleasant, which is located geographically in central Vancouver. It was established in 1959 as an intermediate school. Galloway (2011) notes:

> In 1959 when Tupper opened, it was indeed a facility that was state of the art. It had rooms and programs for laundry and dry cleaning, electricity and electronics, carpentry and millwork, and power mechanics and industrial power.

As demographics changed, Tupper became a secondary school that enrolled students in grades 8 to 12. Galloway (2011) also notes that during the school's early years, the student population was primarily White. Early photographic evidence validates this statement (VSB-Archives-and-Heritage, 2018). In the 1960s and 1970s, the Tupper neighborhood was known for gang activity (Chapman, 2011) and the school was not considered a safe place (Braham, 2017). A member of the ESL Assessment Consortium who was a student at Tupper confirmed that there was gang activity at the school.

Since the 1950s, the demographics of Vancouver have changed rather dramatically as a result of increases in immigration (Historica Canada, n.d.). The number of immigrants from India and Hong Kong, for example, increased dramatically (Gunderson, 2007). The planned return of Hong Kong from the United Kingdom to China resulted in a dramatic increase in immigration that resulted in, among other things, Cantonese-speaking immigrants becoming the largest immigrant group to Vancouver in the mid- to late 1990s (Gunderson,

2007). During the 1980s, the Tupper neighborhood began a process of gentrification as Mount Pleasant changed from an industry-based area to a more residential-based one.

The first author (Lee Gunderson) has conducted long-term research in the Vancouver secondary schools, beginning in the late 1980s (Gunderson, 2000, 2004, 2007; Gunderson & Clarke, 1998). Part of this research included conducting interviews with students and staff in all of Vancouver's high schools from 1995 to 1998, including Tupper, and tracking immigrant students' academic success from their primary years to their graduation (Gunderson, D'Silva, & Odo 2012; Odo, D'Silva, & Gunderson, 2012). Results revealed that Tupper was ranked very low in academic achievement and had a low enrollment of students in academic classes. In addition, its population decreased significantly over the years and there are persistent rumors that the school, presently operating at 60.93% capacity, might be closed (Sherlock, 2015).

Mickleburgh (2003) reported, "The 1,200 students at the east-side school are a microcosm of Vancouver's growing racial diversity, with ethnic Filipinos, Vietnamese, Caucasians, Chinese and Indo-Canadians all well represented." Filipino students had a very high "disappearance" rate from the examinable courses in Tupper (Gunderson, 2007). Examinable courses included math, science, social studies, and English in grade 12, which were required courses for admission to university. The following information is taken from Tupper's 2017 School Plan:

> Sir Charles Tupper has a population of 1013 students. Our school population is ethnically diverse, with home languages that include English, Cantonese, Mandarin, Vietnamese, Arabic, Amharic, Farsi, and Tagalog. Sixteen percent of our students are enrolled in ELL classes, of whom approximately seventy are International Students. We also have a cohort of 34 Aboriginal students representing three percent of our total student population. In addition to a broad array of regular programming in the core academic and elective subject areas, Tupper offers a number of district educational programs for students with distinctly identified learning needs. These programs include:
>
> • The Tupper Mini School, providing student access to accelerated and enriched core academic studies for 150 students from grade 8 through 12.
>
> • The Learning Support Program for a cohort of fifteen grade 8 and 9 students with learning disabilities and an IEP which supports their learning by providing access to an adapted curriculum in a supportive setting.
>
> • The Life Skills Program for thirty grade 8 through 12 students from across the district with moderate to severe cognitive difficulties, or autism.
>
> • The ELL Literacy Program for fifteen refugee students from across the district in grades 8 through 12. Each student works on building his/her English language skills to then successfully transition into ELL studies. Students are also provided many opportunities to help learn about life as a Canadian citizen.

- The ELL Intensive English Enrichment and Development (I-LEAD) Program for fifteen ELL students who are 15 years or older who have experienced little success in school and continue to struggle with English acquisition.
- The Tupper Tech Program focusing on trades based careers and pre-apprenticeship training for 20 grade 12 students from across the district.
- The Cook Training ACE-IT Program focusing on food services and pre-apprenticeship chef training for twelve grade 12 students from across the district
- The Tupper Alternate Program (TAP) which is located on-campus for fifteen grade 8 and 9 students who require support for social-emotional, behavioral or mental health reasons. (Vancouver-School-Board, 2017)

Students in the Mini School are integrated into the school population. They take separate English, math, and science classes, but do take the same classes for electives and other subject areas as other students. There is also a program to support and help teen mothers to graduate; these young women are housed in a separate building (Bellett, 2016; Vancouver School Board, n.d.-e). There is also another program that helps support students from more economically stressed families (Bellett, 2015). Overall, the number of special programs is impressive.

Immigrant and refugee students come to Tupper from different school catchment areas in programs referred to as District Programs. Tupper's ELL programs are designed to "maximize the students' exposure to academic English in order to ensure that they are adequately prepared for senior English courses, for courses that require a high level of English ability, and for success on the examinations that are needed for graduation and for admission to post-secondary schools" (Vancouver-School-Board, n.d.-c).

Tupper has seven specialist ELL teachers. As noted earlier 16% of the school population is designated as needing ESL services. We will describe the significant efforts made at Tupper to improve the teaching and learning of literacy for immigrant students and to establish an inclusive environment for all, regardless of background. Members of the Tupper community urged school personnel to develop a code of conduct for the school population.

A TRAGEDY AT TUPPER

Mickleburgh (2003) reported on news concerning the death of a Filipino student:

Mao Jomar Lanot, 17, described by the school principal as "a bright light in the classroom [with] a sparkle in his eye", was savagely beaten to death Friday night by a gang of youths after he tried to flee across the dark fields of Sir Charles Tupper Secondary School, following an exchange of racial slurs.

The Vancouver School Board (n.d.-d) reported:

"Culture is the root of our lives, and love is the most powerful force." This quote from the notebook of Mao Jomar Lanot features prominently in a 320´ long, 16´ high mural that covers a vast stretch of wall at Tupper Secondary. Lanot was the student killed 13 years ago by gang members around the corner of the building where the mural is now displayed.

Members of the Tupper community have told us that work on the *ROARS* code of conduct preceded the Lanot tragedy, even though the report noted above from the Vancouver School Board disagrees.

SCHOOL ELEMENTS THAT SUPPORT STUDENTS' LEARNING

The acronym *ROARS* stands for Respect, Ownership, Attitude, Responsibility, and Safety. ROARS was developed by members of the community, including students, teachers, administrators, parents, and a school planning council (Vancouver School Board, n.d.-a).

According to the Vancouver School Board (n.d.-a):

> The Tupper Code of Conduct promotes the values expressed in the British Columbia Human Rights Code respecting the rights of all individuals in accordance with the law—prohibiting discrimination based on race, colour, ancestry, place of origin, religion, marital status, family status, physical or mental disability, sex or sexual orientation in respect to discriminatory publication and discrimination in accommodation, service and facility in the school environment.

The Tupper code of conduct is detailed in a matrix that highlights Respect, Ownership, Attitude, Responsibility, and Safety across six contexts: all settings, classrooms, halls, cafeteria, off campus, auditorium, and online.

As illustrated in Figure 3.1, Respect (We care for self, each other, and community) is broken down into components in the six contexts. In the area of "all settings," it is stated in the code that "We will: Respect cultural, religious and individual differences; Communicate with others in a positive and supportive way; excluding putdowns and language of a racist, sexist or homophobic nature, and; Reduce, Re-Use and Re-Cycle." The publication of a code of conduct does not, of course, automatically bring about change. However, Tupper personnel also become active agents of the code. The statement also notes that:

> In order for ROARS to work, the adults in the school role model appropriate behaviours and help the students to make the connection between the individual and the community. Students might point out that an adult is not doing something Roarsy. This is allowed as it is a teachable moment and an opportunity to model ownership. (Vancouver School Board, n.d.-a)

In addition, applying the code of conduct is positively reinforced:

> TLC stands for Tupper Leadership Card. Anytime staff catch a student or staff member doing something roarsy, they can get rewarded with a TLC. Roarsy recipients can either display them proudly in their lockers or their bedroom walls or they can put them in a clear plastic TLC draw box in the office. Every Friday at the end of the last block there is a draw and the winner gets a prize (anything from a t-shirt to a ski pass). (Vancouver School Board, n.d.-a)

There are published consequences for individuals who may be judged to demonstrate behavior in opposition to the code.

A Unified Commitment to ROARS

Tupper is an exciting place to visit and its worn nature is a testament to its age and use. ROARS posters are displayed everywhere. The foyer just inside the main entrance is lined with typical high-school showcases filled with awards, medals, plaques, trophies, and lists of winners of various awards and scholarships. One bulletin board has posters dedicated to the LGBTQ community with pictures of notable representatives. When one visits the main office, the TLC box is full of cards demonstrating that ROARS is an active feature of the school. Tupper's commitment is strikingly demonstrated in a 320′ long, 16′ high mural (Vancouver School Board, n.d.-d). The mural is dramatic evidence of the commitment to ROARS. Inside the school there is additional solid evidence of this commitment.

The School Environment

The ROARS Matrix is both displayed and described in detail on a poster on a bulletin board in a prominent location in the library. The library is a hub of activity, especially during the lunch hour. In addition to being a high school library in the conventional sense, it appears also to be a social space for the student community. We observed groups of students engaged in conversations seated around tables, while computer terminals in the central area were occupied by others browsing the Internet.

A group of eight boys was seated at a table playing a card game. The game involved cards with pictures on them and the objective seemed to be to remember who had which cards and to claim them by correctly naming the individual and the card. When one individual began to speak in Cantonese, he was strongly reprimanded by another, "No cheating; English, English." It was the only incident we saw where the speaking of a L1 was considered a negative feature of communication. It was cheating in this case because some of the players did not speak Cantonese and could not understand what he was saying.

continued on page 41

Figure 3.1. Sir Charles Tupper Secondary School Code of Conduct

All Settings	Classroom	Halls/Cafeteria	Off Campus	Auditorium	Online
RESPECT—We care for self, each other, and community					
We will: • Respect cultural, religious and individual differences; • Communicate with others in a positive and supportive way; excluding putdowns and language of a racist, sexist or homophobic nature; • Reduce, Re-Use and Re-Cycle.	We will: • Encourage mutual respect by listening when others speak, including announcements made on the P.A.; • Respect each others' work and classroom materials; • Turn off cell phones/devices	We will: • Be courteous towards cafeteria staff; • Clean up after ourselves and others; • Be quiet in halls while classes are in session.	We will: • Stay off of our neighbour's property; • Keep the healing garden clean; • Give our seats to seniors and pregnant women on Public Transit.	We will: • Give full attention to the performance; • Respect the "no food or drink" rule; • Respect the "no in/out privileges" rule.	We will: • Use appropriate and respectful language on-line; • Post appropriate items on sites; • Respect site rules.
OWNERSHIP—We are accountable and take pride in positive behaviour and actions.					
We will: • Take ownership of our behaviour and accept the consequences of our actions; • Make amends for mistakes by apologizing, repairing or replacing; • Report any unsafe, dangerous, or destructive behaviour; • Offer help to those in need.	We will: • Do our own work and our own share of group work; • Take ownership of our learning by studying for tests and completing homework on time; • Attend Friday school when we have been late to class twice.	We will: • Use the recycling containers and garbage cans provided; • Make healthy choices; • Take the amount of food we plan on eating.	We will: • Behave in other schools the way we are expected to behave at Tupper; • Be roarsy, realizing that Roars is a philosophy that can be applied n all aspects of our lives; • Conduct ourselves with dignity and integrity.	We will: • Remove hats; • Turn off cell phones, pagers, and MP3 devices; • Ask others to honour our expectations of appropriate audience etiquette.	We will: • Use school computers for school related research only; • Remember that plagiarism is illegal; • Report internet bullying and other unsafe internet activities.

ATTITUDE—We are courteous and committed to doing our best

We will:	We will:	We will:	We will:	We will:	We will:
• Be well mannered, compassionate and helpful; • Be inclusive of existing community members as well as visitors and newcomers; • Promote a positive attitude towards life and remind ourselves that a change in perspective can make a difference.	• Work together to create a positive classroom environment; • Be open to explore new concepts and ideas; • Remember that learning can be fun.	• Wait our turn; • Use inside voices; • Use vending machines before and after school, at break and at lunch only.	• Be gracious, courteous and friendly with our neighbours; • Keep our voices at appropriate levels.	• Be active listeners; • Recognize and show appreciation for the efforts of others by applauding and by asking questions when appropriate; • Support the performers by not calling out their names.	• Sign off our school accounts and sign off for those who have forgotten to; • Remember that the internet is a public forum and that what we do and say creates a permanent record; • Use Facebook/MSN and other sites as a forum for positive interactions with others.

RESPONSIBILITY—We know and meet personal, classroom, and community expectations.

We will:	We will:	We will:	We will:	We will:	We will:
• Return what we borrow and treat others' belongings as if they were our own; • Honour our commitments and manage our time wisely; • Use the student agenda to keep track of our commitments.	• Come to class prepared, on time and ready to learn; • Make up missed assignments and tests at our teacher's convenience; • Be committed to producing quality work and expect to re-submit any assignments that do not meet expectations.	• Keep aisles, doorways and stairways clear, especially in high traffic areas; • Clean up after ourselves; • Eat in designated areas.	• Be good citizens: positive ambassadors of Tupper; • Report vandalism; • Report bullying and unsafe behaviour.	• Refrain from discussing performance or presentation while in progress; • Recycle programs; • Use the aisles to change seats rather than climbing over chairs.	• Abstain from internet bullying and encourage others to do the same; • Take responsibility for what we do and say on-line, and be mindful that feelings can be hurt over the internet; • Prioritize time spent on the computer, making sure that it does not interfere with our success.

SAFETY—We ensure the health and well-being of all.				
We will:	**We will:**	**We will:**	**We will:**	**We will:**
• Follow directions from all staff members; • Communicate with the adults in our lives when we encounter difficult situations and/or problems; • Acknowledge that emotional safety is just as important as physical safety; • Resolve conflicts safely, in non-violent ways.	• Be aware of emergency routines and exits; • Keep classrooms clean and graffiti free; • Pass objects hand to hand rather than throwing them across the room; • Use athletic equipment and tools in appropriate areas and safely.	• Watch where we are going and respect personal space; • Be courteous when navigating through the hallways; • Keep our locker combinations to ourselves.	• Use the buddy system; • Be safe emotionally, physically and sexually; • Respect posted speed limits, paying close attention to school zones.	• Enter and exit in an orderly manner; • Sit in assigned areas with staff; • Protect the emotional safety of performers by acknowledging the risks they are taking and supporting their courage.	• Keep personal information to ourselves and use safety settings; • Be cautious of downloads; • Only add those we know to our facebook accounts; • Keep food and drink away from computers.

Source: go.vsb.bc.ca/schools/tupper/About/Documents/Roars%20Tupper%20Code%20of%20Conduct%202016-17.pdf

Bulletin boards, posters, and fact sheets covered the walls and areas along the walls. Pinned on the walls at a number of places were witticisms such as "Do bald men actually get hairline fractures?" The librarian told us he collected these items from the Internet. We heard conversations in Japanese, Tagalog, Mandarin, and Cantonese.

Secondary school hallways during transition times between classes are often nearly impassable because of the hundreds of students navigating to their next classes. Tupper hallways seem more manageable. The first author makes this claim based on his observations in all of the secondary schools in Vancouver and many across Canada and the United States over 5 decades.

We overheard a student enthusiastically report to a teacher that she had been admitted to a local university. We met an Arabic-speaking Settlement Worker in Schools (SWIS) speaking in Arabic with a refugee student. The worker reported she was taking the student to the hospital. We also met the student, who was a refugee. SWIS workers are supported by federal funds. The program is valued by all of the local school districts. It provides individuals knowledgeable about first cultures who are bilingual and can communicate with individuals at both home and school. The number of SWIS workers is limited by budget considerations; however, individual districts in the area have as many as 25. These workers are expert links between the home and school.

On one of our visits, the school was holding a Pink Shirt Day. Hallways were filled with posters describing the day. One noted:

> The original Pink Shirt Day was organized by David Shepherd and Travis Price of Berwick, Nova Scotia, who in 2007 bought and distributed 50 pink shirts after male Grade 9 student, Charles McNeill, was bullied for wearing a pink shirt during the first day of school. (BCTF, n.d.)

A more complete history can be found at www.cbc.ca/news/canada/bullied-student-tickled-pink-by-schoolmates-t-shirt-campaign-1.682221. The British Columbia Teachers' Federation also has an informative webpage containing lesson plans, posters, and other resources at bctf.ca/SocialJustice.aspx?. There were a number of related posters displayed in the school hallways downloaded from www.ourcityofcolours.com/. These posters feature people of color and bilingual messages. It is noted on the website the purpose is to present "a series of 16 multilingual posters in Chinese, Punjabi, Farsi, Spanish, Russian, French, Filipino, and Vietnamese in order to increase visibility for LGBTQ people in diverse linguistic and cultural communities" (Our City of Colours, n.d.). Figure 3.2 is one of the many posters displayed in the school hallways. Its English, "Study breaks are more fun with my boyfriend," is accompanied by the same text written in Punjabi.

Classroom Teaching and Learning

We visited a District ELL Literacy class, meaning students from outside Tupper's catchment area were enrolled, designed for students from backgrounds with interrupted or no schooling in their home countries (referred to as a late-to-literacy class). There were 11 students from refugee families who spoke four different languages (Spanish, Arabic, Oromo, and Turkish). They were all beginning English speakers, of varying ages (14 to 18), who had no L1 school literacy backgrounds. Two were Arabic-speaking siblings. They had no or interrupted schooling in their home countries. The teacher informed us that one of the main goals was to help students develop the English skills necessary to enroll in regular ELL courses. She was their teacher for four of their six scheduled classes each day.

Word walls, posters, and anchor charts filled the walls of the classroom. A chart with sentence stems such as "May I go . . ." and "Can you help me?" was prominently placed in the center of the classroom on the whiteboard to help learners with basic everyday English language structures. It was clear that the teacher had created a literacy-rich environment for these students.

The beginning of the class involved RAZ-Kids reading (many aloud) their interactive reading texts (see www.raz-kids.com) on iPad Minis. As the reader reads an ebook, the individual words are underlined and the program produces the oral equivalents. The reading is word by word and somewhat monotone. While class members were reading independently, the teacher met with individual students for reading one-on-one activities and asked questions about their reading. We circulated and listened to individual students read aloud. "Braille," "Baseball," and "The Human Body" were among the texts that were being read. The teacher concluded that reading with a human being is superior to reading with a computer program. The reading level of these students, however, did not allow them to serve as buddy readers. Reginald D'Silva, the second author, understands Arabic; conversations between a Moroccan and a Syrian student included the questions: "Who are they?" and "Why are they here?" (referring to the two authors). We concluded that these comments might have been related to the students' perceptions of strangers as potentially being government agents of some kind.

At the end of the class, we participated in a discussion of ROARS conducted in a circle of chairs. The activity began with the participants, including us, introducing themselves and indicating the languages they speak. The ROARS discussion was random in that students were selected from a group of colored sticks with their names written on them. Each student was asked about what ROARS meant to them and to the school. The majority of the responses were things like "safety" and "no fighting." The teacher was able to extend the discussion to talk about "mutual respect" and "understanding." On occasion, a student would laugh at another's response and the teacher interrupted to say, "Are you laughing at her English? That's not Roarsy." Most often, the student would apologize. The session demonstrated the teacher's dedication to the concepts in ROARS and to the students' expanding

Figure 3.2. Diversity Poster

ਪੜ੍ਹਾਈ ਤੋਂ ਛੁੱਟੀ ਆਪਣੇ ਬੋਆਏਫਰੈਂਡ
ਨਾਲ ਜ਼ਿਆਦਾ ਮਨਪਰਚਾਵਾ ਹੈ

**Study breaks are more fun
with my boyfriend**

knowledge and understanding of its related concepts and vocabulary. There were a number of interactions in Arabic as students attempted to communicate English statements about ROARS and needed help—evidence that use of the L1 was not viewed negatively by teachers. There was a focus on both the ROARS concept and oral English language development.

In addition to this course, there is also a District ELL Intensive English Enrichment and Development (I-Lead) class for students 15 years or older who have experienced little success in school and continue to struggle with English acquisition. This population represents students who are in serious potential jeopardy because, by law, at age 19 they are not eligible to attend high school. Programs to assist them after 19 are extremely limited and their potential to acquire employment and to succeed in society is limited by their English ability and their school records.

ROARS and Whole-School Instruction

The total commitment of teachers, administrators, and students to ROARS and their focus on and belief in ROARS were brilliantly exemplified by a half-day schedule of activities designed to explore and reinforce its concepts. We participated in the February 28, 2018, Pink Shirt Day and ROARS activities that included a lesson taught by all of the Tupper teachers and a session in which drama was used to reinforce and demonstrate the goals and learning outlined by the lesson plan developed by Tanya Baron, the English language learners (English as a Second Language) department head, in collaboration with the school's drama teacher and school administrators. As a knowledgeable ELL teacher, Baron designed activities that engaged students in various literacy practices such as formulating questions, recording responses, recording "powerful phrases," writing assessments of how ROARS was represented in the scenarios, and oral language development.

The goals of the day's activities, taken from the common lesson plan, were to "reinforce a high standard of behavior and human interaction, according to our ROARS code of conduct, equip students to be more than just bystanders in unROARSy situations, and expand student awareness around what real ownership looks like" (Baron, 2018, p. 1). The lesson plan begins with an "icebreaker," including items such as "the kindest thing you said to someone this week, what you said the last time someone was unROARSy near you, and how you showed ownership this week." We observed a class involved in this icebreaker and students were enthusiastic and appeared to enjoy participating.

Students are asked to form groups and to act out scenarios such as: "You witness a student in the cafeteria giving a Hitler salute. Their friends are videotaping it. What do you do?" The scenarios include four action alternatives and an open-ended "other" category. The scenario ends with the students questioning one another about what they would do and to identify "Where is ROARS in this situation?" Discussions occasionally included the use of students' L1. The lesson ends with the teacher developing a dictionary of upstander phrases. As groups reported about their scenarios, the teacher asked questions such as "What could someone say here?" The end of the lesson included the teacher naming "ROARSy behaviors they saw" and a final question: "Do you take a risk and speak up? How can you get support?"

One extraordinary feature of this lesson plan is that it was taught by all of the teachers in the school, adapted to the needs and abilities of their classes. However, even more extraordinary is that the goals of the lesson were highlighted and reinforced by a lesson and dramatizations that took place with half of the school population at a time.

The Plays

Some 400 to 500 students came to the session we observed. The school drama teacher "taught," or, more accurately, guided the activities. She began by thanking the students who had worn pink and noted that the activities would all be related to "antibullying day." She reviewed ROARS issues and spoke of respect as important, both for others and for oneself. She discussed the notion of bystanders and how they react to a difficult situation, and reinforced the notion of upstanders. She described the role of bystanders in the Holocaust. An example of prejudice by

surface-level difference— the Sneetches (Seuss, 1953)—was described and discussed, and then the first play was introduced.

Two students read from the Seuss book and six actors, three with large paper
stars attached to the fronts of their shirts and three without, acted out the narrative. The narrative begins with "Now, the Star-Belly Sneetches had bellies with
stars. The Plain-Belly Sneetches had none upon thars" (Seuss, 1953, p. 3). Those
with stars feel superior and do not allow those without stars to participate with
them. A character named "Sylvester McMonkey McBean" enters with a machine
that adds or eliminates stars. After a number of interactions with and without
stars, the narrative ends with "That day, all the Sneetches forgot about stars and
whether they had one, or not, upon thars" (p. 21). The conclusion reinforced by
the story and the drama teacher is that surface-level differences are not important
in judging character. She recounted stories from her life in which she learned from
her mother the damage that ethnic-based jokes can do.

The second play presented was based on experiences of the student actors
themselves—incidents that took place at Tupper. Situations were described in
which, for example, a Sikh student was asked whether or not he had a bomb in his
backpack, a straight student was asked if he was gay because he liked musicals, a
student was repeatedly asked if he was a Filipino, a student was identified as too
skinny, and an Asian student's lunch was questioned.

In each case, five or six students portrayed the incident. After the portrayal,
the actors stopped action by freezing in place. The individual who experienced the
incident in real life walked to the front of the stage and addressed the audience, describing his or her views and asking how he or she should address or confront the
issue in a positive manner. For instance, the student who identified as Sikh spoke
during the stop-action sequence about the misconceptions related to him being
a Muslim and, therefore, being a terrorist. He noted that Sikhs were not Muslims
and that Muslims were not all terrorists. He questioned how he could inform his
school friends of their misconceptions in a positive way.

The drama teacher described the difficulty of confronting issues, of moving
from being a bystander to being an upstander. At the end of each dramatic presentation there was enthusiastic applause. It was clear to us that students were
aware of and applied the ROARS code of conduct as it related to behavior in the
auditorium (see Figure 3.1). Indeed, there was no talking we could hear about the
presentation as it was occurring, as noted in the ROARS code: "Be active listeners,
recognize and show appreciation for the efforts of others by applauding and by
asking questions when appropriate, and support the performers by not calling out
their names." There were 400 to 500 students in the audience who did not know
we were there and in the reduced light of the auditorium we could not see any
monitoring of their behavior by teachers or other adults.

The 1-hour session concluded with everyone in the audience doing the
Macarena, led by the drama teacher. We were amazed because it was not chaotic.
Everyone participated and the dance moves were made in amazing unison. The

first author (Lee Gunderson) has, since the mid-1960s, participated in and observed many school assemblies, but this was the first time he has observed the integration of the goals and objectives of a lesson taught by every teacher in a secondary school with the activities of an assembly.

OUTCOMES

Teachers we spoke to were enthusiastic about the outcomes of Tupper's programs. One long-time teacher approached us in a hallway and, after introducing herself and inquiring about who we were, strongly supported the view that ROARS has resulted in major changes in students' behavior and the way they communicate with and respect one another. We encountered the principal escorting a central office district administrator to the ROARS assembly and they both agreed that ROARS and teachers' commitment to it had improved teaching and learning in many different ways. They noted that achievement, including literacy achievement, had risen as a result of teachers' focus on the code of conduct. The Fraser Institute reported that Tupper's graduation rate was 96%. This is an admirable outcome considering it is higher than graduation rates reported for Canada and the United States (OECD, n.d.).

One testament to Tupper's success success is that a non-English-speaking refugee student from Afghanistan, Somaya Amiri, won a prestigious scholarship from the Federal Government of Canada of $100,000 after 4 years of study. "'She was so anxious to learn and she was absolutely ravenous for more,'" said ELL teacher Sally Ringdahl (Rossi, 2015). Rossi reported that, although Amiri's family lived in a different school catchment area, "school board staff suggested Amiri attend Tupper, on East 24th Avenue near Fraser Street, which provides extra supports to newcomers."

DISCUSSION AND CONCLUSIONS

We are convinced that reports that employ statistics often mask significant underlying differences in the human beings and institutions they attempt to represent: "To be meaningful, statistics must be disaggregated to reveal underlying instances of disturbing inequities" (Gunderson, 2008, p. 185). We have concluded, for instance, that there is an underlying student mobility that renders statistical analyses inaccurate and unreliable (D'Silva & Gunderson, 2014). After exploring Sir Charles Tupper Secondary School, its population, and the statistics associated with it, we are more convinced that statistics—for instance, means and standard deviations—are neither necessarily reliable nor valid.

The mean income level of families in a neighborhood surrounding a school is often used to judge the socioeconomic status of students in the school. Socioeconomic status in many studies is positively correlated to academic achievement (e.g., Gunderson, 2007). The mean family income of the Tupper neighborhood ranks it ninth out of Vancouver's 18 secondary schools. That means it's about average. The difficulty is that this statistic does not take into account the number of district programs offered at Tupper—programs that enroll high numbers of students from economically stressed families from across Vancouver. Tupper is not so average in this regard.

The number (or percentage) of ESL (ELL) students in a school is often used to assess their influence on the achievement of a school, often in a negative way. Jiménez and Rose (2008) argue that "ESL students who succeed in school are no longer counted as ESL and their scores are not reflected in ESL reports" and "This tends to make it seem like there is never any measurable ESL achievement" (p. 186). In British Columbia, ESL students are recognized for 5 years, during which districts receive extra financial support, and after 5 years ESL students are no longer eligible for support and are not counted as ESL. It is not clear to us what effect this might have on the assessment of a school's achievement. The Fraser Institute in Canada collects school data and produces what they call a *Report Card on Schools*. The institute's 2017 report maintains that Tupper's ESL population is 8.5% (Cowley & Easton, 2017), while school-based personnel report that it is 16%. It is not clear, however, how many students are actually emergent bilinguals. The diversity of the school is underestimated in various ways.

Exceptional School and Exceptional Programs

The Fraser Institute in 2017 ranked Tupper as 142 out of 293 secondary schools in British Columbia (Cowley & Easton, 2017). Tupper seems about average, similar to results based on neighborhood family income levels. However, from 1995 to 2000, Tupper was ranked 243, considerably lower. There has been exceptional growth in this ranking and this should impress those who believe in such metrics.

McMahon (2007) suggests that Tupper's ranking has resulted in its decreasing population because parents have enrolled their children in higher-ranked schools in the district, which is allowed by British Columbia Ministry of Education policy. McMahon notes that "Plunging registration due to cross-boundary enrollment comes despite the rise in the number of school-age children in the area." These rankings mask the extraordinary exceptionality of Tupper, its programs, its, staff, and its students.

The Canada Census in 2016 reported that the median income in Tupper's neighborhood was $61,350. Median income in Vancouver varied from $48,383 to $109,452 (Global News, 2016), with Tupper ranking ninth out of 18 school neighborhoods. The school itself is located in a block surrounded by million-dollar single-family homes. Tupper's statistics, however, are somewhat misleading because many of its students do not live in the neighborhood, but they come to Tupper for special educational programs.

The Tupper Code of Conduct

We have painted a glowing picture of the implementation of a code of conduct and immigrant support programs at Tupper. It would be naïve, however, to assume that schoolwide codes of conduct, such as ROARS, are implemented and sustained without an enormous amount of effort. The entrance to the library, for instance, had a poster saying that "after seeing unRoarsy behavior absolutely no food or drinks allowed in the library." The drama teacher also alluded to having heard "unRoarsy" behavior in the hallways. In discussing excessive discipline and suspensions in schools, sociologists have suggested that "when you are in a very punitive environment, you're getting the message that the school is focusing on crime control and behavior control," resulting in lower student achievement (Adams, 2015). Students may similarly view a pervasive web of behavioral rules as repressive, making a code of conduct a greater challenge to maintain. The focus on "building relationships" (Adams, 2015) through acknowledging and rewarding positive behavior appears to be at the heart of the ROARS philosophy, which has made it possible for Tupper to address diversity and inclusion issues successfully. We did not get a sense that students perceived ROARS as repressive. Many students bring with them cultural backgrounds within which there are sets of expectations related to school and schooling that differ from the expectations in schools such as Tupper. In addition to establishing the importance of respecting the rights of all individuals, prohibiting discrimination based on race, color, ancestry, place of origin, religion, marital status, family status, physical or mental disability, sex or sexual orientation, ROARS provides a cultural template for appropriate school behaviors. Indeed, it gives students a sense of what school-based behaviors are appropriate that may differ from the ones they knew before they entered Canada.

The overall commitment to ROARS as a code of conduct is exceptional in our experience. That a uniform diversity lesson would be taught to all students by all teachers in a school is exceptional. That plays and a lesson would be presented to all students that reflect and reinforce the goals of the uniform lesson is exceptional. That overall teachers are committed to teaching and modeling a code of conduct is exceptional. That a school and its staff are dedicated to teaching and learning about diversity is exceptional. That the head of the ELL department would develop a uniform lesson plan in collaboration with the drama teacher is exceptional. That teachers, as a consequence of the language-based lesson plan, would be simultaneously developing students' language through ROARS is exceptional.

Our basic finding is that entire schools, like individuals or groups of human beings, can be reduced to misleading categories, unless the humanizing activities and programs going on within them are recognized. Tupper is exceptional in that its staff and administration are truly dedicated to diversity, inclusion, its code of conduct, and the protection of human rights. It is noteworthy that the individual who led the design and writing of the Pink Shirt Day is an ELL teacher. The ROARS lesson she designed for all of the students at Tupper develops the concepts in ROARS, but in addition, is based on her language teaching background, knowledge, and expertise. The lesson helps students develop oral and written language, use language to explore concepts, and become critical language and literacy users.

It is clear to us that parents, teachers, administrators, policymakers, researchers, and other interested individuals want the best for students. It is also abundantly clear that the meaning of the term *best* varies from individual to individual, group to group, and community to community. Differing beliefs about what is best often result in vituperative public discourse. Differences in views of what constitutes "the best" also affect broadly what is judged to be exceptional. Tupper is an exceptional school as a result of the views of the members of its communities concerning standards of behavior, diversity, inclusion, and the importance of language as the framework within which such issues are integrated. Its model may have important implications for other schools and their communities.

REFERENCES

Adams, J. M. (2015). Study: Suspensions harm "well-behaved" kids. *EdSource*. Retrieved from ed-source.org/2015/study-suspensions-harm-well-behaved-kids/72501

Baron, T. (2018). *Diversity day February 28, 2018: Lesson plan: Where is ROARS in this moment?* Sir Charles Secondary School, Vancouver, British Columbia.

BCTF. (n.d.). *British Columbia Teachers' Federation*. Retrieved from bctf.ca/DayofPink/

Bellett, G. (2015, December 21). Adopt-a-school: Charlie's closet more than a humble storeroom. *Vancouver Sun*. Retrieved from.vancouversun.com/adopt+school+charlie+closet+more+than+humble+storeroom/11605835/story.html

Bellett, G. (2016, November 28). Program at Sir Charles Tupper secondary school helps teen parents graduate. *Vancouver Sun*. Retrieved from vancouversun.com/news/local-news/adopt-a-school-program-at-sir-charles-tupper-helps-teen-parents-graduate

Braham, D. (2017). Teacher Daryl Mutz's legacy lives on in his students and his bequests. *Vancouver Sun*. Retrieved from vancouversun.com/opinion/columnists/daphne-bramham-teacher-daryl-mutzs-legacy-lives-on-in-his-students-and-his-bequests

Chapman, A. (2011). Gangs of Vancouver. *Vancouver Courier*. Retrieved from www.vancourier.com/news/gangs-of-vancouver-1.2374033

Cosslett, R. L. (2017, June 12). Schools don't prepare children for life. Here's the education they really need. *The Guardian: International Edition*. Retrieved from www.theguardian.com/commentisfree/2017/jun/12/schools-children-education-coding-toilet-unblocking-rote-learning

Cowley, P., & Easton, S. (2017). *Report card on British Columbia's secondary schools 2017*. Vancouver, Canada: Fraser Institute.

D'Silva, R., & Gunderson, L. (2014). Teaching to kinetic diversity: Multicultural Canadian classrooms in the 21st century. *Education Canada*. Retrieved from www.cea-ace.ca/education-canada/article/teaching-kinetic-diversity

Galloway, G. (2011). Tupper history—1959–2009. Retrieved from go.vsb.bc.ca/schools/tupper/About/history/Pages/default.aspx

Global-News. (2016). Income by postal code. *Global News*. Retrieved from globalnews.ca/news/370804/income-by-postal-code/

Gunderson, L. (2000). Voices of the teenage diasporas. *Journal of Adolescent and Adult Literacy, 43*, 692–706.

Gunderson, L. (2004). The language, literacy, achievement, and social consequences of English-only programs for immigrant students. In J. Hoffman & D. Schallert (Eds.), *National reading conference yearbook* (pp. 1–27). Milwaukee, WI: National Reading Conference.

Gunderson, L. (2007). *English-only instruction and immigrant students in secondary school: A critical examination.* Mahwah, NJ: Lawrence Erlbaum Associates.

Gunderson, L. (2008). The state of the art of secondary ESL teaching and learning. *Journal of Adolescent and Adult Literacy, 52*(3), 184–188.

Gunderson, L., & Clarke, D. C. (1998). An exploration of the relationship between ESL students' backgrounds and their English and academic achievement. In T. Shanahan & F. V. Rodriguez-Brown (Eds.), *Yearbook of the National Reading Conference 47* (pp. 264–273). Chicago, IL: National Reading Conference.

Gunderson, L., D'Silva, R., & Odo, D. M. (2012). Immigrant students navigating Canadian schools: A longitudinal view. *TESL Canada Journal, 29*(6), 142–156.

Historica Canada. (n.d.). Vietnamese Canadians. *The Canadian Encyclopedia.* Retrieved from www.thecanadianencyclopedia.ca/en/article/vietnamese/

Jiménez, R. T., & Rose, B. C. (2008). English language learners. In S. Mathison & E. W. Ross (Eds.), *Battleground schools* (pp. 228–234). Westport, CT: Greenwood Press.

McMahon, R. (2007, February 14). Student exodus threatens Eastside schools. *The Georgia Straight.* Retrieved from www.straight.com/article-70975/student-exodus-threatens-east-side-schools

Mickelburgh, R. (2003, December 2). Students mourn death of "bright light." *The Globe and Mail.* Retrieved from www.theglobeandmail.com/news/national/students-mourn-death-of-bright-light/article1170009/

Odo, D.M., D'Silva, R., & Gunderson, L. (2012). High school may not be enough: An investigation of Asian students' eligibility for post-secondary education. *Canadian Journal of Education, 35*(2), 249–267.

OECD. (n.d.). *OECD Better Life Index.* Retrieved from www.oecdbetterlifeindex.org/topics/education/

Our City of Colours. (n.d.). Posters. *Our City of Colours.* Retrieved from www.ourcityofcolours.com/page/posters/

Rossi, C. (2015). Sir Charles Tupper student wins scholarship: Somaya Amiri, a refugee from Afghanistan, overcame remarkable odds. *Vancouver Courier.* Retrieved from www.vancourier.com/news/sir-charles-tupper-student-wins-scholarship-1.1769006

Seuss, Dr. (1953). *Sneetches and other stories.* New York, NY: Random House.

Sherlock, T. (2015, June 9). Vancouver's lowest capacity schools. *Vancouver Sun.* Retrieved from www.vancouversun.com/Vancouver-lowest-capacity-schools/11122394/story.html

Staff Writer. (2017). Academic achievement isn't the only mission. *Kappan Magazine Supplement—September 2017.* Retrieved from pdkpoll.org/assets/downloads/PDKnational_poll_2017.pdf

Vancouver School Board. (2017). School plan for Sir Charles Tupper: Year 3. Retrieved from www.vsb.bc.ca/sites/default/files/school-files/03939017.pdf

Vancouver School Board. (n.d.). Our schools. *Vancouver School Board.* Retrieved from intered.vsb.bc.ca/schools

Vancouver School Board. (n.d.-a). Code of conduct—ROARS. *Vancouver School Board.* Retrieved from go.vsb.bc.ca/schools/tupper/About/Pages/Code-of-Conduct.aspx

Vancouver School Board. (n.d.-b). Our district. *Vancouver School Board.* Retrieved from www.vsb.bc.ca/about-vsb

Vancouver School Board. (n.d.-c). Sir Charles Tupper Secondary School. *Vancouver School Board.* Retrieved from go.vsb.bc.ca/schools/tupper/departments/ell/Pages/default.aspx

Vancouver School Board. (n.d.-d). Tupper mural reflects the evolution of a neighbourhood. *Vancouver School Board.* Retrieved from www.vsb.bc.ca/district-news/tupper-mural-reflects-evolution-neighbourhood

Vancouver School Board. (n.d.-e). Tupper young parent program (TYPS). *Vancouver School Board.* Retrieved from go.vsb.bc.ca/schools/tupper/Programs/young%20parent/Pages/default.aspx

VSB Archives and Heritage. (2018). Sir Charles Tupper. *VSB Archives & Heritage.* Retrieved from blogs. vsb.bc.ca/heritage/archives/secondary-schools/sir-charles-tupper/

Westheimer, J., & Kahne, J. (2004). "Good" citizen: Political choices and pedagogical goals. *Political Science & Politics, 38*(2).

PART II

HUMANIZING SCHOOLS THROUGH CAREGIVER AND COMMUNITY COLLABORATION

We need to help students and parents cherish and preserve the ethnic and cultural diversity that nourishes and strengthens this community—and this nation.

—Cesar Chavez

CHAPTER 4

Humanizing Education

Teachers and Caregivers Collaborate for Culturally Responsive Literacy Learning

Patricia Ruggiano Schmidt

It's 2:40 P.M. at the Syracuse Academy of Science Charter School (SASCS), a public nonprofit school that serves students from several economically stressed urban neighborhoods in Syracuse, New York. Around the classroom table sit six teachers and five family members at a first meeting to discuss the implementation of culturally responsive teaching and learning (CRTL). The children are attending music, art, or physical education classes, thus allowing these scheduled monthly grade-level sessions. CRTL is a new concept for teachers and family members, so "ice-breaking" introductions and snacks are offered.

As the facilitator of these sessions, I begin by introducing myself and tell why my parents gave me the name Patricia. The next person continues the game. The meeting formality subsides and is replaced with laughter and engagement. Next, I explain the purpose of the meeting and invite all to join me in talking about their language and cultural origins. These introductions soon turn into more serious conversations about race, literacy learning, and parents' visions for their children's education.

One grandparent expresses her wish that the children discuss differences in skin color during class discussions. Her grandchild's parents are European American and African American. She says, "My child needs to feel proud that he is Black!"

A parent questions whether it is okay to speak Spanish at home: "Should we be speaking our language?"

Another parent, recently from Ghana, who speaks several languages including English, asks: "Is it good that my son learns more than one language?"

The next parent questions: "How many cultures are in this classroom?

This was how our parent–teacher meetings for CRTL began. Teachers didn't have answers to many caregivers' questions, and so the conversation offered a unique space to listen and learn. Questions and ideas that emerged prompted teachers to consider issues of skin tone, multilingualism, nations of origin, stereotyping, and families' traditions. Most important, this initial conversation paved the way for continued exchanges between teachers and caregivers that translated to exciting collaborations. Families were recognized for their lesson contributions in ways they had never encountered in schools. This work resulted in authentic teaching/learning relationships that are not traditionally experienced between teachers and caregivers, especially in schools that serve multilingual students.

I have facilitated similar inquiries in many schools in my career as a teacher educator and researcher. In the fall of 2016, I was invited to serve as a consultant to the school to guide conversations related to CRTL. One of the primary thrusts of the SASCS system is to honor and preserve the cultural and linguistic assets of students while also developing English literacy learning. This chapter describes work with teachers and parents as they began planning culturally responsive–sustaining teaching and learning as a priority in the elementary school and how this effort translated to the educational changes during the first year of implementation. I begin the chapter by describing various components of the SASCS system, and in particular, the elementary school where these culturally responsive literacy sessions took place.

SCHOOL AND COMMUNITY CONTEXT

For more than 50 years, I have worked as a literacy teacher in public schools and as a professor of education at colleges and universities. Newly retired, I was delighted to work with an energetic and committed faculty at SASCS. The system was founded in 2003 as a nonprofit, publicly funded, urban education institution and includes elementary, middle, and high schools. A new elementary school was added in the fall of 2017. Seventy-eight percent of SASCS students receive free and reduced-price meals. Fifty percent identify on applications as African American, African, or Black. Thirty percent claim European American or White heritage. Fifteen percent affiliate as Latino, and 5% claim Asian or Native American heritage, many of whom speak languages other than English in their homes. About 15% of the children's families are refugees or immigrants and their children are developing their English literacy, while speaking other languages at home.

Meeting Economic, Financial, and Education Challenges

Most students live in economically stressed communities. Syracuse was once home to manufacturing companies, such as General Electric, Carrier Corporation, and General Motors. These have been replaced with medical centers, technology companies, and expanding colleges and universities. Consequently, the urban population has decreased because of unemployment and low-paying jobs, while those with high incomes fled to suburbia.

Syracuse Academy of Science Charter School's website (www.sascs.org) states its mission: to "provide support, challenges and opportunities for all students, and

. . . instill the necessary skills and knowledge in math, science, and technology to empower students, through high intellectual standards, preparing them for college, career, and citizenship . . . to graduate students who can think critically and creatively, who are committed to a lifetime of learning and civic involvement, and who are conscious of local, global, and environmental issues."

This public charter school system receives $12,000 per-pupil aid from New York State while the local public city school receives $18,000 per student. From the New York State allowance, SASCS pays for rent, supplies, and teacher/staff salaries. The school's finances are audited by the state more often than regular public schools, and student progress is also scrutinized by state officials. SASCS teachers and administrators make less salary than other public school educators and manage with many fewer district office administrators. Contract compensations include the same pension and health benefits that are typical for New York State public school employees.

The SASCS volunteer board of directors includes a diverse group of men and women who work directly with the superintendent, Tolga Hayali, an educator with exceptional energy and dedication. Dr. Hayali earned a doctorate in education leadership, management, and policy from Seton Hall and holds an executive master's degree in public administration from Maxwell School, Syracuse University. His almost instant responses to questions, comments, and concerns have made him a rare, readily available supervisor who is routinely present in all of the schools. The SASCS student population is determined by parent applications. Annually, through a legally mandated lottery system, with state and local officials present, new students are selected in the spring for the following school year. The lottery ensures that students are drawn from the most underserved communities. There are 1,000 students on the waiting list.

I have spent the greatest amount of time at the elementary school. It is a three-story, red-brick structure with new windows, doors, ceilings, and tiled blue and white bright floors. In every classroom, an educationally themed carpet is placed near a smartboard, allowing students to gather for group lessons, games, and brain breaks. Brain breaks occur in classrooms when students appear to need time to refresh during a lesson or seat work. Students gather on the class carpet and follow children's music exercise videos of 3 to 5 minutes. These videos depict children of diverse language and cultural backgrounds.

Classrooms possess new chairs, desks, small-group tables, smartboards, class and teacher computers, Elmo devices, and phones. Walls are adorned with student work, learning tools, college and university banners, and recently added in 2016, laminated Peter's Projection maps of the world (Peter, 1974).

Efficient air conditioning exists throughout the school, something not typical in central New York urban schools. Lush indoor plants occupy hallways. Bulletin boards, created by teachers and students, display children's latest accomplishments, such as "writing about my future," self-portraits, math and science research projects, letters to famous people, and values messages related to kindness, compassion, and citizenship. Finally, the school takes pride in its playgrounds, landscaped gardens, and large greenhouse where vegetables are planted, grown, and distributed.

The SASCS elementary school serves kindergarten through 4th grade. There are three classrooms per grade level, with a maximum of 25 students in each room, guided by two certified elementary teachers, one dually certified in elementary and special education. The "lead" teacher has the major responsibility for classroom planning. She or he also serves as a mentor for the cooperating teacher and earns a higher salary; both learn from their shared experiences. After a year or two, a cooperating teacher may be promoted to lead teacher. Furthermore, faculty have opportunities to move into school leadership positions and administration. The SASCS system rewards those who are committed to the school.

The faculty and staff in the elementary school include full-time art, music, and physical education teachers, a reading and ENL (English as a new language) teacher, two school counselors, a counselor aide, a dean and associate dean of students, two math teaching specialists, a nurse, an office manager, a custodian, and a security officer. All are involved with the 370 children in the school. A visitor is just as likely to see the security officer walking and chatting with students in the hallway as a teacher or dean. Seven men and 40 women work in the school. One Latinx, seven African American women, three African American and Latinx men, four European American men, and 30 European American women make up the school personnel. Most faculty and staff are under 40 years of age, giving the site a youthful enthusiasm not seen in many educational institutions.

Pamela Smith, dean/principal of the school, is a dynamic young woman who was a math teacher in the SASCS middle school for several years before becoming a certified administrator. She possesses endless energy, great management skills, and a delightful sense of humor. Her work ethic encourages a positive learning environment where attentive, well-prepared, and compassionate SASCS educators and staff implement the best practices for teaching and learning.

ELEMENTS THAT ADVANCE STUDENTS' LITERACY AND LANGUAGE LEARNING

School leaders and teachers support the belief that English literacy learning is developed in a system with several essential components: the expanded school day and year; continuous teacher inservice requirements; student–teacher community involvement; family–school communication; student academic and social recognition; student emotional, social, and academic support; and cultural and language understanding.

Expanded School Day and Year. An expanded school day of 8 hours for students and 9 hours for teachers and a school year from mid-August to the end of June mean that students have more exposure to academic literacies and languages. Monthly meetings within the school day analyze student academic progress to ensure that students receive individualized teaching assistance. Also, regular staff meetings discuss students' social–emotional needs.

Teacher Education and Support. Teachers are prepared to work with cultural-ly and linguistically diverse groups of children. They are required to attend inser-vice workshops regarding classroom teaching and learning during the first 2 weeks in August and throughout the school year. These daily institutes may include data collection and interpretation, students' social–emotional behaviors, teacher be-haviors and practices, team building, lesson planning, learning theory, language learning, specific content areas, and in 2016, culturally responsive teaching and learning. Teachers also may receive tuition assistance for master's, Certificate of Advanced Study, or doctorate degrees.

Home Visits. Home visits are written into each teacher's contract, and in pairs, teachers are expected to visit at least four student homes per month, beginning in September. The visits are scheduled according to parent convenience and the purpose is social. There is no agenda, just opportunities for teachers and families to learn from one another. Parents are free to ask questions or initiate comments about their children; teachers may talk about themselves and their families and interests. Most parents welcome these visits, though some prefer to meet at neu-tral sites, such as the local donut or fast-food site. These experiences help teachers become familiar with homes, neighborhoods, and family dynamics, so they can better understand their students and make connections between students' prior knowledge and the curriculum.

Field Trips. Another beneficial element of this school is monthly grade-level fieldtrips. Children are transported by the SASCS bus to science and art muse-ums, local farms and businesses, musical performances, recreation centers, and other educational venues. These events allow children and teachers to have shared community experiences that stimulate writing, reading, listening, and discussion, further enhancing English literacy learning.

School Celebrations and Events. Monthly award celebrations involving the whole school take place during the school day, as children and classes are rewarded for excellent community service, caring classroom behaviors, and academic achieve-ment. For example, classes are awarded Do Go (pronounced "doe joe") Do Good Points. These celebrations emphasize positive group behaviors, such as contribut-ing gently used clothing and toys, canned goods for the hungry, and pennies for childhood illnesses; making book fair purchases; doing classroom work; and much more. Monthly, classes earn pizza parties with their Do Go points. This recognition presents more venues for listening, writing, reading, discussion and celebration of students from diverse backgrounds. Other school events include "moving up" day, kindergarten graduation, and field days, all taking place at the end of year. Parents attend in great numbers to celebrate their children's achievements.

Supportive Contexts for Differences. Children with social–emotional and/or learning issues are continually assisted in gentle and positive ways so they may return to learning as quickly as possible. If a child appears to be heading for a meltdown or is distraught, a teacher is on the phone to obtain the help needed. A counselor, counseling aide, or dean appears immediately and the child is taken for a "walk and talk" or a calm time-out room to collect him or herself with an adult listening and helping. Similarly, if a child begins to show questionable academic progress, he or she is given timely one-on-one attention. Saturday morning classes are also for special help.

Culturally Responsive Practice. Cultural and linguistic diversity has always been embraced at this elementary school. Administrators and teachers believed there was more to learn and invited me to join them as a literacy consultant for CRTL. I will devote the remainder of this chapter to explaining how CRTL was fostered. First, I will provide a rationale for culturally responsive–sustaining pedagogy.

A CULTURALLY RESPONSIVE TEACHING AND LEARNING (CRTL) PROGRAM

The purpose of a CRTL program is to develop collaboration among, school, family, and community members for literacy learning. CRTL is informed by critical race theory (Ladson-Billings & Tate, 1995), the belief that racism is embedded in many institutions in the United States, including schools. European Western culture is prominent in the curriculum of most U.S. schools, obscuring the histories and contributions of many students from culturally nondominant communities. This lack of recognition compromises individual and group confidence and it undermines how students see themselves and their learning capacities (Delpit, 2002; Igoa, 1995). Culturally responsive instruction is an attempt to reverse this trend through: (1) raising expectations of students and focusing on student achievement, (2) drawing from students' languages and cultural knowledge to make instruction more relevant, and (3) raising students' social consciousness (Cummins, 2000; Ladson-Billings, 1995). The goal of CRTL is not only to make instruction more relevant, but to preserve students' knowledge in the curriculum. As Paris (2012) states, culturally sustaining pedagogy is explicitly about "supporting multilingualism and multiculturalism in practice and perspective for students and teachers" and seeks to sustain students' "linguistic, literate, and cultural pluralism as part of the democratic project of schooling" (p. 95). CRTL is based on a sociocultural theory of learning in which knowledge is socially constructed and shaped by the knowledge, beliefs, and practices of particular discourse communities (Rogoff, 2003). Furthermore, CRTL is a crucial step toward humanizing education. Too often, children are required to leave their homes and families behind when they enter school (Salazar, 2013), thus enabling an inequitable pedagogy (Freire, 2000).

The challenge for educators in the SASCS system is not only to preserve students' knowledge of languages and traditions, but also to connect prior knowledge and experiences to the New York State curriculum (Gay, 2010; Ruggiano Schmidt & Ma, 2006). Culturally responsive–sustained teaching engages and motivates students so they can achieve at higher levels (Ruggiano Schmidt & Lazar, 2011).

Research has demonstrated that a significant factor in literacy development is parent involvement (Edwards, 2016). Therefore, the objective of the SASCS program was to see how parents, educators, and community leaders could work together to enhance literacy learning for culturally diverse and bilingual students.

The program began in August 2016, with daylong staff development workshops designed for elementary and middle school teachers and staff as well as board members and family and community members. The purposes of the workshops are to expose participants to culturally responsive literacy strategies and create various implementations with help from families, students, and community members. All received the text *50 Literacy Strategies for Culturally Responsive Teaching* (Ruggiano Schmidt & Ma, 2006) and a laminated global Peter's Projection (Peter, 1974) map for classrooms and homes, partially funded by a Central New York Community Foundation Grant.

During the school year, I conducted classroom observations and kept records of all meetings, strategy implementation efforts, and schoolwide events. I also studied the state's standardized test scores and conducted parent, teacher, and administrator surveys and semi-structured interviews during and at the end of the school year. Interviews with parents took place at a nearby Dunkin' Donuts and teachers were interviewed in their classrooms after school. Notes were recorded after each parent–teacher meeting. Open-ended questions led to lengthy conversations that demonstrated the importance of continuing the CRTL project. Sample questions include: "Tell me about your thoughts regarding culturally responsive teaching and learning. What did you learn? How can the project be improved?" Sixty-one family members were involved in the meetings, but not all attended every meeting because of work and other obligations.

Parent–Teacher Culturally Responsive Grade-Level Meetings

The dean of the elementary school launched the grade-level meetings and sent out notices to faculty and staff for scheduled sessions during the 10 months of the 2016–2017 school year. Exact dates and times were finalized, and throughout the year, she reminded faculty of the meeting schedule. She emphasized that parents should be contacted several times, not only by email or letters, but face-to-face, and by phone before the meetings. Her leadership set the tone for the significance of the program. She attended meetings, visited classrooms when parents presented possible lessons and units of study, and encouraged teachers to let her know what was happening with culturally responsive teaching and learning.

Multicultural literature played a key role in this initial CRTL program. It is one of the easiest ways to emphasize population similarities and differences in positive ways. "We need diverse books, because we need books in which children can see reflections of themselves" (Sims-Bishop, 2015). Multicultural literature can also be tied to required curricula and connected to the prior knowledge and experiences of children and families. Several parents suggested ideas for lessons regarding diversity and some volunteered to read books that reflected their backgrounds. For example, a parent of Puerto Rican background read a story to the kindergarten class, *Abuela* by Arthur Dorros (1997). An African American parent of a 1st-grader volunteered to read *I Love My Hair* by Natasha Anastasia Tarpley (2001). This involvement inspired teacher-led initiatives as explained in the following examples.

Second-grade teachers surveyed families to discover home languages and invited parents to share languages in class. Third-grade teachers invited parents from Togo, who dressed in special garb and taught about climate, geography, and the flora and fauna of their nation. Fourth-grade teachers discovered a group of parents who initiated numerous ideas and opinions resulting in the classes' creation of an outstanding international cookbook. It included color photos and represented 14 nations and 6 continents. The students typed and designed the book and several added the history of their family recipes. Teachers and parents decided that next year, a feast should follow the recipe book.

Whole-school initiatives included Muffins for Mom and Donuts for Dad, multicultural concerts, a Cultural Cruise, international folktales, and world and nation holiday celebrations, such as Denali, Holi, Chinese New Year, Christmas, Id, Ramadan, and St. Patrick's Day.

Studies of food, national heroes, and holiday multicultural events are often dismissed as the tourist approach to appreciating diversity, representing a cursory recognition of cultural differences (Banks, 1994). This would be the case if these festivities were not followed with sincere efforts to share and shift the power dynamic from educators to caregivers. I have found that these events are necessary first steps to building trust, an essential factor for establishing the collaborative study necessary to foster students' language and literacy learning (Nieto, 2006).

Caregiver–Teacher Collaboration for Literacy Learning

In conjunction with our regularly scheduled teacher–caregiver meetings, teachers at each grade level worked with parents to design culturally responsive lessons related to their literacy curriculums. I offer the following vignette as an example of how the 2nd-grade team worked with caregivers to deliver CRTL.

During the fall of the year, 2nd-grade teachers met with parents and decided that skin tone was a critical characteristic for the appreciation of similarities and differences. One parent of African American and Latinx origins who had attended the summer workshop stated, "There are getting to be more and more Black and Brown people in our country and I want my child to be proud of her chocolate-brown skin and know there are many shades out there." One of the teachers immediately responded, "Would you help the class with the lessons? We have a book you might like to read to the class." Without hesitation, the parent agreed. The teachers and parents chose *All the Colors We Are: The Story of How We Got Our Skin Color/Todos Los Colores: La Historia de Por Que Tenemos Diferentes Colores de Piel* (Kissinger & Bohnhoff, 2014). It seemed to be a match with recently purchased multicultural crayons and individual mirrors. ~~After reading and discussing the book, each child created a self-portrait to be displayed in the school hallway with a written account about the book.~~ This was a positive way to celebrate racial/ethnic differences while inviting students to think and use language. The book also served as a means for introducing scientific understandings with sophisticated vocabulary.

On the first day of the lesson, the teachers put a pack of multicultural crayons and a small hand mirror at each child's place; a pack of crayons contained seven skin tones and one white crayon for shading. The children were seated on the class carpet, ready for the story. The mother had access to the book to prepare the reading. The following is an excerpt from the reading:

> *Teacher:* We have a special guest today who will help us learn about
> ourselves. Gianna's mother will read the book *All the Colors We Are.*
> *Mother:* What color are you?

Students looked at one another and began shouting out: I am Black! I'm White! I ain't Black. I no color."

> *Mother:* What color am I?
> *Children:* You not Black! You Brown! You are tan!

Student enthusiasm was great and the teacher found it necessary to calm them.

> *Mother:* I'll read this book and then you can tell me what color I am.
> (Mother reads the book and stops to answer students' questions as
> suggested by the teacher.)
> *Child 1:* Where did we people live long ago?
> *Child 2:* We live in the sun and got black.
> *Child 3:* My ancestors . . . grammas and gramps didn't live in sun. We live
> where it is cold and not much sun.

Students were excited about the book and began learning new words, such as ancestors and melanin.

> *Teacher:* So, who can tell me what makes our skin color?
> *Child 5:* My mom and my gramma.
> *Teacher:* Yes! And they got their color from your ancestors. Ancestors are
> your family from a long time ago.
> *Mother:* Where did they live?
> *Child 7:* Africa!
> *Child 8:* How about them Eskimos? They live in igloos and it's cold! They got
> brown skin.
> *Teacher:* Yes, but they get a lot of sun. Where do you think their ancestors
> came from? Maybe someplace like Africa with a lot of_____?
> *Several Children:* SUN!!!
> *Teacher:* Yes! It gives us our skin color. Who in this class has lots of melanin?
> Who doesn't have a lot of melanin? We are different, aren't we?

Child 1: I got lots a melanin.

Child 2: I don't got much melanin.

Mother: Who do we call those families that lived long ago?

Child 16: Ancestors!

Teacher: Yes! so we have different skin colors because of the sun, our ancestors, and melanin. We are now going to make a large picture of our faces. We are going to match the color of our skin with the crayons on your desk. You can work with a friend and use a mirror so you can see the color of your skin. We are going to hang our portraits in the hall.

Students returned to their seats and started their portraits. There was a "healthy hum" (Ruggiano Schmidt, 1999, p. 338) of purposeful activity in the room as students shared their work and talked about their skin tones with friends.

The following day, the teacher created an anchor chart on the smartboard and wrote these questions on the chart:

- How do we get skin color?
- How much can we tell about people by just looking at them?
- What is a good way to find out about a person?
- What are our similarities and what are our differences in this class?
- What do we all have in common?

The children read the questions as a group and wrote their answers, in complete sentences, on their individual anchor charts. They then completed their self-portraits. Each portrait was displayed in the hallway with the person's name and the anchor chart below.

This lesson broadened students' understandings about the science of skin color and prompted many to make inferences about the level of melanin in their own skin and think critically about skin color, as exemplified by the child who asked about Eskimo skin tones. They learned new vocabulary, wrote complete sentences, listened, and talked. And, of course, they experimented with skin tones using their multicultural crayon packs. The anchor chart below each portrait also demonstrated learning. The following are samples of contributions by several children:

I got my skin color from my ancestors.

I have lots a melanin. Our skin need protection from the sun.

We all different in this class, but we all like candy.

A lot of us like soccer. We can find out stuff from each other.

The teachers enjoyed teaching this lesson with a parent, and the parent was pleased to be included in the process.

Parents couldn't always be an integral part of lessons, so they sent cultural artifacts from home or simply suggested possible ideas for lessons at the monthly meetings. Teachers became confident as the year progressed and began initiating many questions, hoping the parents would realize the importance of their responses and suggestions.

OUTCOMES

The most significant outcome of this project was that it energized teachers to learn more about students and their families. At the end of the school year, several more teachers created and sent home surveys regarding students' home languages, cultures, and countries of origin. They discovered that the 51 families who responded linked their national and cultural origins to 34 countries from North America, South America, Central America, Europe, Middle East, Africa, and Southeast Asia. Languages spoken at home included Arabic, Dinka, Swahili, Russian, German, Spanish, Hindi, Urdu, Mandarin, Turkish, and many more local dialects. In the past, teachers had paid little attention to the specifics relating to the extent of the cultural diversity in their classrooms. This information surprised them and will have an impact on future planning.

When shared at full-faculty meetings, the survey shaped and reinforced many teachers' pedagogical decisions. The following indicates their developing awareness of CRTL:

1. Requested and ordered bilingual fiction and nonfiction books for classrooms and invited parents to read these texts to the class.
2. Invited parents to share Arabic, French, Swahili, Dinka, and other phrases in the classrooms.
3. Labeled objects in several languages.
4. Played games with laminated maps and globes to learn the names of countries, continents, and oceans.
5. Implemented more paired learning.
6. Used the smartboards for culturally responsive stories.
7. Posted and reviewed the class daily schedule.
8. Saw the significance of authentic, hands-on learning and community fieldtrips.
9. Encouraged drawing/writing for all content-area writing.
10. Studied famous people from diverse cultures.
11. Presented daily opportunities for students to speak their home languages.
12. Invited families to present information or artifacts from countries of origin.

These activities were initial attempts for bilingual curriculum integration.

The project, of course, inspired elements of culturally sustaining pedagogy (Paris, 2012). During the year, classroom lessons and units of study made use of families' knowledge and traditions, along with multicultural literature that reflected diverse backgrounds. Family members came to meetings with teachers and contributed ideas related to the development of racist attitudes, recognition of family cultures, and ways to promote language learning. As profiled earlier, a parent helped several times in the classroom when children compared skin tones and drew self-portraits. In another classroom, a parent told the story of African American stoplight inventor Garrett Morgan and captured the children's interest with a well-planned lesson. Many similar encounters took place in classrooms throughout the school during the year.

Recognizing and validating all students' experiences and histories became the new normal at this school. Each classroom studied and presented a country represented in the school, as part of the whole-school Cultural Cruise. Numerous outstanding hallway bulletin boards demonstrated diversity issues and classrooms competed for recognition. The art teacher took up the lead by featuring artistic styles from around the world. The physical education teacher created end-of-the-year field days where almost 60 parents participated in supervising games whose origins could be traced to other countries. The music teacher researched and taught music of different countries.

Some evidence suggests that the school's climate of inclusiveness and cultural celebration may have played a role in students' achievement. Of the 61 caregivers who participated in the culturally responsive meetings during the school day, 29 had attended the majority of the school meetings. Over half of the children of those 29 caregivers made significant gains of more than 1 year in reading according to the STAR Reading Assessments. These children were in the 2nd and 4th grades. First- and 3rd-grade students whose parents attended the majority of meetings made at least 1 year's growth.

End-of-year anonymous parent and teacher surveys and interviews about CRTL gave strong pronouncements for the continuation of the program. Teachers and parents wanted to learn more about how to implement culturally responsive teaching and learning. Several cultural identity projects were conceived and these explorations of culture translated to greater appreciation of students and their communities.

A few teachers were not pleased with the campaign to involve caregivers, because their phone-calling efforts did not yield the participation they desired. The experience, however, helped them realize that parents' lives were complicated by work and child-care commitments. As one teacher stated, "Obviously, parents have jobs that do not allow them to leave work early." And parents explained, "The fact that we're invited by teachers says that we are important to our children's learning." These teachers suggested that meetings occur at the end of the school day so that children could be supervised in one of the team rooms by a cooperating teacher.

Additionally, the teachers realized that culturally responsive teaching and learning require changes in dispositions. Parents and teachers are placed in new roles of sharing ideas and lessons that may be unfamiliar, so teachers needed to be persistent, patient, and positive while explaining the need for participation.

CONCLUSIONS AND RECOMMENDATIONS

Based on responses from teachers and parents and my own reflection program changes are recommended. First, the school's faculty and staff need to know more about the languages and cultures of their children's families. Second, tone of voice and the ways in which parents are invited may need to be studied to help with more effective communication with diverse groups of people. Third, teachers indicated that they had never been taught how to share lesson ideas with parents. Therefore, they suggested that workshops for creating culturally responsive thematic units take place as part of teacher inservice. Finally, parents had never been asked to participate in a teaching experience and were hesitant about this new way of involving caregivers.

As a possible solution, I recommend that workshops be provided for teachers and parents, based on the ABCs of Cultural Understanding and Communication (Ruggiano Schmidt, 1999), a model that prepares educators and parents to communicate constructively so that powerful relationships can be forged (Finkbeiner & Lazar, 2014; Ruggiano Schmidt & Lazar, 2011).

In the wake of our progress in the first year, I invited four parents (a Latinx, a European American, and two African American parents) to create and present a workshop to a group of teachers, parents, and community members in the fall of 2017. They volunteered and planned to explain to teachers and family members in a new SASCS elementary school what they accomplished in their children's classrooms. They suggested possibilities, such as reading books related to their languages and cultures, presenting information about their countries, teaching a few phrases and words from home languages, bringing in culturally related music and dance, telling stories of famous people from their backgrounds, and inviting other parents to get involved.

Syracuse Academy of Science Charter Schools (SASCS) appear to be a model system for the education of diverse groups of children in economically stressed areas. The educators understand the power of student and family recognition and how it leads to high academic and social expectations. The central administration supports this goal and the resources needed to see it realized. This is not often the case in many schools across our nation. Too often, school systems in economically stressed areas blame poverty, violence, and family indifference for student failures. Consequently, faculty and staff at those educational institutions use societal factors to lower student expectations and create an environment of hopelessness (Ripley, 2013; Smith & Fullan, 2008). Some schools have even lowered student, faculty, and staff expectations related to the Common Core (Ripley, 2013) in order to demonstrate that academic achievement, even though weak, is at least moving forward. Classroom annual goals are formulated at such low levels that minimal effort is needed to reach them, a highly questionable practice. And in other school systems, problem issues may be left to administrator top-heavy district offices. Finally, rather than carefully evaluating issues, schools often adopt expensive and unproven new programs and focus on faculty retraining (Smith & Fullan, 2008). So, what can we do?

This leads to the main implication for this chapter. We know there are for-profit charter schools, excellent charter schools, failing charter schools, excellent public schools, excellent private schools, and failing public and private schools. In the end, what really matters is that schools maximize students' literacy and language learning opportunities. SASCS is doing this by encouraging caregivers and teachers to construct learning opportunities that link students' experiences/heritage to learning goals. SASCS is also a system that recognizes the power of mentoring new teachers. Novice teachers earn less than lead teachers, but the rewards emerge for those who are committed to the school's mission. It is true that SASCS requires a high level of commitment from faculty, administration, and other staff, but student growth and development is made obvious through constant academic and emotional support and the culture of high expectations for parents, teachers and students is maintained. With these elements in place, students will have the best opportunity to grow as literacy and language users. It is no surprise that SASCS superintendent Dr. Tolga Hayali claims: "All students can achieve at the highest levels in life, if recognized and given the power of a challenging education" (Interview, February, 2017).

Our focus this first year was developing students' English literacy through a culturally embracing pedagogy (Cummins, 2000; Gunderson, D'Silva, & Odo, 2014), but our work opened up possibilities for developing students' home languages. When considering the next steps for SASCS, more attention should be paid to multilingualism and students' use of their home language in the classroom. Educators and caregivers can work together to develop a schoolwide philosophy for multilingual teaching and learning. These suggestions, along with those already in use by teachers in several classrooms, include inviting students to speak, read, and write in their home languages. For instance, students could use their home languages in a number of literacy events, such as choral reading, readers theater, writing in personal journals and assignment pads, and assisting parents with language translations. Of course, the school would benefit from the addition of more ENL teachers.

Finally, educational institutions in the United States might learn from the exceptional work of schools like SASCS that are taking significant steps to understand their diverse student populations. The implementation of culturally responsive teaching serves to assist in the goal to develop English literacy, whether English is a new language or the only language. Furthermore, home languages are valuable assets that will enhance educational and social–emotional growth (Garcia, 2009). Therefore, recognizing and appreciating the prior knowledge and experiences of diverse groups, proposed by CRTL, touches students', families' and teachers' hearts and minds. And the results appear to encourage all communities to contribute their talents to the nation's common good (Bellah, 1985), thus making the humanizing of our schools an individual and collective enterprise (Salazar, 2013).

REFERENCES

Banks, J. (1994). *An introduction to multicultural education*. Boston, MA: Pearson, Allyn & Bacon.

Bellah, R. (1985). *Habits of the heart: Individualism and commitment to American life*. Harper & Row: New York, NY.

Cummins, J. (2000). *Language, power and pedagogy: Bilingual children in the crossfire*. Clevedon, England: Multilingual Matters.

Delpit, L. (2002). No kinda sense. In L. Delpit & J. K. Dowdy (Eds.), *The skin that we speak: Thoughts on language and culture in the classroom* (pp. 31–48). New York, NY: The New Press.

Dorros, A. (1997). *Abuela*. New York, NY: Penguin Random House.

Edwards, P. (2016). *New ways to engage parents: Strategies and tools for teachers and leaders (K–12)*. New York, NY: Teachers College Press.

Finkbeiner, C., & Lazar, A.M. (Eds.) (2014). *Getting to know ourselves and others through the ABCs*. Charlotte, NC: Information Age Publishing:

Freire, P. (2000). *Pedagogy of the oppressed*. New York, NY: Continuum.

Garcia, O. (2009). *Bilingual education in the 21st Century: A global perspective*. Malden, MA and Oxford, England: Wiley-Blackwell.

Gay, G. (2010). *Culturally responsive teaching: Theory, research and practice*. New York, NY: Teachers College Press.

Gunderson, L., D'Silva, R., & Odo, M. (2014). *ESL (ELL) literacy instruction: A guidebook to theory and practice* (3rd ed.). New York, NY: Routledge.

Igoa, C. (1995). *The inner world of the immigrant child*. New York, NY: Routledge.

Kissinger, K., & Bohnhoff, C. (2014). *All the colors we are: The story of how we got our skin color/Todos los colores: La historia de por que tenemos diferentes colores de piel*. St. Paul, MN: Redleaf Press.

Ladson-Billings, G. (1995). But that's just good teaching! The case for culturally relevant pedagogy. *Theory into Practice, 34*(3), 159–165.

Ladson-Billings, G., & Tate, W. F. (1995). Toward a critical race theory of education. *Teachers College Record, 97,* 47–68.

Nieto, S. (2006). Solidarity, courage and heart: What teacher educators can learn from a new generation of teachers. *Intercultural Education, 7*(5), 457–473.

Paris, D. (2012). Culturally sustaining pedagogy: A needed change in stance, terminology, and practice. *Educational Researcher, 41*(3), 93–97.

Peter, A. (1974). *Peter's projection*. Amherst, MA: ODT Maps.

Ripley, A. (2013). *The smartest kids in the world and how they got that way*. New York, NY: Simon & Schuster.

Rogoff, B. (2003). *The cultural nature of human development*. Oxford, England: Oxford University Press.

Ruggiano Schmidt, P. (1999). Know thyself and understand others. *Language Arts, 76*(4), 338.

Ruggiano Schmidt, P., & Lazar, A.M. (Eds.). (2011). *Practicing what we teach: How culturally responsive classrooms make a difference*. New York, NY: Teachers College Press.

Ruggiano Schmidt, P., & Ma, W. (2006). *50 Literacy strategies for culturally responsive teaching*. Thousand Oaks, CA: Corwin Press.

Salazar, M. (2013). A humanizing pedagogy: Reinventing the principles and practice of education as a journey toward liberation. *Review of Research in Education, 37,* 121–148.

Sims-Bishop, R. (2015). Mirrors, windows and sliding doors. *Reading Rockets Interview*. Retrieved from www.youtube.com/watch?v=_AAu58SNSyc

Smith, L., & M. Fullan. (2008). *Schools that change: Evidence-based improvement and effective change leadership*. Thousand Oaks, CA: Corwin Press.

Tarpley, N. A. (2001). *I love my hair*. New York, NY: Scholastic, Inc.

CHAPTER 5

Framing Literacy as "Revolutionary"

Creating Transformative Learning Opportunities in a Predominantly Latinx-Serving High School

Steven Z. Athanases and Marnie W. Curry

It is early May, Friday afternoon. The upstairs hallway of Molina High School (MHS) is bustling with clusters of professionally dressed students rehearsing presentations and offering one another encouragement. An annual rite of passage, the Senior Defense, has commenced. This exhibition culminates this small, community-based school's efforts to promote the learning and life chances of culturally and linguistically diverse, mostly Latinx youth in a low-SES urban community. The Senior Defense is a graduation requirement aligned with the school's challenging academic work focused on health issues, community-rich experiences including internships, and transformative learning.

In seven classrooms, spectators have gathered. In one room, several Latinx males report on their research related to health issues facing urban communities. A panel of evaluators in a front row of desks is a diverse team: Wei, a Vietnamese American math teacher and lead advisor for some of the projects; Leonardo, a Spanish teacher, immigrant from El Salvador, and another advisor for projects; Tomás, a Latinx part-time science teacher at MHS; and a White male professor volunteer (first author of this chapter) from a team conducting a 2-year, multisite study entitled Schools Organized for Latina/o Educational Success (SOLES). They sit ready with rubrics that identify criteria: perspective-taking, evidence, logical reasoning, effective communication, and professionalism. Family members, classmates, and professionals who mentored students at community sites are present for support and feedback.

Jaime presents on the Affordable Health Care Act of 2010 and universal health-care access for underserved populations. He references interviews conducted with a doctor and an ICU nurse at his hospital internship. During Q&A, Wei presses Jaime to explain a graph on a slide. Jaime confesses, "I don't really know what you're asking." Wei probes, and Jaime repeats that he doesn't understand the question. He looks panicked. Wei asks Jaime to reconstruct the graph at the board with chalk, shifting the Q&A to an intense one-on-one scene, scaffolding with a series of questions for Jaime to demonstrate graph knowledge. As Jaime's advisor, Wei appears confident that he can press for elaboration. He keeps the bar high but tailors scaffolding to narrow the zone of proximal development (Vygotsky, 1962), closing the gap between what Jaime demonstrated and what he needs to rethink and articulate. Though it takes time, Jaime works through the language to satisfy Wei's inquiry. After more panelists' questions, Jaime appears crestfallen, defeated.

After deliberation yields scores denoting more work needed, Jaime receives the verdict—low-pass. Jaime's internship mentor, an African American hospital health-care professional, offers support but tells Jaime he appeared defensive in Q&A and needs to work on that. Jaime's mother says something softly in Spanish and Leonardo translates for the group: "Jaime's mom said, 'You knew it all at home when you practiced. What happened?'" A plan is proposed for Jaime to write a reflection to satisfy expectations. Jaime resists. He is proud of his work, disappointed he did not display his best, and wants to redo key parts. Wei promises to negotiate next steps with Jaime.

Rafael's defense follows. Though it is Friday late afternoon, Rafael's peers pour into the room. Rafael reports on adolescent Internet addiction. His defense goes smoothly and ends with resounding applause. Evaluators suggest that a data display would have made the findings more compelling. Members of a technology business where Rafael interned probe a bit and praise him. His mother also pays tribute in Spanish (aided by Leonardo's translation to English), saying that Rafael's impressive presentation was the greatest Mother's Day gift she could imagine. When evaluators announce pass-with-honors, Rafael (who has been composed throughout) bows his head, puts his hands over his glasses, and sobs in apparent relief and pride. His mother embraces him and they sob together.

This vignette is a scene from SOLES, a study conducted at Molina High School, a school serving mostly low-SES Latinx youth. This culminating event includes literacy learning opportunities aided by school elements that we describe. We begin with the context of the school and our study, then turn to these elements, followed by outcomes.

COMMUNITY AND SCHOOL CONTEXT

MHS is a small, urban, Title 1 public California high school. At the time of our study, approximately 90% of MHS students received free/reduced-price lunches, 76% were Latinx (predominantly Mexican descent), and 33% were emergent bilinguals. MHS teachers were diverse, roughly half teachers of color, half Spanish-English bilinguals. MHS emphasizes health sciences and boasts a well-attended, site-based extended-day program (EDP). When enrolling, students and their families commit to participate in after-school activities and internships.

Our analyses arise from a multiyear, multisite project on high schools with documented success in serving urban Latinx students (e.g., Achinstein, Curry, & Ogawa, 2015; Athanases, Achinstein, Curry, & Ogawa, 2016). Our 16-person research team was ethnically and linguistically diverse, more than half overall Latinx, and many bilingual. The authors of this chapter are White researchers, with some degree of bilingual fluency and long involvement with culturally and linguistically diverse urban youth in low-SES schools and communities. In prior work, our team documented how MHS cultivated permeable boundaries between school and community to expand learning opportunities (Achinstein, Curry, Ogawa, & Athanases, 2016) and immerse youth in "authentic *cariño*," profound care to nurture students' whole selves (Curry, 2016). Through such efforts, MHS resists the insidious effects of poverty, foregrounding health as empowering.

SCHOOL ELEMENTS THAT ADVANCE STUDENTS' LITERACY AND LANGUAGE LEARNING

Four elements helped create engaging learning in literacy and language at MHS.

Sustained Vision of Community-Engaged Schooling

A foundational element was a coherent vision of a community-based school. This included schooling within community contexts, with community wealth and health as goals (Achinstein, Athanases, Curry, Ogawa, & de Oliveira, 2013). By wealth, we mean ways programs managed reciprocal relationships with communities, tapping resources of families, community-based organizations (CBOs), and institutional partners. School programs accessed local capital for youth engagement, learning, and empowerment to make changes in and contribute to community wealth.

By health, we mean how MHS focused academics on health. This included internships for 11th- and 12th-graders in contexts such as hospitals and clinics. Science teachers developed internship-aligned curriculum; others designed interdisciplinary projects on health themes including mental illness and public health disparities. Our opening vignette of Senior Defense reflected this focus in a capstone event and research paper that incorporated science, health-oriented internships, and community focus. The presence of the hospital employee, Jaime's internship mentor, on the panel of caring, critical evaluators (supported by peers and family) communicated to students that their performance and education mattered to their community. Through these activities, MHS sought to prepare nondominant youth for college, en route to medical careers.

Supporting these goals was a vision of transformative learning to interrupt patterns of injustice and inequity for underserved communities. Professional development (PD) sessions began with reading the MHS mission. It appeared on rubrics for Senior Defense evaluators and students. The principal, Braxton, a White male, explained that the mission mattered in hiring: "The first question will always have to be, 'Is this person a powerful educator and aligned with the school's mission and vision?'" He noted how the hiring committee—comprising himself, teachers, students, and parents—sought to maximize cultural and linguistic resources for youth:

If they are a person of color that represents our school community and our demographic at the school, even better . . . because there absolutely is a way that being bilingual or being a teacher that has a similar background as our kids [matters]. Kids connect differently with them. To watch Leonardo with students, he is like a father figure to those kids.

MHS's hiring not only ensured that recruits understood and embraced the mission, but also that they prioritized cultural and linguistic diversity. In this way, MHS joined other effective schools that recruit and amplify diverse voices to better serve emergent bilinguals (Menken & Solorza, 2015).

Faculty supported MHS's mission to empower nondominant youth through transformative learning. On a teacher survey (100% response rate) with Likert scale prompts (1–5, 5 meaning "strongly agree"), teachers affirmed that "This school has a clearly stated goal" (4.82 mean) and "The school is doing a good job in reaching its stated goal" (4.41 mean). Faculty agreed that the MHS goal had support of instructors (4.53), support of parents (4.12), and support of students (4.0).

Distributed Leadership for Literacy Activity

Schools serving many emergent bilinguals can benefit from distributing leadership among teachers and unofficial leaders (Ascenzi-Moreno, Hesson, & Menken, 2016). At MHS, distributed leadership was widely in evidence. An Instructional Leadership Team comprising the principal, a community partner, and two teachers charted the school's course with assistance from teacher committees. At a retreat, teachers discussed shared leadership. Paul, a founding teacher, impressed upon new hires, "It's an expectation in this school that you will become a leader." His colleague Audrey echoed this: "Every staff member is expected to lead and find and use his/her voice."

MHS administrators tapped faculty and staff for various roles. At one PD workshop, with the principal offsite, a humanities teacher led a session on cooperative learning and roles in complex instruction (Cohen, 1994). He focused on pairing emergent bilinguals in activity to support language practice, stating, "Studies show that ELs speak only 12–13 seconds in a full school day, so it's important to elicit oral language." In interviews, numerous faculty reiterated this point. Wei noted an emphasis on English language acquisition and literacy for the "large nonnative-English-speaking population" at MHS: "We focus on having our students gain literacy. . . . [M]ath teachers and science teachers realize that we will be expected to be literacy teachers as well and work with vocabulary development." These comments highlight how faculty embraced responsibility to promote literacy learning.

Distributed leadership required staff investment. Orchestrating the Senior Defense program required human resource and capital. With seven rooms for defenses, three per room over several hours, times 3 days, these events required focus to keep mission and goals running through the work. Managing moving parts was

Ashley, a biology teacher who also served as internships coordinator. She recruited community members for evaluation panels and ensured that they were prepared. Her 30-minute orientation included clarification of goals, evaluation criteria and rubric language, and procedures. Ashley also oversaw the distribution of teachers as evaluators, noting how in one case she partnered a novice with a veteran: "She needs to be calibrated." In this way, Ashley guided faculty to hold the bar high and hone Senior Defense scoring through interrater practice.

MHS also benefited from Wanda, a veteran ESL and reading instructor, who served as a literacy coach/instructor. She noted at MHS that "Not everything is on the principal":

> Teachers are taking on a lot of leadership roles. . . . A lot of times I think I'm going to talk to the principal about something, and people will say, "Talk to Audrey about that; she's organizing that." I don't go to a lot of their PD meetings, but I know teachers really are in charge of a lot of those areas of PD, too. I think that's really strong at that school.

Managing such leadership required robust communication, including an email listserv and an online documents repository. Wanda noted, "I've never heard of any school with this much email. . . . Everyone's in the loop. I know what the 11th-graders are doing, 12th-graders are doing."

An informal but key leader was Luz, a Colombian-born immigrant, who described herself as having been on the run from "*la migra*" (immigration police) for years before gaining legal status. As the EDP site coordinator hired by the CBO Community Action, she was the de facto vice principal. She spearheaded a "Parent Academy" to help parents navigate the system and support youth academic success; obtained and allocated extramural funds to support rigorous college-prep classes, such as AP Spanish and college writing; hired teachers to provide intensive after-school intervention for struggling students; and pressed emergent bilinguals to embrace literacy as "the tool of liberation."

Braxton, the principal, valued Luz for her competence, humor, passion, and caring—"stuff that resonates with families"—and also valued parents' response to Luz as a bilingual Latina:

> When we walk into the room together, people know I'm the principal. There's no doubt in their mind. . . . They all turn and look at Luz and they love Luz. They respect me and they know I'm a good principal. But there's a love and appreciation for Luz that is deep.

Luz embraced this shared leadership also. She joked and reflected:

> I married the principal. Have you seen our relationship? There is a level of trust, literally, and comfort and creativity that we both have in each other that's not typical. That is at the center of it, literally. It's not just collaborating. . . . We co-create all the time.

Luz co-created and funded activities supporting literacy, including a digital journalism program with skill development and a college writing class, informed by her experience: "If the kids are to survive the first year of college, their writing skills need to be at proficiency. I'm an immigrant. You have seen my emails. I know the struggle of this. . . . I remember how long it took me." Luz's EDP coaching team never lost sight of MHS's mission, always promoting "high-engaging academics" and larger goals: She helped create an annual Nerd Bowl ("Being bright is cool") and fostered liberatory literacy among emergent bilinguals. Luz's participation illustrates how MHS's embrace of distributed leadership yielded powerful relationships that created literacy opportunities. Luz reflected: "I refused for 20 years to work in public schools because I thought schools were rotten, teachers were disengaged from people's needs, the administration was evil. MHS completely flipped that." Luz was a key player in MHS's leadership, considered by many to be the one maintaining *la cultura* of the school.

Literacy as Transformative and "Revolutionary"

Literacy at MHS was designed as purposeful disciplinary activity, supportive of learning, success, and community engagement. Students chanted the mantra "Reading and writing are revolutionary" in assemblies. Vera, a humanities teacher, conveyed this message to students:

> To make revolutionary change, you have to know how to read and write. And that's how you're going to change how the world works and looks right now. You cannot change it unless you can read and write, unless you can participate in that discussion.

Luz also championed this cause, calling after-school study halls and academic interventions "revolutionary time."

In statistics, teacher Marcus's students designed surveys to gather real-life data. Seeking to sharpen critical perspectives of math as a living discipline, Marcus wanted youth to be able to say:

> I can see why polls are important. I read the newspaper yesterday. I understand what it means. I understand how someone's trying to deceive me with statistics. I understand how to read graphs. I can look at a newspaper, a magazine, I can understand all these charts.

Such real-life application of math concepts could support engagement with community issues and development of a voice in sociopolitical contexts.

MHS students regularly used oral and written argument to advocate positions on issues including immigration, health disparities, and nuclear arms. A Habits of Mind (HOM) model (Meier, 1995) framed such activity and a visual of it was posted, used to guide learning targets and rubrics, and distributed to Senior Defense panelists. HOM included inquiry, evidence, reasoning and analysis, perspective, and metacognition as processes that once acquired and developed would allow students to participate effectively in struggles to overcome oppression. One teacher noted:

> There is a social justice element to teaching using HOM. When you can think critically, you're not just accepting society for the way it is. People who think critically can see the ills, can analyze the ills, can break them down, and are the ones who advocate ultimately for social change. That's part of the mission.

Braxton explained that such work arose in the context of pressure to "go to direct instruction on everything, go down to fine-grained skills, get your test scores up," an approach that was not engaging: "Particularly for students of color and Latino students in this neighborhood and African American kids it had to be connected to a greater context." He added:

> If we were going to change their overall vision of where they saw themselves going and even seeing themselves as viably going into a health career, they had to connect their learning to something bigger that changed the way they saw themselves.

This critical orientation to HOM pervaded MHS activity, linking literacy with revolutionary potential for self-inquiry and critical perspectives on society.

Health internships and equity focus in health concerns, exemplified by Senior Defense, added authenticity to literacy endeavors. Both students in our opening vignette disclosed deep personal connections and convictions related to their research and academic and professional goals. Jaime spoke of encountering patients unable to pay for medical services. Rafael revealed his own Internet addiction. These young men, both formerly labeled according to state tests as "English learners," and later "reclassified" as fluent English proficient, tapped their passions to undertake sophisticated literacy activity. In this way, personal, community, and larger societal concerns suffused literacy activity, elevating students' college and community readiness.

To enable these expansive explorations, MHS structured success. With Senior Defense, months of research guidance, tailored support, and tough probes during defense Q&A demonstrated high challenge and high support (Athanases, 2012; Hammond, 2006). This is especially important in work with linguistically diverse students in low-SES contexts, including emergent bilinguals who often experience too little challenge and support for complex language and literacy activity. Wei's one-on-one dialogue with Jaime during Q&A illustrated how one teacher worked with a student on a topic that mattered to him deeply. Using interactional scaffolding (Athanases & de Oliveira, 2014; Gibbons, 2009), Wei probed to elicit Jaime's problem-solving and elaborated understanding. Such probing had an element of risk, as Jaime was pressed to deliver in front of others. However, these moments were part of a long, scaffolded process guided by Wei, set within the context of MHS where students understood the web of social supports and collective commitment to success.

Senior Defense culminated a 4-year sequence of "transformative learning" that often began in class and extended to dialogic encounters elsewhere where students grappled with issues together. Freshmen in science, English, and math investigated biological, environmental, and social implications of fast food and discussed how companies target poor people of color and how this contributes to health disparities. Drawing from these explorations, students developed digitized public service announcements they showed to middle schoolers.

A hallmark of MHS learning events was how they ignited engagement in tasks themselves, minimizing busywork and pursuit of grades. Juniors anticipated an after-school event called the War Room where after several weeks of studying 20th-century U.S. military conflicts, teams cast as doves or hawks entered the "East Wing of the White House" to discuss whether the United States should engage in military intervention. After one 90-minute War Room, the "U.S. president" (Marcus, a math teacher) stepped out of role, sharing how he "enjoyed" the opportunity to witness a "good, heated debate" with passion, argumentation, and unexpected turns. Still exhilarated from the discussion, a student blurted out, "That was fun!" This visceral, emotional pleasure speaks to ways MHS activities frequently enabled students to revel in and relish *real* idea exchanges. In such settings, literacy activity was unfettered from "doing school" and displaying "academic language," and instead was embodied experience fostering meaning-making and expanded understandings of the world. These events helped students view themselves as learners capable of unpacking complex ideas and influencing people in power (even the U.S. president!).

Multilingualism Valued Across School Spaces

MHS staff celebrated linguistic diversity, regarding bilingualism as an asset and heritage languages as resources. In classrooms, hallways, internships, assemblies, PD, parent gatherings, listservs, and after-school activities, Spanish surfaced repeatedly. A student explained, "They don't isolate us from talking Spanish. They actually want us to show and express where we're coming from." One teacher observed, "Latino culture lives very presently in our school. . . . English and Spanish are spoken interchangeably . . . parents are very present . . . so Latino culture is enmeshed in MHS support structures." As illustrated in our opening vignette, Jaime's and Rafael's mothers knew their contributions in Spanish were valued and welcomed. Leonardo's translation for non-Spanish speakers also ensured that their voices were centered in the discourse of the room.

Throughout MHS there was a fluid mix of languages, with many acts in classrooms and elsewhere of shuttling especially between English and Spanish. Leonardo, who taught Spanish for heritage speakers and AP Spanish, championed language fluidity, invoking a knight's sword:

It's double-sharp. . . . I tell students, "You become a very strong Latino/a because you can handle Spanish very well. And on the other side of the sword you handle English very well. You become a very strong Latino/a person. You can face the world and be able to overcome a lot of the obstacles, just because you're bilingual."

Leonardo and colleagues recognized interconnections of bilingualism, identity, and confidence. Understanding Anzaldúa's (1987/2012) argument, "I am my language. Until I can take pride in my language, I cannot take pride in myself" (p. 81), MHS teachers validated students' cultural identities and their Spanish as an essential foundation for humanizing the school.

MHS benefited from the presence of many bilinguals on staff. Half of the teachers and key players, including the secretary, parent liaison, extended-day coaches, and college counselors, spoke Spanish. It was not uncommon for a student to be greeted with, "*Hola, mi hija. ¿Cómo puedo ayudarte hoy?*" (Hello, my daughter. How can I help you today?); for Spanish lyrics to boom during social breaks; or for students to receive Spanish versions of program evaluations. In daily instruction, translanguaging practices (Bartlett & Garcia, 2011) were common. Teachers used Spanish and English flexibly and intentionally in bilingual arrangements to advance bilingualism and biliteracy. Leonardo, who epitomized this stance, shared:

> I don't care if they're thinking in English or Spanish, I still want them to learn the two ways. If a kid is talking to me in English, I let him or her finish and then I say, "Okay, now tell me in Spanish," or vice versa.

Such practices were not confined to Spanish class; a faculty survey indicated that students spoke Spanish in class activities several times weekly. The humanities department's vocabulary development model emphasized word-attack strategies where students drew upon Spanish to decode English words. Other teachers reported interview assignments with family and community members in which students were free to use their native language. These assignments culminated in syncretic products such as digital stories or published books in which Spanish, Spanglish, and English were intermixed. Such translanguaging occurred informally, too. It was not uncommon to see a student recruited to serve as translator in a community meeting or hear pairs of students engaged in informal tutorials and translating unfamiliar vocabulary to peers with less English fluency. The physics teacher reported how an emergent bilingual student exploited the daily advisory period to review material with a bilingual peer and returned to class "much stronger."

The value of multilingualism also surfaced in attention to code-switching. Teachers coached students to employ language for different audiences. One humanities teacher shared:

> I talk about it [code-switching] every day: "This is how you need to write. You need to write as you would for a college professor, as you would for

an educated audience, not because your culture is less valued, but because this is the way the culture of power operates." I think I expose them to the culture of power as much as possible.

By making transparent how it is possible and desirable to master standardized discourses to navigate the dominant world while still valuing home culture, teachers sought to heighten students' metacognitive understanding of the sociopolitical dimensions of language.

In a focus-group interview, Jaime (from our opening vignette), demonstrated this language awareness, noting challenges in mastering "professional" discourse:

Here we have the proper English, and then we have the slang English. . . . We have *pueblo* Spanish and then professional Spanish like *averiguar* ("to find out, to research, to know"). *[laughter]* . . . I've never been taught that word. They're tryin' to teach us words we've never heard in our life! . . . But I understand, too, they are trying to prepare us to sound more intelligent. . . . I ain't gonna lie. I hate my teacher sometimes, but I'm thankful for what he's doin'. 'Cause it's hard for me, but I'm actually thankful.

Jaime's gratitude demonstrates how he and his peers valued access to "ways of talking, ways of writing, ways of dressing, and ways of interacting" (Delpit, 2006, p. 25) that equipped them to participate in the dominant culture on their own terms. Through multiple pathways, MHS worked to expand students' communicative repertoires and bilingual fluency to exploit unique advantages of being bilingual. One Senior Defense community panelist repeatedly told students:

how much more valuable they'll be because they're bilingual . . . how much smarter they are than monolingual people because they're able to do this in two different worlds, [how] they're able to create community, [how] they are pivotal persons who can bridge the gaps between two different communities.

MHS clearly departed from a deficit treatment of bilinguals (Valenzuela, 1999).

OUTCOMES

Success on Conventional Metrics, Despite Contempt for Standardized Tests

Although test scores frequently judge school performance, MHS staff critiqued high-stakes accountability. Braxton stated tersely, "We're not teaching to the test." School documents, reiterating this point, stressed, "We want MHS students to be transformed into lifelong learners who are engaged and excited about learning. Tests do not transform students, learning does!" Wanda, MHS's literacy coach, noted how staff rejoiced when students tested well, but the primary focus rested on "what's real, what the students are really learning, what they're really producing."

Despite the school's rejection of "test prep," MHS students on average outperformed district and state peers on graduation rates, college preparatory coursework completion, and high school exit exams. From 2011 to 2015, 69% of MHS Latinx graduates completed California coursework requirements for admission to the University of California or California State University systems (expected to include academic challenge, analytical thinking, and all language arts), compared to only 40% countywide and 31% statewide. Also, 84% of MHS 2012 graduates (including Jaime and Rafael) were college-bound. Results underscore ways MHS's humanizing approach did not undermine students' capacity to perform well on standardized assessments or jeopardize their college eligibility.

Expanding Communicative Repertoires

At MHS, we observed students using language fluidly for varied purposes. This is an important process outcome enabled by beliefs about language as resource. Fluid shuttling between language varieties illustrated efforts to value home language and culture and expand communicative repertoires: "the collection of ways individuals use language and other means of communication (gestures, dress, posture, accessories) to function effectively in the multiple communities in which they participate" (Rymes, 2010, p. 528). Ways classes and activities marshaled diverse language forms for learning aligned with evidence that varied linguistic resources support meaning-making and displays of understanding (Enright, 2011; Moschkovich, 2007). At an assembly, an alumna talked about college-going using a rhythmic spoken-word performance. In the War Room, when challenged to rebut an argument, students tapped whatever language forms they could in the heat of the moment. In this way, students drew on diverse linguistic resources for academic purposes (Bunch, 2014)—vital, as schools serving low-SES youth of color often police language deemed nonstandard as nonacademic, providing immediate correction (Orellana, Martinez, Lee, & Montaño, 2012).

The second kind of language activity as outcome was disciplinary language practice. At another school in our larger study, an English teacher reported that she could not engage disciplinary literacy forms such as figurative language, as her students needed "basic English" (Athanases & de Oliveira, 2014). In contrast, at MHS, a school of similar size and demographics, we observed a humanities Socratic seminar focused on figurative language in *The Joy Luck Club* (Tan, 1989). Students took up disciplinary terminology, located evidence to support claims in discussion, and mixed language forms. This was not a "faux conversation" with students robotically spouting academic discourse and "parroting the sorts of words and phrases that their teachers want[ed] them to use" (Glazer, 2018, p. 57); instead, this conversation featured lively, organic exchanges where students thoughtfully analyzed and co-constructed understanding of how figurative language illuminated characters' bicultural identities and relationships. Academic extension activities also provided opportunities to expand communicative repertoires. Students formulated positions on issues, developed evidence, rebutted ideas, narrated immigration stories, spoke on panels, prepared arguments for protests, and explained graphs to evaluators, community members, and peers.

For emergent bilinguals and Latinx students in low-SES communities, curricula often feature formula over purpose, prescriptive and limited strategies, few opportunities to try out genres, and rules and forms overwhelming real communication (Enright & Gilliland, 2011; Valdés, 1999). Such hyperfocus on basics, vocabulary, mechanics, and errors minimizes deeper content knowledge development (Bruna, Vann, & Escudero, 2007; Mohan & Slater, 2006). In contrast, we found a language ideology at MHS of *leveraging* and *expanding* linguistic resources, essential for students who are emergent bilinguals and speakers of nondominant languages, and whose language uses frequently get cast as deficient (Banes, Martinez, Athanases, & Wong, 2016; Palmer, 2011), typically using practices framed by an ideology of remediation (Gutiérrez, Morales, & Martinez, 2009), with nondominant students assumed to be deficient, needing repair.

Becoming Community Ready

MHS's mission featured altering inequities and preparing students as "agents of change in their own lives and their community." Although many schools stress college and career readiness, MHS placed equal value on cultivating "community-ready" graduates. Staff envisioned youth interested, invested, and capable of identifying, analyzing, and solving pressing problems of their community and beyond. Informed by this vision, MHS cultivated students' critical civic praxis (Ginwright & Cammarota, 2007) and long-term aspirations to contribute to their community.

Through critical pedagogy and community-impact projects conducted in EDP, students examined real-world issues such as immigration, violence, poverty, environmental degradation, and college access. Such activities elevated students' critical consciousness of oppressive structures shaping their lives and spurred them to fight for social justice. Luz boasted how students demonstrated a "sense of community and . . . ownership that the problems not just of the school, but the city, are for them to solve." A senior reflecting on her MHS years reported:

> I learned to not be indifferent and don't be shy. Use your voice . . . say what you feel. Don't go with the flow. Just 'cause there's a lot of people on one side, don't feel like you have to go there. Go where you believe is right.

Her stance of advocacy, engagement, righteousness, and resistance surfaced in a wide range of civic action undertaken by students.

One illustration of such activism was a California ballot initiative, which arose when seniors examining escalating college tuition brainstormed policy remedies in government and math classes. After debating ways to make college more afford-able, students crafted a ballot initiative to make college free. The process involved taking voters' perspectives, hashing out eligibility requirements, calculating tax increases to offset lost tuition, drafting legal language, and submitting a proposal to the California secretary of state. Once certified, students engaged in grassroots activism to obtain the 807,615 signatures necessary for final approval. Although these efforts fell short, students gained invaluable exposure to political processes and to a system where industry or millionaire-backed, paid-signature campaigns have overshadowed citizen-initiated efforts. Ultimately, these students exercised their voices, stood for what they thought was right, increased community aware-ness, and challenged negative portrayals of nondominant urban youth.

Students also expressed interest in future community uplift. In focus groups, they shared aspirations to become surgeons, nurses, oncologists, medical inter-preters, pediatricians, psychologists, clinical lab specialists, and anesthesiologists. These vocations reflected MHS's emphasis on preparing medical professionals who would address inequitable health-care delivery and thereby enhance community health. Jaime, from our opening vignette, noted how MHS reshaped his vision:

> I actually wanted to be a mechanic, because I already knew a thing or two about cars. I already started working on them. I was already exposed to that environment. But coming here, I got a new mentality, and I kind of want to be a nurse.

Jaime's reference to his "new mentality" demonstrates ways MHS opened up possibilities and identities for students. Given accounts of urban youth be-ing groomed for service-sector jobs as janitors, waitresses, and clerks (Dabach, Suárez-Orozco, Hernandez, & Brooks, 2018), MHS students' ambitions to be med-ical professionals defied master narratives and signaled their interest in contribut-ing to community uplift.

CONCLUSIONS AND RECOMMENDATIONS

Our examination of literacy practices at MHS uncovered structural and normative elements that coalesced to make the school a humanizing place for students to embrace learning. First, the school espoused a mission to engage nondominant students in transformative learning anchored in community and aimed at social justice. This mission grew from grassroots activism and was sustained through hiring practices, community outreach, and vigorous efforts to align school activi-ties with the mission.

Second, responsibility for enacting the mission was distributed across admin-istrators, teachers, community youth developers, mentors, students, and families. This web of players fostered reciprocal relations between MHS and its communi-ties, while catalyzing an ethos of mutual investment and commitment.

Third, MHS adopted a view of literacy predicated on the idea that reading, writing, and speaking are revolutionary tools enabling one to challenge and transform oppressive conditions. All MHS teachers, regardless of subject-matter expertise, considered themselves literacy teachers. They leveraged and expanded linguistic resources in ways that supported students, especially emergent bilinguals, to participate in purposeful, intellectually rich, embodied activities where literacy moved beyond "doing school."

A correlated fourth element was MHS's celebration of multilingualism as a source of power and possibility. This shared value meant that students engaged in translanguaging, flexibly moving between Spanish and English in a range of registers from professional to "*pueblo*." It meant that students' facility with their heritage languages was considered a source of strength, cultural identity, and intelligence.

Together, these four elements contributed to a culture of engaged learning where boundaries between school and community faded and students were encouraged and supported to become "more fully human as social, historical, thinking, communicating, transformative, creative persons who participate in and with the world" (Salazar, 2013, p. 126). These elements enabled language-rich opportunities for linguistically diverse students to explore issues that matter. There remains, in the United States and beyond, a proliferation of basic-skills approaches to language development as compliance with standards. Such approaches often feature decontextualized skills that barely approach the disciplinary literacy activity youth need: "Skills-based literacy teaching that is abstracted from purpose and value reduces disciplinary concepts to 'stuff' to be mastered and disciplinary literacy practices to forms and procedures to be memorized" (Moje, 2015, p. 255). Moje (2015) argues for a reinvigoration of the human, social dimensions of disciplinary discourse communities in which imagination and creativity are vital. This is the kind of activity we found frequently at MHS.

Because extrapolating recommendations from a case study of a single school is risky as a result of social, political, historical, and economic particularities of settings, we offer questions, informed by our study (Figure 5.1), to ignite conversations we hope might illuminate ways to promote literacy and language development of nondominant youth in varied contexts.

MHS continues to search for ways to support nondominant students' literacy development. Staff grapple with tensions in how best to provide humanizing spaces for engaged learning. Tensions related to detracking, scaffolding, assessment requirements, reading recovery, funding shortages, and Senior Defense evaluations surface repeatedly. There also are students who have not fully bought into MHS's *cultura* and embraced the learning opportunities painstakingly engineered for them. Against this backdrop, those of us who seek to expand the orbit and efficacy of sanctuary schools must commit to living the questions together, pressing forward to humanize education.

Figure 5.1. Questions to Guide Development of School-Based Humanizing Literacy Opportunities

Element	Guiding Questions
Community-centered mission focused on transformative learning	• Does our mission explicitly outline a path toward humanizing education? • Do stakeholders share a common commitment to the mission? • Are school activities and decisions aligned with the mission?
Distributed leadership	• How can we involve diverse stakeholders? • What CBOs might support youth's academic engagement?
Literacy as purposeful and revolutionary	• How can literacy activities involve youth in real-world issues and problems? • How can we design language-rich opportunities for youth to dialogue with one another, as well as with authentic audiences?
Multilingualism	• How can academically challenging work draw on students' linguistic resources? • How do we support students to value heritage and home-based funds of knowledge and also understand/master codes of power?
Academic extension activities	• How are culminating assessments and the instruction leading up to them "transformative learning experiences"? • How can we engineer activities to engage students' Habits of Mind, identities, imagination, and creativity? • Can we liberate ourselves from "egg-crate" classrooms and expand learning into innovative configurations?

ACKNOWLEDGMENT

The study reported in this chapter is part of a research program entitled Schools Organized for Latinx Educational Success (Betty Achinstein and Rodney T. Ogawa, PIs) funded by grants from the William T. Grant Foundation [Grant #10935] and The Flora Family Foundation [Grant # 2010-1830]. Views expressed here are not those of the funders. The authors acknowledge support of MHS staff, students, and families who shared their experiences. We also thank our multi-campus research team for assistance and insights: Betty Achinstein, Rodney T. Ogawa, Luciana C. de Oliveira, Paulina Moreno, Serena Padilla, Etmae Brinkers, Jose Rosario, Marina Castro, Everett Au, Adriana Escarega, Mercedes de la Riva, Reynaldo Rodriguez, Victor Lagunes, and Naficeh Dastgheyb.

REFERENCES

Achinstein, B., Athanases, S. Z., Curry, M. W., Ogawa, R. T., & de Oliveira, L. C. (2013). These doors are open: Community wealth and health as resources in strengthening education for lower-income Latino youth. *Leadership* (May/June), 30–34.

Achinstein, B., Curry, M. T., & Ogawa, R. T. (2015). (Re)labeling social status: Promises and tensions of developing a college going culture for Latina/o youth in an urban high school. *American Journal of Education, 121*(3), 311–345.

Achinstein, B., Curry, M. W., Ogawa, R. T., & Athanases, S. Z. (2016). Organizing high schools for Latina/o youth success: Boundary crossing to access and build community wealth. *Urban Education, 51*(7), 824–854. doi: 10.1177/0042085914550413.

Anzaldúa, G. (1987/2012). *Borderlands/la frontera: The new mestiza*. San Francisco, CA: Aunt Lute.

Ascenzi-Moreno, L., Hesson, S., & Menken, K. (2016). School leadership along the trajectory from monolingual to multilingual. *Language and Education, 30*(3), 197–218.

Athanases, S. Z. (2012). Maintaining high challenge and high support for California's diverse learners. *Leadership, 42*(1), Theme issue: Learning & the Classroom, September/October, 18–22, 36.

Athanases, S. Z., Achinstein, B., Curry, M., & Ogawa, R. (2016). The promise and limitations of a college-going culture: Toward cultures of engaged learning for low-SES Latina/o youth. *Teachers College Record, 118.*

Athanases, S. Z., & de Oliveira, L. C. (2014). Scaffolding versus routine support for Latina/o youth in an urban school: Tensions in building toward disciplinary literacy. *Journal of Literacy Research, 46*(2), 263–299.

Banes, L. C., Martinez, D. C., Athanases, S. Z., & Wong, J. W. (2016). Self-reflexive inquiry into language use and beliefs: Toward more expansive language ideologies. *International Multilingual Research Journal, 10*(3), 168–187.

Bartlett, L., & García, O. (2011). *Additive schooling in subtractive times: Bilingual education and Dominican immigrant youth in the heights*. Nashville, TN: Vanderbilt.

Bruna, K. R., Vann, R., & Escudero, M. P. (2007). What's language got to do with it? A case study of academic language instruction in a high school "English Learner Science" class. *Journal of English for Academic Purposes, 6*(1), 36–54.

Bunch, G. C. (2014). The language of ideas and the language of display: Reconceptualizing "academic language" in linguistically diverse classrooms. *International Multilingual Research Journal, 8*(1), 70–86.

Cohen, E. G. (1994). *Designing groupwork: Strategies for heterogeneous classrooms* (Rev. Ed.). New York, NY: Teachers College Press.

Curry, M. W. (2016). Will you stand for me? Authentic cariño and transformative rites of passage in an urban high school. *American Educational Research Journal, 53*(4), 883–918.

Dabach, D. B., Suárez-Orozco, C., Hernandez, S. J., & Brooks, M. D. (2018). Future perfect?: Teachers' expectations and explanations of their Latino immigrant students' postsecondary futures. *Journal of Latinos and Education, 17*(1), 38–52.

Delpit, L. (2006). *Other people's children: Cultural conflict in the classroom*. New York, NY: New Press.

Enright, K. A. (2011). Language and literacy for a new mainstream. *American Educational Research Journal, 48*(1), 80–118.

Enright, K. A., & Gilliland, B. (2011). Multilingual writing in an age of accountability: From policy to practice in U.S. high school classrooms. *Journal of Second Language Writing, 20*, 182–195.

Gibbons, P. (2009). *English learners, academic literacy, and thinking: Learning in the challenge zone*. Portsmouth, NH: Heinemann.

Ginwright, S., & Cammarota, J. (2007). Youth activism in the urban community: Learning critical civic praxis within community organizations. *International Journal of Qualitative Studies in Education, 20*(6), 693–710.

Glazer, J. (2018). The power of hmm . . . : Bringing life (back) to words in the classroom. *Phi Delta Kappan, 99*(5), 56–60.

Gutiérrez, K. G., Morales, P. Z., & Martinez, D. C. (2009). Re-mediating literacy: Culture, difference, and learning for students from nondominant communities. *Review of Research in Education, 33*, 212–245.

Hammond, J. (2006). High challenge, high support: Integrating language and content instruction for diverse learners in an English literature classroom. *Journal of English for Academic Purposes, 5*, 269–283.

Meier, D. (1995). *The power of their ideas: Lessons for America from a small school in Harlem*. Boston, MA: Beacon.

Menken, K., & Solorza, C. (2015). Principals as linchpins in bilingual education: The need for prepared school leaders. *International Journal of Bilingual Education and Bilingualism, 18*(6), 676–697. doi: 10.1080/13670050.2014.937390

Mohan, B., & Slater, T. (2006). Examining the theory/practice relation in a high school science register: A functional linguistic perspective. *Journal of English for Academic Purposes, 5*, 302–316.

Moje, E. B. (2015). Doing and teaching disciplinary literacy with adolescent learners: A social and cultural enterprise. *Harvard Educational Review, 85*(2), 254–278.

Moschkovich, J. (2007). Examining mathematical discourse practices. *For the Learning of Mathematics, 27*(1), 24–30.

Orellana, M. F., Martinez, D. C., Lee, C., & Montaño, E. (2012). Language as a tool in diverse forms of learning. *Linguistics and Education, 23*(4), 373–387.

Palmer, D. (2011). The discourse of transition: Teachers' language ideologies within transitional bilingual education programs. *International Multilingual Research Journal, 5*(2), 103–122.

Rymes, B. (2010). Classroom discourse analysis: A focus on communicative repertoires. In N. H. Hornberger & S. L. McKay (Eds.), *Sociolinguistics and language education* (pp. 528–546). Bristol, England: Multilingual Matters.

Salazar, M. (2013). A humanizing pedagogy: Reinventing the principles and practice of education as a journey toward liberation. *Review of Research in Education, 37*(1), 121–148.

Tan, A. (1989). *The joy luck club*. New York, NY: G. P. Putnam's Sons.

Valdés, G. (1999). Incipient bilingualism and the development of English language writing abilities in the secondary school. In C. J. Faltis & P. M. Wolfe (Eds.), *So much to say: Adolescents, bilingualism and ESL in the secondary school* (pp. 138–175). New York, NY: Teachers College Press.

Valenzuela, A. (1999). *Subtractive schooling: U.S.-Mexican youth and the politics of caring*. Albany, NY: SUNY.

Vygotsky, L. S. (1962). *Thought and language*. Cambridge, MA: The M. I. T. Press.

CHAPTER 6

Creating Welcoming Environments for Latinx Families in New Latino Diaspora Schools

Melissa Pérez Rhym

[In my country] I was always involved with what my daughters were doing. I felt frustrated here; I thought that there was going to be a parent and family meeting, but there was never anything. I came in here totally uninformed. I lived uninformed, not only because of the language, but because there were no meetings, just the one that you did later on. We really need to start the year off with meetings like this one we had where you gave all of the information. It was so wonderful, but that was when I really thought to myself, how come it wasn't like this at the beginning of the year? So that we could have this information? It was a horrible shock. I thought there would be a meeting with all the parents and families to be able to hear or at least understand or at least a sheet with the rules for the school. A schedule, when classes start, when they finish, how many classes they would be taking, what it takes to graduate? And then they still don't explain [things] to me and I still don't know what it is. You see what I'm talking about?

The *testimonio* above from Raquel, one of the mothers who participated in a study I conducted at Blue Ridge High School[1] (BRHS) highlights the frustration many Latinx parents felt toward the barriers that prevented them from being more involved in their students' education. Over the course of the study, I heard from various parents who shared similar stories of the multiple roadblocks they encountered as they tried to be more engaged in the education of their students. Many of the parents and caregivers turned to outside resources or other forms of agency to get the answers they needed for their children. Recognizing the need to address the increasing Latinx population at the school and the issues Latinx parents were having with gaining access to the school and its resources, Blue Ridge High School responded by implementing key changes to make the school more welcoming to its Latinx families. This chapter will examine the process one school undertook to examine the practices it had in place to help Latinx families gain access to the school and the services available there. I conducted interviews with Latinx families as well as teachers and administrators. Using this information, my colleagues and I created additional support systems. To measure the effect these new systems were having, I interviewed Latinx families and students, and gathered other comments and anecdotal information from teachers and administrators. Continuously examining our practices to gauge their effectiveness is especially critical as the population of the school continues to change demographically.

FROM CULTURAL INSIDER TO OUTSIDER-ACTIVIST

As a first-generation Cuban American raised in Miami, Florida, I never had the idea that I was an "other." Everywhere I went, everyone was Latinx. Whether it was in the bodega to purchase that night's dinner or at the doctor's office, not only were most of the faces of professionals and working-class people like mine, but we all also spoke in a beautiful mix of Spanish, English, and something in between the two. If my mother needed to talk to one of my teachers, language would not have been an issue. Nor would any of my teachers ever consider the fact that I was Cuban American or bilingual a hindrance to my desire to continue my education. Moreover, because at the time Cuban immigrants were protected under special immigration laws, my immigration status and that of my parents was never something I had to take into account when considering my educational and career options. My culture and my bilingualism were celebrated in my schools and in my community.

Moving to Georgia in my late 20s was quite a shock to me. Not only did I realize that most of the country labeled me as a minority (I was most definitely *not* the minority in Miami), but speaking Spanish served as an additional marker that stigmatized me. My first jobs as an educator in Georgia were in mostly rural counties where I was the only Latinx at the school, and sometimes, the district. When I was called upon to help translate, others would remark on how well I spoke English, or how articulate I was, never considering that I could have been born and educated in this country. When I began my teaching career, teachers complained to me about their Latinx students and how they did not know what to do with them or how to help them learn English faster. They were frustrated at their inability to effectively communicate with students' parents. When parents failed to contact teachers or attend school functions, teachers assumed they were unconcerned about the well-being and education of their children. The teachers I interacted with conceded that unless I took the time to translate materials for them, it would not be done. There was little to no funding to provide these services consistently, nor was there anyone available to answer parents' questions if they were to call the school. The situation was one in which materials and information were sent home to parents in a language everyone knew they couldn't understand, yet these parents were questioned and judged for their lack of involvement. This irony seemed lost to many school staff. The contrast between the world I grew up in and the one I now inhabited could not have been starker.

COMMUNITY AND SCHOOL CONTEXT

New Latino Diaspora

Georgia is in a geographical part of the United States known as the New Latino Diaspora (NLD). The term was first used in the 1990s to refer to the increase in Latinx settlement, both temporary and permanent, in areas not historically associated with Latinx immigration. These changing immigration patterns were driven principally by changing labor markets in areas of the workforce that historically attracted Latinx immigrants, such as construction, landscaping, and agriculture, among others (Hamann & Harklau, 2015). Whereas areas of the United States accustomed to receiving Latinx immigrants have established networks of support for recent immigrant arrivals, areas in the NLD are less likely to have bilingual residents or services available to non-English speakers. Teachers in these areas are also less likely to be culturally or linguistically educated to interact with Spanish-speaking parents and students (Harklau & Colomer, 2015).

The rapid rise in Latinx immigration in NLD states has resulted in problems of inclusion and discrimination for many Latinx families (Hamann & Harklau, 2015). This is evident in xenophobic policies, practices, and laws aimed directly at Latinx immigrants and youth. In Georgia, one way that this has manifested is in the form of discriminatory educational laws. The 2010 Georgia University System Board of Regents passed legislation that bans un(der)documented[2] students from attending universities in Georgia that have competitive admissions policies. This same governing body declared that undocumented as well as un(der)documented students (those who fall under the protection of Deferred Action for Childhood Arrivals [DACA]) do not have a legal presence in the state. By extension, the state ruled that these individuals cannot make use of the state's tuition programs for high-performing students, known as the HOPE scholarship, nor access federal aid to defer college costs, such as the Pell Grant or Stafford Loan (Board of Regents Policy Manual, n.d.). These discriminatory policies prevent thousands of students, many of whom were brought to the United States as young children, from continuing their education (Acosta, 2013).

Concurrently, the incidence of immigration raids targeting the Latinx community in Georgia has risen (Floyd, 2015; Gomez, 2016). This compromises Latinx parents' involvement in their children's schools, as many parents are afraid to leave their homes or otherwise possibly expose their documentation status to strangers. The confluence of these factors has created a hostile environment for Latinx families and a sense of frustration and helplessness for many Latinx students in the area.

Latinx Families at Blue Ridge High School

As one of few Spanish-speaking teachers at my high school in a small school in northeastern Georgia, I was often called upon to translate. This was not unusual, as I had previously served in this capacity in other schools in the state. As Harklau and Colomer (2015) note, most schools in Georgia rely on their Spanish teachers to translate, interpret, and at times provide counseling services for their Latinx students. What was unusual about the circumstances at this particular school was that while Latinx students constituted almost 30% of the student body, there were few resources available in Spanish when I began teaching there.

BRHS was a Title 1 school in a small, urban county. In 2017, 56% of students affiliated as African American, 27% Latinx, 13% White, 2% Asian, and 2% multiracial. Over the past 10 years, the Latinx population at Blue Ridge High School had more than doubled, with the largest gains occurring over the past 5 years (Georgia Department of Education, 2017). Similar demographic shifts occurred in the county's feeder middle and elementary schools, which indicated that the Latinx student population would continue to increase at BRHS.

The teachers, staff, students, and parents of BRHS were keenly aware of these demographic changes. Jennifer, a retired teacher who taught at BRHS for 30 years, recounted how in the 1980s the school was predominantly White. At that time, communication with parents was minimal because the modern online database systems used to house student information was not yet available to teachers. Teachers did not have telephones in their rooms and the use of email was not yet prevalent. The lack of Latinx school personnel or teachers who could interpret for parents was irrelevant. The rise in the Latinx population between the late 1990s and early 2000s coincided with an increased nationwide focus on parental engagement. Given limited resources, teachers relied on siblings or students to interpret.

When I began my study, the county employed one interpreter to serve 13 schools and the district office. The school and district relied on volunteer interpreters for parent conferences with no services available at other times. Although well meaning, these volunteers often lacked an understanding of educational terms and concepts. The parents' frustration with the lack of language access at school was reflected in a community needs assessment conducted by local university personnel which found that "language is one of the most common barriers cited . . . when describing access to basic services like health care, legal aid, and employment seeking" (Calva & Helmey, 2016, p. 16). In that assessment, only 29.5% of respondents received language assistance when seeking health-care services and 7% at police, courthouse, or other government agencies. They also found that schools in the area did a better job than other public services, with 51% of parents with school-age children reporting that there was an interpreter available at school events. However, parents also noted that relying on volunteers meant that the interpreting was inconsistent and not always helpful. In fact, 43.9% of the parents said they would rather rely on their own children, family members, or friends to interpret at school functions.

The postsecondary educational limitations placed on many Latinx students at BRHS, together with parental lack of access to the school, created an unwelcoming environment for Latinx parents. This is significant given the strong correlation established between parental engagement and a student's academic achievement. Henderson and Mapp's (2002) review of 51 studies related to family involvement and student achievement determined that as a whole, there is a positive relationship between family involvement and beneficial student outcomes. These positive results were consistent across families from a variety of economic, racial, ethnic, and educational backgrounds.

As the Latinx population at BRHS increased, with this growth projected to continue, it became apparent to me that the school needed to examine the barriers preventing Latinx parents from feeling welcomed in our schools. I presented our demographic information along with some anecdotal information (conversations with parents and teachers) to our administration to draw attention to the need for more support for our growing Latinx population.

A Commitment to Support Our Latinx Families

Our administration that year was mostly new to the area, coming from a school district with a larger, more established Latinx population. The principal of the school, Ms. Leon, was surprised at the lack of Latinx representation on a district level and disappointed that more conversations were not taking place about the needs of Latinx families in the community. She had previously worked in a school with a much larger population of multilingual students and was used working with parents to meet their students' language and cultural needs. Despite the differences in our school district, she never felt unsupported in the changes she initiated. As a new administrator in the district, she felt the district and community were invested in her success.

The segregationist educational policies enacted by state and university governing bodies created a sense of exclusion and resentment among the un(der) documented Latinx students growing up in the shadow of a university they were prohibited from attending. The presidential election of 2016, and the anti-immigrant rhetoric that prevailed during that time, created fear and uncertainty as many Latinx students faced possibly losing the limited protections that DACA afforded. Ms. Leon and I, together with teachers and counselors at the school, felt that as our Latinx families continued to be politically and emotionally attacked, the school's role in providing assistance and support needed to be examined. We engaged in an assessment of our practices including a faculty survey and surveying and interviewing our Latinx parents.

EXAMINING OUR PRACTICES

In the spring of 2017, we hosted a *Cena de Padres* at BRHS. The purpose was to disseminate information to the school's Latinx parents and to provide a positive, welcoming experience for Latinx parents. Students from the school's Latinx club helped secure food donations from area restaurants and volunteered at the event.

Latinx Parent Survey. At the *Cena*, parents were asked to complete a survey that included questions about which current school practices they found helpful and what areas needed improvement. The majority of parents indicated that the most impactful change the school could make was to hire more Spanish-speaking staff, have calls home be done in Spanish, and provide informational materials in Spanish. For example, in response to the question, "Are you satisfied with the frequency with which the school and teachers communicate with you?" one parent commented that she was unable to communicate directly with her child's teacher and said, "It was complicated to know how our children are doing." Another stated that although she appreciated having interpreters at conferences, she needed them at other times as well. One parent said, "I have no idea what's going on in my daughter's classes." A fourth respondent stated, "No, I am not satisfied. We need direct communication in our language."

From parents' comments, it was clear that many were unaware of the services offered at the school, such as onsite mental health counseling and assistance to families in financial crises. One survey question asked, "What types of events would you like to see at the school?" Parents responded with a variety of suggestions, such as phone calls when their child was absent from a class and information on how to monitor their children's grades, how to find tutors for their children, and how to gain access to psychological services. All of these suggestions already existed at the school, but many of the parents at the meeting were not aware of them. This highlighted the lack of access Latinx parents had to the school and its resources and the feeling of exclusion many of them felt.

Faculty Survey. In May 2017, the faculty at BRHS completed a survey on how welcoming they found the school to be to our families and students. Although the Latinx families at the school were not the exclusive focus of the survey, the faculty noted the need to add bilingual signage in the front office area. The faculty survey also highlighted the need for increased access to translation and interpretation services so they could share information such as syllabi, class rules, and regular communication home in Spanish as well as English.

Parent Interviews. From those who responded to the survey administered at the *Cena*, I solicited volunteers to participate in interviews. I interviewed five parents, all mothers of students at BRHS. All of them differed in the length of time they had been living in the United States, immigration status, English proficiency, educational background, and country of origin. Despite these differences, their experiences and frustrations were similar.

DISCOVERIES

The Language Barrier

All of the Latinx parents interviewed reported that language barriers—namely, not being able to communicate with the school and the school sending information only in English—were obstacles to becoming more involved in their students' education. Language barriers are an issue not only in NLD communities, but nationwide (Poza, Brooks, & Valdés, 2014). Though 11 million schoolchildren in the United States speak a language other than English at home, primarily Spanish (U.S. Census Bureau, 2015), over 82% of the teachers in public schools are White and monolingual (Aud, Hussar, Kena, Bianco, Frohlich, Kemp, & Tahan, 2011). Many educators falsely believe that they are meeting the needs of parents who need interpreters. However, the reality is that these efforts are concentrated around special events, with daily needs left unmet (Lowenhaupt, 2014).

One of the participants interviewed, Loli, described her experience at her children's school: "I couldn't find anyone to help us; I started distancing myself from the school because of the language. Because there wasn't anyone who could translate for me. At that time, my son was being bullied and I didn't have anyone who was supporting me." The language barriers that prevented Loli from approaching the school for basic information led to a dangerous situation for her family. When she turned to resources outside the school, she was able to get her son the help he needed. She recounts:

> I started getting support when . . . I was stopped for driving without a license and I had to do court-ordered community service. I talked to them and told them what was going on and they got me a psychologist, they gave me help and support, and he started getting the help that he needed. But [at] that school, I was pushed away because of the language and because of the bad way they treated the parents.

Another participant, Nena, recalled the difficulty many of her friends had approaching the school for information:

> I tell them ask for someone who knows Spanish. At schools, you can always find someone who speaks a little Spanish, and if not go to the district. There are a lot of parents who do not come because they can't understand. They leave just like they came. So then, why should we come to these events?

Cultural Differences

Cultural differences between educators and caregivers also undermined parental involvement. Many teachers assumed a type of engagement from families that did not always match what Latinx parents believed was necessary or appropriate. In the United States, teachers have an expectation that parents will read to their children and engage them in literacy activities, whereas many Latinx parents believe that literacy education is something that should be left to the school and educational experts. Instead, they believe that character and moral education, religious activities, and participating actively within family activities are crucial aspects of a home education, and that these aspects should not be covered in school (Trumbull, Rothstein-Fisch, Greenfield, & Quiroz, 2001). These cultural differences do not mean that Latinx families believe they should not be involved in their students' education, but that their concept of school involvement may not match that held by the mostly White, middle-class educators in U.S. schools.

Immigration Status

The undocumented parents interviewed discussed their fears of being asked about their documentation or being stopped by police when traveling to the school. Issues surrounding documentation status and "hostile immigration policies challenge school efforts to develop meaningful family engagement practices" (Lowenhaupt, 2014, p. 525).

Although the other barriers addressed so far are more visible, the emotional, psychological, and physical impacts of being un(der)documented are not as obvious. Parents living in states that do not allow undocumented individuals to obtain driver's licenses risk being stopped or detained every time they drive to school for conferences, meetings, or school functions. Another consequence of parents' documentation status is that, in many cases, it limits them to low-skilled, hourly labor. These jobs often have less flexible work schedules and parents fear asking for time off to attend school events. As Nena recalled,

> Unfortunately, a lot of Latino parents, sometimes because they have a problem with language and also because they work, they don't want to lose their jobs, they don't want to involve themselves in school things . . . many say, "Well if my daughter is doing well, why am I going to go in?" or, "No, I'm not going to go. They will kick me out of my job if I miss a day."

MAKING CHANGES

After examining the parent and faculty surveys together with the parental interviews, the unmet needs the Latinx families became clearer. We knew we would need to make several changes to make our families feel more welcomed. Ms. Leon stated she felt there was a need not only to create temporary solutions for addressing the families' needs, but to work together to "develop leaders within those communities who can advocate for those who don't know yet how to navigate an American school system."

We decided to address the language barriers and those related to the documentation status of parents and students because they were most frequently cited barriers. As I explain the steps that we took at our school, it is important to keep in mind that these changes took place in a school within the NLD. The practices described may be obvious or routine in other areas of the country, but they were not in ours. Practices considered innovative relating to family engagement and educational practices are contextual and dynamic.

Language Access

One of the first changes made was to hire a bilingual staff member for the front office as well as for the newly created position of parent director. This new position served as a liaison between the parents and the community as a whole, not specifically the Latinx families. However, the person hired for this role was bilingual. Now, when parents called the school, came in to ask a question, or needed to speak to their students' teachers, they had at least two individuals who could assist them. Moreover, students who were more comfortable speaking Spanish knew that they could seek out one of these individuals if they had any questions or concerns.

Once we started improving communication with parents, we realized that the calls that went home alerting parents about student absences were only being made in English. These calls went out between 5:00 and 6:00 P.M., when many parents were still working, so the calls were redirected to their voicemails. This was problematic because those with economy plans for their phones did not have voicemail features and only registered a missed call from the school. Those who had voicemail received a recording in English that mentioned their student's name, and parents had no idea why they were called. This caused confusion and concern among our Latinx families, who had no way to discern whether calls were because of an emergency or a teacher calling home with a concern. We addressed this easily through the software used to generate the calls. Once the technicians at the district became aware of the issue, they were able to have these calls go home in Spanish and English for all of the schools in the district.

To reach a wider audience, we established social media accounts in Spanish and English. To ensure parity, any content posted on the English accounts was also posted on the Spanish accounts. We asked our Latinx parents from which social media sources they received news and information. We learned about Spanish language social media pages created specifically for and by the Latinx members of BRHS. We began publishing activities and special announcements on these pages.

Programs and Initiatives

The *Cena de Padres* was the first event of its kind held at the school exclusively for Latinx parents. We developed several workshops and programs based on the requests of parents and the feedback from the surveys given at the *Cena*. The most requested workshop was adult ESL classes. We established a weekly adult ESL class, held both in the mornings and in the evenings with free child-care available. We also offered resume building and job search workshops, also held in the mornings and in the evenings. Lastly, we provided workshops on utilizing technology and keeping teens safe on social media, held during parent–teacher conferences.

Bringing the School to the Community

Many of our undocumented Latinx parents stated that the inability to procure a license in Georgia prevented them from coming to the school. Therefore, we decided to take several measures to bring the school to the community. We increased the number of home visits for our Latinx students. Because home visits are associated with absentee parents or truant students, we were careful to avoid approaching these from a negative, deficit perspective. We began by visiting the homes of rising 9th-grade Latinx students to bring them information in Spanish about the school, their student's schedule, and to give them a point of contact at the school with whom they could communicate (Pérez Rhym & Gordon, 2015). Building on the home visit program we started in 2015, we continued conducting these visits to disperse information about social services available through the school and to keep parents informed of their students' academic progress, address attendance concerns, and answer their questions.

We also hosted events in the communities where our Latinx families lived. First, we met with community leaders and parents to determine what the community's concerns were. Then invited representatives from school transportation, technology services, after-school programs, as well as teachers from various departments to the event. We advertised the event at the previously mentioned social media sites, our weekly parent newsletter, the automated calling system, and with paper flyers at the locations most frequented by our Latinx families.

Increased Community Support

In the wake of the presidential election of 2016, a group of local educators and activists met to brainstorm ways they could show support for Latinx and immigrant students and families. Among other actions, the group organized and held a forum in September 2017. The event was advertised to educators in surrounding districts and open to the public. Plenary sessions included round-table discussions with students of various documentation statuses discussing their experiences in school, and a panel discussion with the county sheriff, school superintendent, school board members, and immigration attorneys. There were workshops on topics ranging from the language rights of parents in our schools to the social services available to our families. Several parents shared their experiences as well; however, many were scared to talk in a public setting, and helped instead by providing homemade lunches for the attendees and volunteering at the event.

Ms. Olive, a forum organizer and local educator, believed that in addition to the information shared at the forum, one of the greatest impacts was that it empowered students. Whether they sat on panels, informational tables, or co-presented at sessions, the students realized "that their voices were the most important part of the event. It was centered on them and their experiences and in having the opportunity to tell educators what it was that they needed from us," Ms. Olive said. The presidential election left many of the students feeling powerless, but the forum "gave them an opportunity to advocate for [themselves]. They realized that when things like this happen, you are not powerless."

Three school board members and the superintendent of schools attended the forum. Their attendance precipitated conversations between them, local activists, and educators as to what the school board could do to help our Latinx families feel safe in their schools. In December 2017, the school board passed a Safe Schools Resolution. The resolution supports the right of all children to an education, "regardless of their or their parents' actual or perceived national origin, citizenship or immigration status" (Board of Education Passes Safe Schools Resolution, 2017). The resolution further states that students need an environment where they can focus on their education, free from concerns about their safety because of their own or their families' immigration status, ethnicity, national origin, race, or religion. The resolution requests that members of the board convene to examine board and county policies as well as those of local law enforcement agencies and immigration policies to make recommendations to the board on how to better serve our families. Lastly, the board requested that this resolution be shared with parents at all of the district's schools in all the predominantly used languages.

OUTCOMES

It is difficult to measure the impact these measures had on Latinx families' sense of belonging to the school community at BRHS. We relied on anecdotal evidence to help guide us as to what still needed improvement. We again turned to informal interviews and parent comments to ascertain what was working and what still needed improvement. I also interviewed students who had been at BRHS for the past 4 years and could attest to the differences, if any, they had witnessed. As the principal, Ms. Leon, stated, "Sometimes we think we are making an impactful change but if the perception is not that it has done what we intended it to do, then we really haven't made a change at all."

In reflecting on the changes that have taken place at the school, Loli stated, "I feel more connected here [now]. . . . There are a lot of Latina teachers. They try to give us a lot of support. Now I am more involved; I try to be more aware of what's going on." Another participant, Barbara, also felt hopeful about the direction the school was taking. Although she felt her English skills were sufficient to communicate with her children's teachers, she had several friends who struggled to communicate with the school. She shared that she believed things were slowly improving. She stated, "Now the parents get the phone calls in Spanish. It's just starting. It's small changes, but little by little."

The students reported feeling the changes made at the school. One student, Yesel, reflected that since starting at BRHS, she has noticed that Latinx parents are more comfortable coming to the school. Compared to her freshman year, she said, "Now, you see parents coming more often and asking more questions." For Yesel, this meant that her parents could participate in her education in a way they never could before. Instead of apologizing for being unable to help her with her work, they now know what is going on because "they can come to school and figure out what the problem is. Now they can help me solve the problem." This increased involvement has been important to Yesel because "now they know that the things that they worked so hard for are paying off." She pointed to the bilingual staff available to parents and the communications going home in both languages as two major changes that have helped her family.

Another senior at BRHS, Monica, also witnessed the changes at the school and the effect on Latinx families. In her freshman year, she never saw Latinx families at school events or even in the main office waiting to talk to someone. Now she sees Latinx families involved in activities and coming to school to get information. She attributes these changes to the increased number of Latinx personnel at the school, especially in the front office. Parents know that they can come and someone will be able to answer their questions. Monica feels that her mom is now more aware of the progress she is making at school because she knows how to get information about her grades and attendance.

When asked about the board of education's resolution, none of the students or parents interviewed was aware of it, despite each school having a poster-sized version of the resolution in Spanish and English. I showed the students interviewed the resolution and asked them to comment as they read it. Yesel commented that she felt it was important that students become aware of the resolution. She felt strongly about the part that mentioned providing an education for all students, something she felt has not always been the case for Latinx students. Both Yesel and Monica mentioned the acknowledgment of the threat of deportation and the stress that it places on students as particularly meaningful to them. Monica felt that teachers at the school were not comfortable talking about immigration status and deportation, failing to acknowledge the stress that immigrant students face. Having it stated in the resolution, Monica felt, was a recognition of the reality students were dealing with. Both Yesel and Monica suggested ways for disseminating the resolution, like posting it on the school's social media sites in both languages, sending copies home, and making posters for teachers to place in their classrooms.

CONCLUSIONS AND RECOMMENDATIONS

In our information gathering, it became obvious that many of our Latinx families were not familiar with the services available at the school. Students and parents also suggested that we create a brochure or other easily accessible document listing all of the services available at the school and distribute it at community centers and other centrally located sites. We determined that we needed to collaborate with feeder schools, particularly with middle schools whose graduates attended BRHS. The transition from middle school to 9th grade was especially concerning for families. Research corroborates these concerns, showing that successfully completing 9th grade is a critical indicator of graduating high school. Yet this transitional period is associated with lowered parental engagement, decreased communication between school and home, and increased parental anxiety as they learn to navigate their student's desire for independence with a desire to remain involved in their student's education (Simon, 2004).

We also acknowledged the need to look beyond meeting the immediate needs of the school and community and create longer-term solutions from the community itself. Although the school had a small Spanish for native speakers program in 2012, by 2016 the program had more than tripled, with the feeder middle schools also beginning similar programs. By continuing to encourage the development of this program, the school was making a statement about the value that it placed on bilingualism and the development of those skills from within the community. These programs have been in place for decades in states such as California and Florida. However, in Georgia, the bilingual skills of immigrants and their children are rarely viewed as assets, but rather as a deficit and hindrance to successful integration into U.S. schools and society (Harklau & Colomer, 2015). Investing in and promoting the bilingualism of students in BRHS showed a commitment to the Latinx community and a respect for the preservation of their language.

The recognition by schools of the barriers that prevent Latinx parents from being more involved in their student's education is an important step. However, it is not enough to acknowledge the issues and take a few token steps toward addressing them. Having occasional interpreters or access to language interpretation phone lines are perfunctory services that fall short of creating truly welcoming spaces where families are empowered to engage in the educational experiences of their students. By critically examining the systems that undermine families' engagement, the school and community can work together to create both immediate and long-term solutions, ultimately benefiting all.

NOTES

1. The names of individuals and locations have been changed to protect their identity.

2. The term *un(der)documented* refers to those who, despite being granted legal presence by the federal government through the Deferred Action for Childhood Arrivals program, are not afforded the same status by the state of Georgia.

REFERENCES

Acosta, C. (2013). Pedagogies of resiliency and hope in response to the criminalization of Latinx students. *Journal of Language and Literacy Education, 9*(2), 63–71.

Aud, S., Hussar, W., Kena, G., Bianco, K., Frohlich, L., Kemp, J., & Tahan, K. (2011). *The condition of education 2011 (NCES 2011–033)*. Washington, DC: U.S. GPO.

Board of Education Passes Safe Schools Resolution. (2017, December). Retrieved from www.clarke. k12.ga.us/site/default.aspx?PageType=3&DomainID=4&ModuleInstanceID=31&ViewID=6446 EE88-D30C-497E-9316-3F8874B3E108&RenderLoc=0&FlexDataID=7&PageID=1

Board of Regents Policy Manual. (n.d.). Retrieved from www.usg.edu/policymanual/section4/C327/

Calva, A., & Helmey, S. (2016). The Hispanic/Latinx community of Athens-Clarke County, Ga. in 2016: A comprehensive needs assessment and recommendations for service providers. Retrieved from lcfgeorgia.org/wp-content/uploads/2017/01/acc-latinx-needs-assessment-report-final-11.pdf

Floyd, A., (2015, June 17). Broken families: Raids hit Athens' immigrant community hard. *Athens Flagpole*. Retrieved from flagpole.com/news/news-features/2015/06/17/broken-families-raids-hit-athens-immigrant-community-hard

Georgia Department of Education. (2017). Enrollment by race/ethnic and gender—Fiscal year data report. Retrieved from oraapp.doe.k12.ga.us/ows-bin/owa/fte_pack_ethnicsex?pub.entry_form

Gomez, A. (2016, January 4). Raids target undocumented immigrants in Georgia, North Carolina and Texas. *USA Today*. Retrieved from www.usatoday.com/story/news/nation/2016/01/04/ice-raids-immigration-central-america/78265144/

Hamann, E., & Harklau, L. (2015). Revisiting education in the new Latino diaspora. In E. Hamann, S. Wortham, & E. Murillo, Jr. (Eds.), *Revisiting education in the new Latino diaspora* (pp. 3–8). Charlotte, NC: Information Age Publishing.

Harklau, L., & Colomer, S. (2015). Defined by language: The role of foreign language departments in Latino education in Southeastern new diaspora communities. In E. Hamann, S. Wortham, & E. Murillo, Jr. (Eds.), *Revisiting education in the new Latino diaspora*. (pp. 153–170). Charlotte, NC: Information Age Publishing.

Henderson, A., & Mapp, K. (2002). *A new wave of evidence: The impact of school, family, community connections on student achievement*. Austin, TX: National Center for Family & Community Connections with Schools. Southwest Educational Development Lab.

Lowenhaupt, R. (2014). School access and participation: Family engagement practices in the New Latino Diaspora. *Education and Urban Society, 46*(5), 522–547.

Pérez Rhym, M., & Gordon, A. (2015, October). Reconceptualizing home visits: How schools can promote language rights and access for Latino parents. *Journal of Language and Literacy Education*. Retrieved from jolle.coe.uga.edu/wpcontent/uploads/2014/01/SSOOctober_FINAL.pdf

Poza, L., Brooks, M. D., & Valdés, G. (2014). Entre familia: Immigrant parents' strategies for involvement in children's schooling. *School Community Journal, 24*(1), 119.

Simon, B. S. (2004). High school outreach and family involvement. *Social Psychology of Education, 7*(2), 185–209.

Trumbull, E., Rothstein-Fisch, C., Greenfield, P. M., & Quiroz, B. (2001). *Bridging cultures between home and schools: A guide for teachers*. Mahwah, NJ: Lawrence Erlbaum.

United States Census Bureau. (2015). Detailed Languages Spoken at Home and Ability to Speak English for the Population 5 Years and Over for United States: 2009-2013 [Data file]. Retrieved from www.census.gov/data/tables/2013/demo/2009-2013-lang-tables.html

PART III

PORTRAITS OF HUMANIZING SCHOOLS

When you learn something from a people, or a culture, you accept it as a gift, and it is your lifelong commitment to preserve it and build on that gift.

—Yo-Yo Ma

The Effects of Humanizing School Culture on the Literacy Engagement of Bilingual Students

Portrait of a High School in South Texas

Suniti Sharma and Usha Gurumurthy

John's story: I am a twelfth-grade Hispanic bilingual student. My father graduated as an agricultural engineer from the Autonomous University of Tamaulipas in Mexico but left his managerial position to move to the United States. In the United States he started as a butcher, then became a welder for Kiewit Offshore Services. Once my mother graduated from middle school she went into the workforce and received her GED while she was pregnant with me. She worked as a waitress for years and is currently unemployed and it is difficult for her to find another job with Spanish being the only language she knows. All of these factors have contributed to how I was raised. Immigrants such as my parents are not familiar with the U.S. education system, as opposed to a native student's parents whose children follow and understand the steps that must be taken to go to college. Children of immigrants may not get the opportunity to receive this level of education due to unawareness that automatically puts them at a disadvantage. With help from school, through my teachers, and a determination to succeed, I found what I need to graduate high school and go to a university. Whether SAT exam preparation, AP class enrollment, or extracurricular activity involvement, there are many obstacles and automatic disadvantages students with non-native parents, like myself, struggle through that students with native parents probably do not face. I am who I am today because my parents, my teachers and I didn't let disadvantages keep me from engaging with school work and activities. (Autobiographical Profile of Student at Big Spur High School, 2018)

Elva's story: I was born, raised, and educated in South Texas. My family has lived in this area for generations as Mexicans before 1848 and as Americans after the expansion of American borders into Mexican land. So I am an

American of Mexican descent. In the sixties, we use to identify as "White" till the government decided to put us down by separating us from those who are Anglo-White and since then, I have been called Mexican, Latina, Mexican American, and now "Hispanic." In third grade we were about 5–6 bilingual-Mexican children in each class and were spanked on our calves each time we spoke to each other in Spanish. Teachers and Anglo children didn't want anything to do with us as we were Mexican, spoke Spanish at home, and lived in project housing. In eighth grade we were moved to separate academic tracks and the Spanish speaking students were sent to a lower track. Ten years after graduating high school I realized that separate tracks meant we could not go to college and were not given any information on college like Anglo students. I took college classes ten years after graduating high school. In college I was told to take two speech courses to "get rid of your Mexican accent." Professors told us to our face that we were Mexicans as if it was a bad word, and that our accents had to be "cleaned up" or we should go home to Mexico. I did not go to BSHS but my grandchildren do and they are very fortunate. The school teaches them to honor their U.S.-Mexican-Indigenous history, teachers show they care by making my grandchildren feel proud of their bilingual heritage, the principal is a very dynamic lady, and I am happy to see the school respects Mexican and other cultures. (Interview with a Grandparent of Big Spur High School and Teacher Educator, 2018)

THE HUMAN FACE OF BILINGUAL EDUCATION IN SOUTH TEXAS

We begin this chapter with two human stories behind bilingual education in the United States to highlight how a humanizing school culture and climate of authentic care is critical to the affective well-being, academic success, and equitable college and career opportunities of language-minoritized students. In presenting the personal narratives of John and Elva, we bring to the forefront stories of generational, linguistic, and educational experiences of bilingual students—the human side of courage, care, and the struggle for justice in teaching and learning. John and Elva's narratives tell us much more than why a particular high school has raised their test scores or is categorized as Title 1 or on the brink of closure. Their narratives are testimonials on what it means to be minoritized while straddling multiple linguistic and cultural spaces and some of the educational transformations that are possible in the everyday experience of schooling in the United States.

According to Salazar (2013), "narratives can be powerful tools for illuminating and challenging the inhumanity that marks the oppressed" and compels educators to pay attention to the struggles of minoritized students as they navigate "the discourse of whiteness" (p. 122). Elva's narrative is powerful as it sheds light on areas of change reflected in the marginalization of language-minoritized students, the politics of language, culture, and identity, and the history of "subtractive schooling" (Valenzuela, 1999, p. 93) in the education of U.S.-Mexican students. Speaking of public education in Texas, Valenzuela (1999) describes the experience of U.S.-Mexican students as the "interplay between subtractive cultural assimilation and student disaffection" (p. 93) with a negative impact on their educational futures. Elva's narrative sheds light on the history of subtractive schooling, the devaluing of bilingualism under English-only norms, and the determination of those affected by the marginalization of their culture and language.

Valenzuela's (1999) ethnographic study of subtractive schooling of U.S.-Mexican students has drawn attention to inequitable schooling conditions and the underachievement of language-minoritized groups, especially Latinx students who comprise the largest bilingual student population in the country. According to Valenzuela (1999), the Texas public education system offers subtractive schooling to U.S.-Mexican students through "academic tracking, a curricular bias against Mexican culture, the Spanish language, and things Mexican" (p. 16). Elva's testimonial is a firsthand account of the experience of minoritized schooling that has led to what Gándara (2010) refers to as the Latino education crisis, which is the consequence of failed social and educational policies. Valenzuela and Gándara also highlight how the dynamics of power and language have been used to dehumanize Latinx students, denying them the right to high-quality education, and they urge educators to fight against the educational and systemic barriers to their academic success.

John's life story also touches on the systemic factors that operate as barriers to academic success for Latinx students; however, his testimonial highlights some of the transformations that are possible and need to be brought into conversations and debates on the education of language-minoritized students in public schools. John's educational experience testifies that there are schools that care about the education of bilingual and bicultural students and work hard at establishing a humanizing culture of inclusion without compromising on academic standards. Such schools empower language-minoritized students through humanizing teaching that counter subtractive schooling and positively influence their academic outcomes.

John's experience is supported by a body of research that sheds light on the wealth of language practices of language-minoritized students and families (García & Wei, 2015), the advantages of culturally responsive teaching (Ladson-Billings, 1994), and the role of authentic *cariño* (care) in minority education (Bartolomé, 2008). Research also sheds light on the positive correlation between humanizing school culture and academic outcomes facilitated by school and classroom leaders (Acker-Hocevar, Cruz-Jansen, & Wilson, 2012). Hunt's (2011) research on the role of governance in schools serving bilingual students provides evidence that a culture of care is established through effective leadership practices, close school–parent–community relationships, student empowerment, and classroom instruction responsive to the sociocultural context of students.

We situate our research within the literature of authentic care and culturally responsive teaching to explore how an urban school in South Texas creates and enacts a humanizing culture and climate of care for bilingual and multilingual students. First, we begin with a brief outline of our research followed by a profile of Big Spur High School (BSHS). Next, we elaborate on the school's leadership practices in establishing a culture of care, present evidence of how the school has created spaces for student empowerment, and offer a few examples of teachers' humanizing and culturally responsive pedagogies that engage students in language and literacy. In conclusion, we summarize the outcomes of our study, discuss the implications, and make a few recommendations for future research.

RESEARCH DESIGN AND A FRAMEWORK OF AUTHENTIC CARE

Much of the literature on language-minoritized students offers critiques of the current system of education in the United States or proposes theoretical models for emergent bilingual education at the early childhood and elementary levels. A developing body of research explores the linguistic needs of students in secondary grades and offers examples of effective teaching and learning in bilingual and multilingual classrooms (García, Flores, & Woodley, 2012). Our study builds upon this developing body of research by highlighting how an urban high school in South Texas creates a humanizing culture of care for the literacy engagement of bilingual and multilingual students. Participants in the study comprised the principal of the school, a dean, six teachers, eight students, four parents, a grandparent, and two teacher educators for bilingual education who serve as faculty at a local university. Data consisted of a survey; response to open-ended statements; interviews; autobiographical statements; district documents on student demographics, language policy, and school Annual Report Card for 2016–2017; school documents on programs offered; school website; and student assignments. In keeping with district policy, pseudonyms have been used for the school and all participants in the study.

This study draws from Freire's (1998) praxis of humanization as "armed love" (p. 41), Bartolomé's (2008) notion of authentic *cariño* and respect in minority education, and Valenzuela's (1999) advocacy for authentic care. In his *Pedagogy of the Oppressed*, Freire (1970) critiques the "banking concept of education" (p. 73) by which schools enforce assimilation to Eurocentric norms through transmission of dominant knowledge and values that simultaneously dehumanize the cultural systems of those who are dominated and oppressed. Freire identifies a number of reasons why current practices in education are dehumanizing: Knowledge transmitted to students is separate from their cultural experiences, the role of students is as passive learners rather than as critical inquirers, and ahistorical knowledge is memorized rather than contextualized in cultural and human relations.

Freire (1970) describes humanizing pedagogy as a revolutionary approach to instruction that "ceases to be an instrument by which teachers can manipulate students, but rather expresses the consciousness of the students themselves" (p. 51). As Freire explains, humanization as praxis is developing a critical consciousness toward social issues that dehumanize, replacing the banking concept of education with problem-solving, and coproducing knowledge that is cultural and historical through critical inquiry. Valenzuela (1999) draws from Freire's (1998) notion of humanizing education and armed love to urge teachers to go beyond aesthetic care to authentic care, beginning with analyses of educational policy and school practice in relation to power and knowledge. Similarly, when teaching students who are minoritized, Bartolomé (2008) advocates authentic *cariño*, which is reflected in thoughtful leadership, the kinds of programs offered, and the value placed on students' language and culture.

According to Salazar (2013), authentic care requires teachers to balance humanizing pedagogy that values students' "linguistic, cultural, and familial resources" (p. 121) with high expectations in academic performance. Salazar (2013) shares her personal experience with schools that "privileged whiteness through the English language and U.S. culture" and "excluded all that was native" (p. 122). Salazar locates such exclusions within the banking model of education perpetuated through standardization of knowledge and measurement of student learning while excluding culture and language in the schooling process.

In the classroom, a humanizing culture of care translates into culturally responsive pedagogies, an inclusive set of practices and beliefs that recognize the sociocultural context of students and teachers' experiences (Ladson-Billings, 1994). Ladson-Billings advocates culturally responsive pedagogy in the teaching of minoritized students as it "empowers students intellectually, socially, emotionally, and politically by using cultural referents to impart knowledge, skills, and attitudes" (pp. 17–18). This study draws from scholarship on the theory and praxis of authentic care to highlight the effects of a humanizing school culture on the literacy engagement of bilingual students in a high school in South Texas.

SCHOOL AND COMMUNITY CONTEXT

BSHS is a large urban public school under one of the independent school districts in South Texas and is situated between low-income neighborhoods on one side and luxurious oceanfront homes on the other. District information states that the school serves 2,117 students from grades 9–12 and the student body reflects the community demographics. The school consists of 80.7% Hispanic, 13.3% White, 2.7% Black, 0.01% American Indian, 2.3% Asian, 0.01% Pacific Islander, and 0.7% two or more races. There are 112 full-time faculty members who are 53.2% White, 39.1% Hispanic, 3.4% African American, 3.4 % Asian, and 0.9% two or more races. The school is designated Title 1, with 63.8% categorized as economically distressed. According to the school's annual report for 2016, some 8% of the students were in special education, 10.9% in gifted-and-talented education, and 1.9% were identified as English language learners. The graduation rate for the same year was 82.2% under the recommended high school program; 52% of students attained proficiency in English and 73% in math. Although the state average for class size is 18–19 students, at BSHS the average is 24 students per class.

Regarding college, 37% of the school's 2016 graduates enrolled in 4-year colleges/universities, and 41% in 2-year colleges. Since 2010, the school has been designated as a World School by the International Baccalaureate Program (IB), which draws students from all income groups. BSHS is the only high school in the district that offers the IB Program and a program for gifted-and-talented students. The IB Program is open to all students in and outside the school district; it graduated its inaugural class in 2013. The principal, teachers, and students have worked hard to make the IB Program successful, and since it began, graduates have been accepted into Harvard, MIT, Yale, Columbia, Georgetown, NYU, Stanford, Rice, and Duke, among others.

The district's motto is "Developing Hearts and Minds," and the mission of the school is to "develop the hearts and minds of all students, preparing them to be lifelong learners who continue their education, enter the world of work, and become productive citizens" (BSHS.ccisd.us). Because BSHS is a public school, all curricula, instruction, and assessment in the district are governed by policies defined by the Texas Education Agency (1995), which recognizes the needs of bilingual and multilingual students, stating, "Experience has shown that public school classes in which instruction is given only in English are often inadequate for the education of those students" (tea.texas.gov). In accordance, school districts are required to provide bilingual instruction in elementary grades, transitional language instruction in postelementary through grade 8, and English as a Second Language (ESL) instruction to students in grades 9 through 12 who are identified as English language learners (ELL). By state policy, emergent bilingual students at BSHS are supported with an ESL teacher, ELL paraprofessional, online resources, and language accommodations for immigrant newcomers for the first 3 years after moving to the United States.

SCHOOL ELEMENTS THAT ADVANCE STUDENTS' LITERACY AND LANGUAGE LEARNING

Humanizing School Leadership and Culture of Care

BSHS is headed by Dr. Mari-Lou, who has served as the school's principal since 2009. Mari-Lou grew up in a small town in South Texas, identifies as Hispanic, and is bilingual. She is certified as a teacher and administrator, has a doctoral degree in educational leadership, and has served as principal at all levels: elementary, middle, and high school. She was offered this position to lead BSHS out of its designated "low-performing/unacceptable" status for not meeting state academic standards and was assigned the task of improving the school's annual performance. Under her leadership, the school has made a complete turnaround by raising academic performance levels in all content areas and increasing school attendance, graduation rates, college admissions, and student engagement in extracurricular activities.

Mari-Lou was named the state of Texas's principal of the year in 2014 by the Texas Association of Secondary School Principals. She attributes the improvement in the school's performance to her team of teachers and staff. When interviewed, Mari-Lou stated that the success of the school starts with the "positive impact a principal can have on hundreds/thousands of lives in a school community." Mari-Lou elaborated that she practiced a philosophy of school leadership that makes every student feel welcome through caring relationships, values students' culture and language, strengthens students' social and cultural capital for postsecondary education, watches out for students who fall behind, pays special attention to parents of first-generation college-goers, supports teachers and staff, and values teamwork.

According to Mari-Lou, the students should feel welcome when they enter the school, as it creates the conditions for a nurturing environment conducive to learning. To this end, the Student Council maintains a "Take What You Need Wall," which is placed at the main hallway with sticky notes of encouragement, gratitude, respect, love, and other messages that put a smile on students' faces. A student described the messages as "compliments that lift your spirits and boost your morale as you go to class. Sometimes we need help coming to school and on tough days the notes remind us that the school cares."

As the school principal, Mari-Lou is conscious of her leadership role and combines academic rigor with building close working relationships with students, teachers, and staff. As she says, "My role is key. I must model, every single day, the characteristics I expect from my teachers/staff to ensure that we are developing relationships with our students." When asked to describe her leadership style, Mari-Lou explained, "One of my mottos is: Know Your Students; No Excuses." Mari-Lou is also aware that teachers are school leaders who must be given opportunities for showcasing their innovative pedagogies and supported in their professional development. To this end, she encourages teachers to advance their education through programs offered at the Advanced Placement Summer Institute and Advancement Via Individual Determination (AVID).

According to the teachers who participated in the study, the principal advocates for teachers and staff, appreciates the work they do, and gives them autonomy on how they teach in the classroom. For example, the principal has introduced a Staff Appreciation Week to honor those who work as custodians, in the cafeteria, and as instructional paraprofessionals. Another change that Mari-Lou has made is the special allotment of time to the school's third period dedicated to teachers and students to get to know one another. In practice, Mari-Lou shows that humanizing spaces are built on authentic caring relationships nurtured through collaborative engagement with her teachers and staff.

When speaking of college readiness and the pressure on students to raise their test scores, Mari-Lou critiqued the culture of standardized testing as oppressive to many students and families because the "content does not reflect the students' cultural contexts or experiences." This sense of oppression reminded Mari-Lou of Freire's "banking form of education and divide and rule theory" built on an educational system that "rewards those who have cultural capital and leaves the others behind." Mari-Lou added that she works with the school district, teachers, staff, students, and families to address these pressures and is always looking for strategies to balance the demands of testing with authentic caring for the whole child. As one student stated, "Dr. Mari-Lou always makes sure to tell us how much she cares for us all the time. She always takes action."

When asked about students' literacy engagement, the teachers were quick to point out that literacy goes beyond reading and math scores to creating spaces for transforming students' school experiences. A teacher who participated in the study stated that Texas Education Agency focuses on standardized tests such as State of Texas Assessments of Academic Readiness (STAAR) to improve the quality of education in Texas, which has led to "less creativity and problem-solving in the classroom, and more of rote-learning." According to the teacher, in spite of Texas's reputation as a state with test fatigue, classroom leaders maintained a humanizing and culturally relevant pedagogical approach to teaching literacy despite budget cuts and reduced support from the state.

An important component of school leadership and organization is communicating with parents, enlisting parental engagement in school events, and holding PTAs, booster club meetings, and information sessions for first-time college-goers and their families. As Freire (1998), Valenzuela (1999), and Salazar (2013) have reiterated, a humanizing culture of care means developing a critical consciousness toward issues of power, privilege, and justice. Conscious of the student body and parent community, Mari-Loul is mindful that many of the students are first-generation high school graduates, saying, "Parents feel truly burdened as they must not only close the college-readiness gap but also build social and economic capital to compete with more affluent students or students who have college-educated parents." Recognizing the information gap, teachers hold frequent information sessions for parents in English and Spanish that outline the process of college admissions.

Some of the teachers stated that teamwork is visible in how the school nurtures its relationship with parents through consistent and timely communication. Parents who were interviewed stated, "The teachers are ready to talk and explain things and give a lot of information" and "The principal makes sure everything is communicated in English and Spanish, which is very helpful." Throughout the year, parent–teacher conferences and information sessions are held where parents can discuss their concerns and play a role in the decisionmaking process. At BSHS, family serves as a cultural resource that contributes toward the school culture of care and influences students' engagement with school.

According to Fránquiz and Salazar (2004), a humanizing pedagogy that is transformative uses students' cultural resources to build social capital and pedagogical materials. At BSHS, the bulletin boards, flyers, and artifacts on display reflect students' home cultures—a point that three of the parents in this study noted. According to one parent, "The school cares. You can see children's work displayed everywhere. Makes me feel my culture is respected." Interpersonal relationships are built with team efforts, as seen from the school's Freshman Mentoring Program, which is collaboration among teachers and students. Teachers train juniors to become freshman mentors. Selection is not based on academic performance; rather, the program encourages all students to apply. The mentors host the Freshman Orientation; put on the Texan Showcase, which is a night for incoming 8th-graders and their parents; and conduct a peer-mentoring program in which Latinx high school students mentor Latinx junior high and elementary students at neighboring schools.

According to the principal, strong and supportive school and teacher leadership has brought back many students/families who had previously left the high school "when it was rated 'unacceptable' to attend private schools or nearby out of district schools have returned because of the turnaround we made in academics." The principal was thankful to her teachers and staff for transforming the status of the school from "unacceptable" and "low performing" to being a Texas Education Agency Recognized Campus that has earned six Gold Star Distinctions, the maximum number of academic honors awarded to a school in the district. She also attributed the success of the IB Program to teamwork and the perseverance of the teachers and students. The school's academic performance for 2015–16 and 2016–17 show a definite climb in the percentage of students who meet grade-level indicators in all subjects. It is not surprising that school attendance and graduation rates have also risen.

Although the principal plays a key role in defining the school's direction, teachers as classroom leaders actualize the school's mission and trajectory of success. Theories of educational leadership confirm that principals lead the way in building a culture of authentic care by bonding with students, teachers, staff, and community to address school issues (Acker-Hocevar, Cruz-Jansen, & Wilson, 2012). Research in educational leadership also confirms that teachers as caring classroom leaders have the power to effect change through curricula and pedagogical initiatives operationalized through teamwork and close school–parent–community partnerships.

Student Empowerment and Voice

At BSHS, most teachers recognized that cultural and civic engagement is the pathway to literacy engagement. In the opening narrative of this chapter, Elva recalls her school experience of being "spanked on our calves" for speaking in Spanish and teachers' low expectations that placed students who were of Mexican descent in "separate academic tracks." Her thoughts echo Salazar (2013), who writes about her experience of being "la Morena, the dark-skinned girl" who was dehumanized, having to leave her "Spanish language, Mexican culture and familia" in exchange for English and the U.S. culture (p. 121). On the other hand, John's experience with school is positive, showing the transformations that are possible. He speaks of how school and personal determination have transformed his "automatic disadvantages [of] students with nonnative parents" into AP classes, the IB Program, and a pathway to college.

BSHS has brought about several transformative changes that empower students and involve them in critical thinking, group problem-solving in real-world contexts, and teaching that is contextual and historical rather than universal or standardized. Findings from student data showed that the school had grown from 7 to 40 student clubs, creating opportunities for engagement in academics, sports, fine and performing arts, and social activism. Students stated that they were encouraged by teachers to join several clubs, such as the Amigos Spanish Club, BSHS Feminist Society for the Underaged, Audio-Visual Production, Gay–Straight Alliance, French Club and French Honors Society, and International Cultures Club and the Spanish Honors Society.

Students in this study articulated a great sense of pride toward their Mexican, Korean, African American, and Indian culture and felt the school encouraged them to celebrate their identity through art and crafts, creative writing, and autobiographical expressions. While some students felt empowered to express their culture through self-portraits, others were honored to present cultural artifacts they had created. A few of the students earned the privilege of having their self-portraits on display at the Texas A&M University Library, and others were simply happy to be able to articulate their history, identity, and culture through art, crafts and poetry. For example, one of the students was thrilled to display a dress she had tailored and embroidered that brought her Mexican heritage into the classroom.

At BSHS, cultural literacy goes hand in hand with social activism that is supported by school leaders, teachers, and the parent community. Following the Marjory Stoneman Douglas High School shooting tragedy in Florida on February 14, 2018, students' civic engagement was evidenced when they held talks with school leaders on school safety, which prompted the principal to organize a talk with legislators. On March 6, 2018, students met with local state legislators Todd Hunter, Abel Herrero, and Juan Hinojosa to present their concerns and held their state legislators accountable for improving school safety. The students who met with legislators represented the school armed with 2,000 letters from their fellow students. The school facilitated the meeting by creating a space for students to hold this conversation under the guidance of a faculty mentor. The Editorial Board of a community newspaper, the local *Caller Times* (March 12, 2018), stated that the school "is setting an especially fine example for how to engage the topic of school safety, post-Florida. Much credit is due, starting with the students. They wrote more than 2,000 letters. . . . The letters are a measure of their assertiveness, their awareness and their respect for the school's leadership."

A critical component of a humanizing school is creating safe spaces for students to share their personal struggles and empathize with some of the personal experiences of their peers. One of the students spoke of how the school had empowered him and created a safe place to be able to share his life-changing experience of a parent battling cancer. By sharing his experience at school, he was also able to spread awareness among the education community about some of the concerns of children who encounter similar struggles at home.

As seen from the above examples, a humanizing school culture of care is a process of empowerment that is cultural, political, and educational. As one of the teachers who was asked what a humanizing education meant to him stated in an interview, "The Texas system targets standardization. But children are not test scores, as teachers we celebrate students' knowledge. This way, students don't feel alienated or weighed down with problems." Our findings show that critical to students' literacy engagement is fostering a sense of belonging and creating a school culture where students feel included and take pride in sharing their cultural experiences with the school and the outside community.

Culturally Responsive Teaching in Multilingual Classrooms

At BSHS, secondary-grade teachers use a diverse range of humanizing and culturally responsive pedagogies that attend to the literacy engagement of bilingual and multilingual students. According to Ladson-Billings (1994), culturally responsive pedagogy aims at developing teachers' sociopolitical consciousness of self in relation to students, and places value on culture as a dynamic asset in the construction of classroom knowledge. Findings from data on teachers' curricula and instruction underscore the importance of humanizing and culturally responsive pedagogies for teaching bilingual and multilingual students.

According to a teacher at BSHS, "deficit thinking is the largest roadblock to equity . . . so ELLs are relegated to special ed and underrepresented in gifted and talented." The teacher added, "You can't teach English by teaching English"; hence, he uses dual-language instruction because "students need the tools to make them successful." An ESL teacher explained that most of the students in her class spoke Spanish, so she used their home language as a tool to help them learn English and allowed students to process new knowledge in their home language, even though the final written work is in English.

In the ESL class, one of the tasks that students have fun with is reading a text in English and scavenger hunting for cognates they recognize. In an autobiographical reflection, one of the students stated that "using Spanish to recognize big words in English like *primary-primario* and *experiment-experimentar*, helps me in math and science." Processing new information using cognate lists/walls is well documented in dual-language educational research that supports building cognate awareness as a bridge between a familiar and an emergent language (Baker, 2011). The use of two languages also makes curricular room for strengthening students' proficiency in both the home and the new language (García & Wei, 2015).

One of the teachers summed up students' use of two languages when processing new knowledge, saying, "Students have to be comfortable with language engagement so there's code-switching, translanguaging, translation, even trilingual language interaction. . . . It is fascinating how older students communicate." Speaking of translanguaging, the teacher explained that when the district provides fewer resources for bilingual students in high school and increases testing demands, teachers who "are concerned must fill in those gaps, allowing translanguaging in the classroom." García and Wei (2015) describe translanguaging as "transformative pedagogy" that enables students to think through one language and write in another. The use of multiple languages in the classroom served as a tool for engaging emergent bilingual students in ways that were culturally responsive to strengthen their use of the home language and help them learn a new one.

What stood out in our findings was how culturally responsive teaching was the norm in most classrooms. An English teacher at the school stated that the "exciting part of critical reading is more than comprehension and fluency; it is the experience of literacy shaped by the reader's social and cultural knowledge that allows for multiple interpretations of a given text." Palmer and Martinez's (2013) research on teacher agency in bilingual spaces suggests that educators shift their understanding of teaching English by broadening their curricula to include international texts, and translations, and to open learning to the dynamism of dual-language practices.

Evidence of this dynamic space was applauded by a student who described how her English teacher's "multiculturally responsive teaching" had made her realize the importance of reading "world literature to get to know other cultures." This particular class consisted of 80% Hispanic and 20% White, Asian, South Asian, Southeast Asian, Native American, and African American students. Accordingly, the class compiled a global reading list that consisted of several translated works. Reading *Rickshaw Boy* (Lao, 2010) transported students into the political and social history of China in the 1930s, which led them to conduct historical research that extended to Southeast Asia. At one point, *Rickshaw Boy* took an innovative turn as students transformed the traditional text by fast-forwarding the characters in the novel into the 21st-century digital world of social media and text messages.

In another class, after reading Bao Ninh's *The Sorrow of War* (1996), set in Vietnam, students said they felt "transformed" and "changed" because it provided them with the Vietnamese perspective on the Vietnam War and connected the conflict to the wars in Middle East. While reading Gabriel García Márquez's *Chronicle of a Death Foretold* (2003), students generated a multicultural discussion on virginity in different cultures, gender equality, the notion of *machismo* (masculine pride), and domestic violence in today's social context. Student reflections written as class assignments signal their multicultural awareness. For example, a Hispanic student spoke of the experience of reading multicultural literature, saying:

> I think that reading texts from around the world has widened my global view and enhanced my perception of world affairs. For example, when I read news articles, I am able to understand the cultural context of gender, the role of men and women, and to see how they matter in my life. When meeting international students in college, I will be able to better communicate and be more open-minded about other cultures.

As seen from the above examples of culturally responsive pedagogies in classrooms at BSHS, teachers recognize that there is no blueprint for English instruction for bilingual and multilingual students in a secondary classroom. Rather, literacy engagement is a sociocultural process of teaching and learning that is dynamic, contextual, and relational to the multicultural and multilingual experiences of students, teachers, and their communities. Findings from the data indicate that all of the parents and students who participated in the study considered the teachers caring and supportive and believed this was a key factor in turning around the school's academic performance and school attendance.

OUTCOMES

We hope the outcomes of this study will be useful to teachers, teacher educators, educational researchers, as well as school and district leaders and policymakers when conceptualizing and making decisions on how to advance students' literacy and language learning. Key outcomes of this study include the following:

- A humanizing culture of authentic care across the school is an effective framework that advances language-minoritized students' language and literacy learning.
- Students' literacy and language learning must be supported by strong leadership, student empowerment, close-knit school–parent–community relations, teamwork, and culturally responsive teaching.
- Effective school leadership implies caring about minoritized students and taking initiatives to create a culture of inclusion by introducing programs such as mentoring, information sessions for parents, resources for teachers' professional development, and acknowledgment of staff contributions.
- Schools committed to empowering language-minoritized students create spaces for showcasing students' cultural knowledge through art, creative writing, and civic engagement.
- Empowerment of language-minoritized students leads to their emotional well-being, which leads to higher levels of literacy engagement, improved academic outcomes, and greater college and career readiness.
- Language and literacy learning of language-minoritized students is enhanced through pedagogies that balance high academic standards with culturally responsive teaching.

CONCLUSIONS AND RECOMMENDATIONS

This study presents a multidimensional portrait of BSHS with several examples of how a humanizing school culture of care promoted the literacy engagement of bilingual and multilingual students. School leadership practices, school–parent–community relations, student voice and empowerment, and teachers' culturally responsive classroom pedagogies constitute a humanizing culture of authentic care. Many urban schools serve minoritized communities that struggle with issues such as economic hardships, unemployment, inadequate housing conditions, and lack of structural support needed for their children's education. Minoritized communities, especially Hispanic and African American, suffer the consequences of racism and segregation perpetuated by misconceptions and stereotyping that alienates their children from schools and compromises their right to high-quality education.

In contemporary contexts, the education of bilingual and multilingual students has become a politically charged issue that affects school policy, classroom practice, and public perceptions. Besides focusing on high-quality education for all students, public schools have an added responsibility of countering public perceptions that dehumanize bilingual and multilingual students and communities. This dehumanization influences policy, which, in turn, affects minoritized communities to unimaginable extents, as evidenced in the plan to build the border wall, end the Deferred Action for Childhood Arrivals Act, and continued support to "make America White again." Schools are in a central position to fight for equity and equal opportunities for their students, take a stand, advocate for change, and act against misconceptions, stereotyping, and xenophobia that lead to unequal academic outcomes.

Today, it is more important than ever that we support public education by showcasing humanizing schools and the enormous efforts by their principals and teachers to create a safe environment for minoritized students and work toward their affective and academic well-being. Effective school leaders create spaces for transformations by listening to the voices of students and legitimizing their experiences as knowledge worth knowing. By serving as role models and promoting a humanizing culture, school leaders connect with minoritized parents and families and provide teachers with the autonomy needed for culturally responsive teaching.

In fostering a humanizing culture of authentic care, teachers are the glue that holds the fabric of schools together. Working through the political and testing landscape of education, caring teachers make this possible through culturally responsive teaching, not by standardizing curricula or fulfilling testing mandates that criminalize minoritized families and communities. Caring teachers recognize literacy engagement goes beyond interaction with reading and writing or taking tests to creating classroom opportunities for collaborative relationships with peers and the time and space for extracurricular activities, participation in sports, and civic action for bringing educational change.

Teacher education and educational leadership programs play a critical role in creating and facilitating a humanizing culture of care through intentional coursework and as part of continuing professional development for district, school, and classroom leaders. This research suggests that future teachers would benefit from working with bilingual and multilingual students and communities as part of their field experiences. This study also suggests that future research might explore some of the innovative strategies teachers employ when working with secondary bilingual and multilingual students. We conclude with the promise that more secondary educators conduct research on their pedagogical practices and share their transformative work so that schools across the United States can make the humanizing culture of care a top priority in the quest for equitable education for all students.

REFERENCES

Acker-Hocevar, M. A., Cruz-Jansen, M. I., & Wilson, C. L. (2012). *Leadership from the ground up: Effective schooling in traditionally low performing schools.* Charlotte, NC: Information Age Publishing.

Baker, C. R. (2011). *Foundations of bilingual education and bilingualism* (5th ed.). Bristol, England: Multilingual Matters.

Bartolomé, I. L. (2008). Authentic cariño and respect in minority education: The political and ideological dimensions of love. *International Journal of Critical Pedagogy, 1*(1), 1–17.

Editorial Board. (2018). In Corpus Christi, a national model for engaging school safety. *Corpus Christi Caller Times.* Retrieved from www.caller.com/story/opinion/2018/03/12/corpus-christi-national-model-engaging-school-safety/416285002/

Fránquiz, M., & Salazar, M. (2004). The transformative potential of humanizing pedagogy: Addressing the diverse needs of Chicano/Mexicano students. *High School Journal, 87*(4), 36–53.

Freire, P. (1970). *Pedagogy of the oppressed.* New York, NY: Continuum.

Freire, P. (1998). *Teachers as cultural workers: Letters to those who dare to teach.* Boulder, CO: Westview.

Gándara, P. (2010). The Latino education crisis. *Educational Leadership, 67,* 24–30.

García, O., Flores, N., & Woodley, H. H. (2012). Transgressing monolingualism and bilingual dualities: Translanguaging pedagogies. In A. Yiakoumetti (Ed.), *Harnessing linguistic variation for better education* (pp. 45–76). Bern, Switzerland: Peter Lang.

García, O., & Wei, L. (2015) Translanguaging, bilingualism, and bilingual education. In W. E. Wright, S. Boun, & O. García (Eds.), *The handbook of bilingual and multilingual education* (pp. 223–240). Chichester, England: John Wiley & Sons.

Garcia Márquez, G. (2003). *Chronicle of a death foretold.* Trans. Gregory Rabassa. New York, NY: Vintage Books.

Hunt, V. (2011). Learning from success stories: Leadership structures that support dual language programs over time in New York City. *International Journal of Bilingual Education and Bilingualism, 14*(2), 187–206. doi:10.1080/13670050.2010.539673

Ladson-Billings, G. (1994). *The dreamkeepers.* San Francisco, CA: Jossey-Bass.

Lao, S. (2010). *Rickshaw boy.* Trans. Howard Goldblatt. New York, NY: Harper Collins.

Ninh, B. (1996). *The sorrow of war.* Trans. Phan Thanh Hao. New York, NY: Riverhead Books.

Palmer, D., & Martínez, R. A. (2013). Teacher agency in bilingual spaces: A fresh look at preparing teachers to educate Latina/o bilingual children. *Review of Research in Education, 37*(1), 269–297. doi:10.3102/0091732X12463556

Salazar, M. D. (2013). A humanizing pedagogy: Reinventing the principles and practice of education as a journey toward liberation. *Review of Research in Education, 37*(1), 121–148. doi:10.3102/0091732X12464032

Texas Education Agency. (1995). Texas Education Code (TEC) §29.051 -29.064—Bilingual Education and ESL Programs. Retrieved from tea.texas.gov/bilingual/esl/education/

Valenzuela, A. (1999). *Subtractive schooling U.S.-Mexican youth and the politics of caring.* Albany, NY: State University of New York Press.

CHAPTER 8

"I'm Multilingual"

Leveraging Students' Translanguaging Practices to Strengthen the School Community

Ivana Espinet, Brian Collins, and Ann Ebe

Manuel, a 16-year-old student from the Dominican Republic (DR), came to the United States three years earlier. Although he had consistent schooling in the DR, when he first began at "Knowledge and Power Preparatory Academy" (KAPPA) International, his reading level was at 3rd or 4th grade in Spanish, and he did not speak or read much English. Nevertheless, Manuel was very motivated to learn, consistently attended school, and was engaged and persistent in his approach to learning. Since beginning school at KAPPA International, he has been part of the bilingual program, where many of his classes were conducted in Spanish. Teachers at the school provided specific strategies to support Manuel's development in language and content areas. For example, when he first came to the school he struggled with using Spanish language for academic purposes, so teachers worked with him on how to annotate certain words, ask what they mean, and look for meaning within context to figure out complex texts. Manuel was able to raise his Spanish reading abilities quickly to grade level and read at grade-level academic Spanish. The school offered after-school support as well, which Manuel consistently attended. After 3 years in the school, Manuel also made progress in his writing and understanding of English, although he remains somewhat hesitant to speak. As a result, he has been very successful at passing all the required state exams to graduate (Regents) and doing well in most of his classes. Manuel has even begun to tutor other students in Spanish who did not pass or struggled with the Regents. Manuel also was involved in many extracurricular programs, including the student-created multicultural club in which home languages and cultures in the school were represented. He participated in student-led conferences, which KAPPA International hosts during the year for students to reflect on their learning and discuss what they need to do to continue to grow as learners. Several students at the school have been separated from their families who are in their home country. For these families, the school video-records the student-led conference in their home languages for the parents to see from home. Samantha Heiderscheid, the school's ENL coordinator, explained that they began to videotape the conferences for parents "because they won't have access to this American high school experience for their child otherwise."

This vignette exemplifies how a school with a humanizing philosophy can create a space that reaches beyond the school walls so students and families can work together. It takes an educator who knows about her students' lives beyond the school, and who respects and cherishes their languages and cultures, and who reaches out to families so the students can reflect and share their successes, challenges, and plans for how to continue to learn. In this chapter, we focus on KAPPA International, a high school in the Bronx that embraces translanguaging practices in its work with emergent bilinguals. We describe how a school's model of distributed leadership of the English as a new language (ENL) support team has supported faculty to find creative ways of working with emergent bilinguals and their families. Throughout the chapter, we highlight and discuss the work of the three teachers in the ENL team: Samantha Heiderscheid, Tammy Wang, and Sarah Van Etten. Following Salazar's (2013) descriptions of humanizing pedagogy, the philosophy of the school's focus on meaningful, purposeful, student-centered education also builds upon the sociocultural realities of students' lives. To demonstrate how KAPPA International embraces this philosophy, we begin by describing the context of the school and the community in which it is situated. Next, we analyze how the school philosophy, structures, and translanguaging pedagogies have advanced students' literacy and language learning. We end with concluding points and provide recommendations.

COMMUNITY AND SCHOOL CONTEXT

KAPPA International School is a public high school (grades 9–12) in the Bronx, New York City. The school is colocated with five other small schools within the building and shares a floor with another school. With close to 500 students in the school, space is always an issue in making decisions about structuring and supporting student learning.

The student population is primarily Latinx (60%) and Black (33%), including a cohort of newcomer African students who are English speakers but also speak various African languages. The majority of students in the school speak a language other than English, predominantly Spanish, but also Arabic, Bengali, Urdu, and several African languages. Most classes include anywhere from 10 to 100% of students who speak a language other than English at home. Approximately 15% of students have been identified as English language learners (ELLs) and are entitled to accommodations and additional language support. Approximately 10% of students are "newcomers" or students with interrupted formal education (SIFE) who are placed in cohorts with dedicated classes to support their learning. The majority (90%) of students receive free/reduced-price school meals.

SCHOOL ELEMENTS THAT SUPPORT STUDENTS' LEARNING

Committed Staff and School Leadership

The school has a committed staff and principal, as well as 39 teachers, including three ENL teachers and 12 teachers who speak a language other than English (Spanish, French, Arabic, German, and Chinese). The school staff is also multilingual. Two out of three ENL teachers grew up in immigrant families and spoke languages other than English at home. The principal of the school was previously a bilingual (Spanish/English) math teacher before becoming the KAPPA principal in 2007. She believes in a model of distributed leadership where activities and interactions are shared across multiple people and situations (Harris, 2008). Teachers take the lead in different areas and the staff works collaboratively in planning and designing programs.

New York State Initiative on Emergent Bilinguals (NYSIEB)

The school was selected to participate in New York State Initiative on Emergent Bilinguals (NYSIEB), a collaborative project with the City University of New York (CUNY) and the New York State Education Department (NYSED) working toward improving the education of emergent bilingual students across the state. During school visits, researchers from CUNY-NYSIEB, including the authors, interviewed school staff and conducted classroom observations. Through this data collection process, researchers identified specific practices that these schools used to support emergent bilinguals. In addition, an emergent bilingual leadership team (EBLT) was created at the school to lead efforts to increase support and improve the academic achievement and outcomes for emergent bilinguals. The team included teachers, students, and administrators. Part of the support provided to the school included translanguaging strategies to meet communicative and academic needs in English and other languages, and to learn challenging new content. Translanguaging refers to the use of a learner's full linguistic repertoire—including features from multiple languages—to make meaning from the complex interactions that are enacted by different human beings and texts in our globalized world (Sánchez, García, & Solorza, 2017). We describe specific examples of translanguaging in the sections below. The EBLT participated in professional development and support from the CUNY-NYSIEB project over a period of 3 years.

Celebrating and Supporting Bilingualism

Although the school had a philosophy about teaching and learning that was grounded in humanizing pedagogy, its involvement in the CUNY-NYSIEB initiative shifted this philosophy to focus even further on the school's emergent bilingual population of students. As a result, a key aspect of the school's philosophy is to truly celebrate bilingualism. The principal described the school's thinking as they began implementing the CUNY-NYSIEB initiative: "The whole philosophy is moving and we are having those open conversations with our staff and with our students. Learning more about what it means to be an effective educator who is trying to promote multilingualism. How do we get better at that? What does that look like in a school that is promoting the program?" KAPPA's goals were to create spaces for students to use home language, develop professional development for all school teachers to learn strategies of translanguaging, and build multilingualism and multiculturalism into the curriculum design. These goals were created to develop student voice and empowerment as well as to support the school's multicultural student group. The EBLT met regularly to discuss and define the language policy of the school and also included students in the planning.

Having students develop bilingualism or multilingualism was a key aspect of the school's language policy. The students created a survey for their classmates to respond to on how their home languages and cultures were represented in the school and what they would like to improve. As a result, the school started an after-school multicultural club. The administration and school staff embraced the goals of CUNY-NYSIEB and worked toward enriching the multilingual ecology of the school to have the students' languages visually represented in the school environment. New signage around the school included the students' home languages and teachers created multilingual word walls in their classrooms. Teachers were provided time for teams to meet and plan how to incorporate translanguaging in the classroom.

The school organized community events that celebrated the languages and cultures of the families in the school and made efforts to reach out to bilingual families in the community. For example, during Open House Night, student ambassadors communicated with prospective parents in various home languages. The school principal recalled, "Our own students acted as translators and because we have various groups within our school community, the parents are impressed when they see how the students articulate the vision of the school in their native language and that has given a sense of familiarity and trust, so those parents, and the students as well, are quick to identify our school as a safe environment and a communal environment, and it's because our own students have taken a leadership role and they want to reach out." Following the Open House, students also volunteered to be translators for Parent–Teacher Night. The school also started a bilingual bulletin board with information targeted to parents in the school.

Perhaps the most powerful example of the school's focus on celebrating students' languages were the school T-shirts with the KAPPA logo and the slogan "I am multilingual! Are you?" Many of the students wore the shirts proudly in the school (Figure 8.1) The principal explained that when they gave the T-shirts out to the emergent bilingual students in the school, "that just piqued the interest of the other students. 'How do I get that T-shirt? What do I have to do?' and it was nice to see how they wanted to recognize a language other than English, not just to receive the T-shirt but because then they were curious about the languages that other students spoke, again, doing more things as a school community that unite us rather than divide us."

Figure 8.1. I Am Multilingual T-Shirt

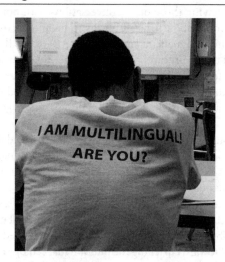

Open Enrollment International Baccalaureate Program

The school philosophy of celebrating diversity is also reflected in their International Baccalaureate (IB) Program, which is open to all students. This program strives to value and support all cultures and the use of all languages present in the learning community. The program explores broad questions, providing students with the opportunity to demonstrate what they know and foster cross-cultural understanding. To implement these ideals, the school includes information, literature, and history from multiple cultures in its content and curricular design.

The International Baccalaureate Program, which fosters cross-cultural understanding, includes, among other things, visits to other countries and exchanges with students from different communities. As the assistant principal described in an interview, the school's program is one of a few programs that has open enrollment in New York City:

> IB is usually viewed as a gifted-and-talented program, you need a 90% average to get in; you know, it's for the elite. It was started in the 1960s for the children who studied over in Europe. We know that it's good pedagogy, right? We know that students who undergo this program, even if they don't get the highest marks, even if they don't take the full program, just a course here or there, they're going to be more prepared for the rigors of college.

The school has done an excellent job of getting students excited about taking IB classes and has created a culture of students wanting to push themselves. Though the school makes this opportunity available to all its students, there are indeed challenges in implementing open enrollment. The assistant principal goes on to explain:

In so many schools, it's "I'm a senior, I only have three classes that I need to graduate, you can't make me take any more than that." Our seniors are asking if they can take IB classes. That's the easier part. And I think we've done a really fantastic job with getting students very excited about pushing themselves in that way. The hard part is the academic part, and the fact that if a kid is coming to us in 9th grade, reading at a 5th-grade level, and by the end of 12th grade, they need to be doing this complex analysis, how do we fill those gaps?

The school prides itself on providing classes based on the population of students it receives each year and their various needs.

Flexible Programming

The school has offered a range of programs for bilingual students, and these programs have changed from year to year, depending on the needs of the incoming students. Most recently, the school applied to New York City Department of Education to open a bilingual program that started in the 2017–2018 school year. In this new bilingual program, additional content courses (math, science, and social studies) are offered in Spanish and English and are aimed at building bilingualism and biliteracy. An ongoing challenge that the school faces, however, is personnel. The school has encountered difficulty finding content teachers who are bilingual or are certified to teach in a bilingual program. Given the limited number of teachers who speak Spanish in the school, in the past the school has offered bilingual sections of a few courses for the students in grades with the largest numbers of newcomers. In the other grades, the school offered classes with bilingual support from ENL teachers who speak Spanish.

Regardless of whether students are part of the bilingual program, the school expects all students to work toward multilingualism by developing their home and additional language literacies. The ENL department incorporates bilingual methodologies across core content classes to build emerging English language acquisition and literacy.

Collaborative Team Teaching

The school employs a collaborative team-teaching model in which ENL and bilingual teachers co-teach within subject-area classes with large numbers of emergent bilinguals. Home language instruction and materials are provided in these classes and students are often grouped by shared home language and encouraged to work together in both languages to complete assignments. This model also includes specific supports for the social–emotional and linguistic needs of newcomers and SIFE students.

In 2017, the administration and a few teachers began to participate in a Learning Partners Program focusing on improving co-planning and co-teaching as a school, hosting and visiting other schools, and examining their shared practices as a triad school team together. As a school, they have been exploring and experimenting with six various co-teaching models (Friend & Cook, 1992). Samantha, the ENL coordinator, explained: "Alternative and station teaching[1] has become more prominent in our ENL practice as we drill down to target skill gaps in co-taught classes with special attention to our EBL students' groups. It's becoming a whole-school topic rather than an ENL and co-teacher conversation, which is tremendously exciting!"

KAPPA began its work with CUNY-NYSIEB with the goal of addressing the needs of emergent bilinguals and capitalizing on their strengths in all the classrooms. Because the culture of the school has always been very collaborative, teachers co-planned and shared resources to incorporate translanguaging strategies in their classroom. In the following sections, we highlight some of the specific examples of how translanguaging was used as a resource in the classroom.

TRANSLANGUAGING FOR TRANSFORMATION IN THE CLASSROOM

A translanguaging perspective in creating student programming and developing classroom curricula focuses on what bilingual learners do with language to produce and interpret their social and academic worlds. This comes with the understanding that students are incorporating new features of languages into their developing linguistic repertoires. Sánchez, García, and Solorza (2017) write about spaces in which translanguaging is used in the classroom intentionally for three purposes: "(a) to have a more holistic understanding of the child as learner (translanguaging documentation), (b) to scaffold instruction for individual students (translanguaging rings), and (c) to transform the normalizing effects of standardized language in school and the hegemony of English (translanguaging transformation)" (p. 7). This framework is useful in analyzing how educators at KAPPA provide students with translanguaging affordances that empower the diverse group of emergent bilinguals that are part of their school community to meaningfully participate in classroom instruction.

Translanguaging Documentation

The ENL team keeps track of the students' language development, not only in English, but also in Spanish in formal and informal ways. SIFE students are assessed at entrance using New York State's Multilingual Literacy Screener (MLS) to determine their home language literacy levels in order to design appropriate instruction. In addition, the ENL team also makes an effort to observe and document the practices of all students' home language use and to assess their understandings in a holistic way.

For example, when Jaime, a student with interrupted formal education, entered the school, his MLS test placed him at a 2nd-grade level in Spanish literacy. Although the initial test informed the school how to place him and the kinds of supports that he might need, Tammy, who works with him in language skills class, continued to observe him and document his language practices for classroom communicative and academic purposes in both languages. She noted that he was very strong in expressing his ideas orally when he shared in class discussion and small groups, which showed that he was capable of complex thinking, but he struggled to write his ideas. Tammy's assessment was based on his oral language practices mostly in Spanish, because he was at an "entering level" in English according to the New York State English as a Second Language Achievement Test (NYSESLAT). She also noted that Jaime didn't write in complete sentences in Spanish. So, she started to teach him strategies that could be applied to both languages, such as using part of the question to begin writing a response. Her understanding of what Jaime could do, regardless of the language, helped Tammy focus on which skills he had and which skills he needed to build, and this helped her determine the scaffolds she used with him in order to support his development.

Documenting students' fluid language practices provides invaluable information to support emergent bilinguals' growth as learners and help them fulfill the external demands that high school students face, such as passing New York State's Regents exams.[2] For example, Samantha, who provides support for a science class, explained: "We use a lot of translanguaging methods since we pre-identify in private conferences that they would be more successful taking the test in Spanish." The class supports the students in learning the content, and developing their language both in Spanish and English, but with the understanding that the students in this specific class will perform better on the test if they are given the chance to take it in their home language.

Translanguaging to Scaffold Instruction

The teachers at KAPPA try to differentiate the design of instruction and provide instructional material and strategies that support individual students. Members of the ENL team shared that determining the appropriate scaffolds for different students in each class is one of the biggest challenges that they face. Sanchez, García, and Solorza (2017, p. 10) explain that translanguaging rings "act as a temporary scaffold until bilingual students have acquired new features that expand their repertoire to the necessary level, and until they gain confidence leveraging their own translanguaging to perform with whatever linguistic features they do have in their repertoire." These translanguaging rings might include the use of bilingual materials or technology such as Google Translate.

In Tammy's literacy class, students read the fantasy novel The Lighting Thief, by Rick Riordan. Though all the students are engaged with the same novel, some students read the English and Spanish versions side by side, others have the English version and the graphic novel in English, while a student like Jaime, who is developing his reading skills in both English and Spanish, have the graphic novel in English and Spanish, as well as the novel in Spanish. Tammy explained that the pictures and the images, as well as the language used in the graphic novels, help students like Jaime follow the storyline and the context: "I'm trying to help him understand the book as a whole, through these different resources." Using different kinds of texts is embedded in a guided process. As Tammy explains:

> I don't give them all the books at the same time. We practice short snippets of each kind of text for a particular purpose. For example, we might use the graphic novel to move through the book and learn specific vocabulary words in both languages, but we would also close-read a few paragraphs of the novel itself to analyze characters or a conflict which requires more complex thinking. It is important to use each kind of text purposefully.

Tammy's design of the translanguaging rings that support Jaime in reading this novel along with his peers is based on the understanding that translanguaging also involves the use of multimodal communication. Jaime was able to utilize not only linguistic signs, but also images, lines, drawings, and other conventions used in graphic novels.

In addition to the individual rings that teachers provide, they also use whole-class instructional practices such as lesson scaffolds that build students' language competence in both languages. The following example describes a lesson in a co-taught living environment class in a heterogeneous classroom, with some emergent bilinguals who are newcomers, some who have had interrupted formal educations, as well other experienced bilinguals who are comfortable moving fluidly between both languages.

As the students enter the room, a "Do Now" (warm-up activity) is posted on the smartboard in English and Spanish: What are fossil fuels? What impact do they have on our planet? The prompt also displays a picture of oil wells to provide a visual clue to the students. The "Do Now" activity is designed to help students make connections to the content that they learned previously. The students take a minute to jot down their ideas in either language and share them. Sarah, the ENL teacher, writes down notes on the board. One of the students shares in English that fossil fuels "are made of ancient organisms." Sarah writes it down and asks: "What does the word *ancient* mean?" A student responds in Spanish: "*Anciano, muy viejo.*" She points out that *ancient* and *anciano* are cognates. Many Spanish words that are part of everyday language are encountered, in English, in the context of language used for academic purposes. In this short exchange, Sarah demonstrated using Spanish cognates to make sense of vocabulary that they might find in academic subjects in English. As the lesson progresses, the content-area teacher introduces key concepts, such as global warming and greenhouse effect, in English, but also provides the definition in Spanish and images that support the main idea. The students watch a short video, in English with Spanish subtitles, about fossil fuels' contribution to global warming and about alternative sources of energy. When they are finished, the students work with a partner. Each pair gets two copies of a short article, in both Spanish and English, about alternative sources of energy. The students take notes about the pros and cons of each source of energy, translanguaging as they make sense of the article and negotiate what to write. When they finish the task, they discuss with another pair of students: What kind of alternative energy would you choose for your home? Why is it better than fossil fuels?

In this lesson, the teachers taught content, the students learned about fossil fuels, expanded the students' subject-area vocabulary—in both Spanish and English—and they provided the students with metalinguistic translanguaging strategies that they could use to support their learning. For many emergent bilingual students, translanguaging is also transformative, providing possibilities to learn and engage meaningfully and authentically with lessons.

Though these examples focused on bilingual Spanish support, for the students who speak lower-incidence languages in the school, such as Bengali or Arabic, the ENL team provides scaffolds to access content, such as strategic partnerships with students with the same home language (if available) and access to home language dictionaries. The students also learn to use their home language strategically during reading and writing such as note-taking in their home language when reading a text in English or brainstorming in their home language before writing.

Translanguaging Transformational Spaces

It has been well documented that the effective teaching of emergent bilinguals allows for opportunities for students to use their full linguistic and cultural repertoires of practices (Collins & Cioè-Peña, 2016; García & Wei, 2013; Freeman, Freeman, Soto, & Ebe, 2016; Seltzer & Collins, 2016). Furthermore, researchers have documented that the social and cognitive aspects of learning are inextricably bound together (Jones & Doolittle, 2017; Walqui & Van Lier, 2010). Cognitive processes develop through rich, challenging, and well-supported activities. For example, Walqui and Van Lier (2010) write about how "language is learned primarily in the process of developing a 'voice' in the language, an ability to desire to be heard while claiming the right to be listened to" (p. 57). In working with emergent bilinguals, KAPPA teachers leverage the knowledge that students bring to the school and create opportunities for them to expand and build on their strengths.

Building students' social competencies is an integral component of KAPPA. Tammy, in a language skills class in which most of her students are at an "entering" or "emergent" level, leveraged students' experiences in class activities where students brainstormed questions in Spanish, English, or both that they wanted to ask people in the community about their professions. Next, the class interviewed community members. Given the diverse community that surrounds the school, they found individuals who only spoke English, some who only spoke Spanish, and others who felt comfortable moving between both languages. After approaching individuals and introducing themselves, they had to decide how to ask the questions. In some cases, they had written the questions in Spanish and had to switch to English with the help of a peer. After doing a few interviews, students came back to the classroom and debriefed their experiences, sharing the information they had gathered, as well as how they fluidly moved between their linguistic repertoires.

As a follow-up activity, students chose one person in their family or their community to interview about their work. Students chose the language of the interview, keeping in mind what they knew about the interviewee's language practices. The students created the questions, practiced asking them in class with their peers, thought of possible follow-up questions, and conducted the interviews as homework. After the interviews, they used the information that they had gathered to write an article and create a newsletter that they shared in the school community.

This project extended learning beyond the classroom with students using their knowledge of members of the community to choose an interviewee and their full linguistic repertoire to conduct interviews and write about them. Pauline Gibbons (2015) writes about how spoken language and written language are better understood as a continuum rather than as two discrete forms of language. She recommends that classroom activities should be planned to move along this spoken–written continuum, so that the teaching and learning builds on language that occurs in a face-to-face context toward the written language of school that uses language for academic purposes. In Tammy's classroom, her students translanguaged as they moved fluidly between language modes, writing questions, asking them, listening to the interviewees, taking notes, and reading their answers, in order to write an article. The tasks were grounded in a real-world project of creating a newsletter, in which they could share their knowledge about community members.

USING STUDENTS' LINGUISTIC AND CULTURAL RESOURCES TO ENRICH THE SCHOOL COMMUNITY

One of the challenges that school newcomers face is having to adapt to a new culture, learn a new language, and understand the demands of schools in the United States. High school is a time when young people are developing their identity, establishing friendships, and building social skills. For this reason, it is important to create a caring, supportive environment. It is essential for adolescents to make connections to young people who share their experiences and have a deep understanding of what it is like to be in a new school, in a new country, speaking a new language (Cloud, Lakin, Leininger, & Maxwell, 2010).

KAPPA International places an emphasis on supporting the social–emotional development of each student. Salazar (2013) has written about how strong relationships with adults and peers that are grounded in students' cultural funds of knowledge impact their academic resiliency and help them build strong academic identities. Furthermore, the chance of academic success of newcomer students is strengthened when there are friendships and integration with academically engaged students with and outside of their own cultural background (Conchas,

2001). KAPPA has set up two significant ways in which students provide peer support: through a buddy system that connects individual students on their first day with an older student who is also an emergent bilingual, and through student mentors who provide academic and emotional support during class and after school.

The Buddy System

Before the beginning of the year, all freshmen, including newly enrolled emergent bilinguals, come to KAPPA for orientation to review the school's expectations and to participate in community-building activities. For the students who come during the school year, the ENL coordinator connects each of them right away. Samantha explains: "No new student should eat lunch alone. The most important thing to a teenager is the social–emotional aspect of being a student. We connect them on day one with a buddy who takes them to lunch and gives them a school tour." The buddy, who shares the same home language, shows the new student how to get lunch, takes him or her on a tour of the school, and walks the new student to class. As a result, many of the students also begin new friendships that support them throughout their school career.

The ENL faculty brainstorms with the students who will become buddies about what students need to know about the school because, as Samantha explained, "They know best because they have gone through the same process." The buddy system helps build community and responsibility among the students and allows the older emergent bilinguals to be the expert for the newcomer. In addition, the newcomers who are newly enrolled are invited to an after-school outing with a group of older bilinguals so they have a chance to socialize and discuss how to adjust to their new schools and homes. This buddy system is particularly useful for SIFE students who often need more explicit explanations from their peers about how school works.

Student Mentors

In a meeting with the student mentors, Samantha, the ENL coordinator, told the group: "Diana is the reason why I learned to teach a better Global Prep for the bilingual juniors. I never had taught that before. This was a new thing for me. She would give me feedback at the end of each lesson and then they all passed." Samantha shared her experience with other mentors to illustrate to them that they are not only valuable resources to other students, but also to the teachers who are learning from them how to become better teachers. In setting up opportunities for peer support, teachers at the school are disrupting the adult–child and teacher–student binaries of classroom hierarchy, creating an "in-between" space in the class community and forming relationships with the students who are not subject to those binaries.

The ENL team pairs emergent bilinguals to become mentors for newcomer students who speak their home language. Among other things, the mentors share their work with the new students as peer-led exemplars. They talk through their work samples with their mentees to show what the target looks like. The mentors help "demystify" the academic process, which is particularly important for students who have interrupted formal education.

Camila, one of the student mentors, explained, "I was in the same situation [as the newcomer students] 3 years ago. It's important that we address the language and the content, because if we teach them the words in both English and Spanish, they are gonna do better in the classroom. It's important to explain the content, but also it's important to keep track of the key words that they need to know in English." Camila reflected on her own experience as a learner so she could share strategies to help the newcomer students. In turn, the process of reflecting on her linguistic practices built her metalinguistic awareness.

From a sociocultural perspective, development is an active and dynamic process, as students change their ways of understanding, perceiving, and thinking along with other people, while building on the cultural practices and traditions within communities of practice (Lave & Wenger, 1991). The mastery of knowledge requires moving toward full participation in the sociocultural practices of a community. Wenger-Trayner and Wenger-Trayner (2015) also use the concept of landscape of practice to describe the social body of knowledge that stretches beyond an individual community of practice. Learning is not merely acquisition of knowledge; it is the journey to become a person who inhabits the landscape with an identity whose dynamic construction reflects the trajectory through that landscape. In order to become mentors, the young people at KAPPA needed to reflect on their trajectories as learners so they could strategically leverage them to help new students become members of the community. During the first mentor's meeting, Samantha asked the students: "Thinking about the juniors, what are some things that you can bring to the table to help them?" Some of the suggestions from the students included the following:

- Establishing a relationship with the students, but at the same time setting up boundaries
- Including them in the process of creating a plan
- Giving them the opportunity to explain content to others, because I feel that when I was in freshman year, it was really rewarding for me to actually teach something to other people in the classroom

The student mentors recognized their own expertise: knowledge of bilingual language practices and of what it feels like to be a student. The mentoring process is rooted in an understanding of young people as active participants and contributors to educational communities. It conceptualizes young people as agents who are not only being transformed by their experiences in and out of school, but who are also involved in transforming the communities in which they participate.

One of the student mentors, Javier, was comfortable speaking in English when he started KAPPA but needed to improve his writing skills. He did not want to be in classes with bilingual support. His oral and written skills in Spanish were at about grade level, but he did not want to do schoolwork in Spanish. Over time, Javier started to value his bilingualism and eventually became a tutor in 11th grade, helping younger students in Spanish. In framing students' bilingualism in a way that showcases students' linguistic resources as a source of strength, the peer mentors program offers a space for students to regain, reshape, and assert their identity as bilingual scholars. Javier worked with a small group of boys and tried to be a role model for them. When he talked about his job as a bilingual tutor, he said: "*Me gusta porque uno aprende como tratar con diferentes personas*" (I like it because I learn how to work with different people). Javier had to figure out how to reach out to different personalities and inspire them, a task that many experienced teachers often struggle with.

The mentors program benefited not only the newcomers, but also the student mentors. They learned to see their bilingualism as a source of pride, disrupting linguistic hierarchies and creating a space that can transform students' stigmatized bilingual identities and help them build new bilingual subjectivities that validate their multilingual practices and identities.

OUTCOMES

Diana was a peer mentor for newcomers in English and history classes. She used her personal experience to create strategies to help other emergent bilinguals understand the work. One of her teachers described how having her in class was invaluable because of her ability to move fluidly between Spanish and English to help her peers. Diana came to the United States at the end of elementary school from the Dominican Republic and speaks Spanish at home. When she first started at KAPPA, she was at a beginner level in English. Diana preferred bilingual content instruction in particular for high-level processing and demanding content areas. She made excellent progress and passed her English Regents exam. She will be graduating college ready for both ELA and math and has applied to 4-year universities. She reflected: "Everything takes time and through time, I learned how to put my thoughts together in order to turn something simple into something more advanced using many writing strategies. . . . This year I am really confident. At first, I didn't want to do essays, but now I'm inspired to write. As days passed, I got better at it and it makes me proud how much I've improved since I came to the United States not knowing English and I've gotten so far."

Diana's vignette as well as the others that we shared in this chapter represent some of the many stories of emergent bilinguals who arrived at KAPPA looking for a place where they could belong and grow. Although graduation rates and test results don't tell the full story of a school, 90.6% of KAPPA International students graduate in 4 years (compared to 72.6% citywide). For emergent bilinguals, 58.3% graduate in 4 years (compared to 30.8% citywide) (NYC DOE, Graduation Results, Cohorts 2001–2012).

CONCLUSIONS AND RECOMMENDATIONS

KAPPA International has created a community that supports and embraces students and their families using the strengths that young people bring with them to grow and succeed. The school fosters an environment that celebrates bilingualism and embraces students' languages and cultures. It has designed school programming and classroom instruction with emergent bilinguals at the core. While we recognize that every school/community is unique, there are many lessons that we can learn from the school's success.

In many middle and high schools, emergent bilinguals are often fitted into the existing programming of the school, responding only to the demands of the existing scheduling. Schools need to reexamine the structures and procedures they use, reflecting a philosophical shift in which course offerings and schedules are designed around the needs and strengths of emergent bilinguals. Also, one of the most important aspects of a humanizing space is to create formal structures in which students can support one another. These structures recognize students as agents who have important contributions to make to the school community.

We propose that teachers use a framework in which they document what students can do, regardless of their language (translanguaging documentation), and that the teachers use their knowledge of their students to design translanguaging scaffolds for individual students (translanguaging rings). It is important to create a space within the language structures of the classroom in which emergent bilinguals are encouraged to be creative and analytical language users. Creating a transformational space involves incorporating the linguistic practices that exist beyond the walls of the school and bringing the language and culture of the community into the school space.

NOTES

1. Marilyn Friend and Lynne Cook proposed six approaches to co-teaching: One Teach, One Observe; One Teach, One Assist; Parallel Teaching; Station Teaching; Alternative Teaching; and Team Teaching. In the Alternative Teaching model, one teacher takes responsibility for the large group while the other works with a smaller group. In Station Teaching, teachers divide content and students. Each teacher then teaches the content to one group and then repeats the instruction for the other group. If appropriate, a third station allows students to work independently.

2. The Regents Exams were originally honors exams to evaluate college readiness, but to fulfill NCLB requirements, the state required students to pass the tests to receive a high school diploma.

REFERENCES

Cloud, N., Lakin, J., Leininger, E., & Maxwell, L. (2010). *Teaching adolescent English language learners: Essential strategies for middle and high school*. Philadelphia, PA: Caslon Publishing.

Collins, B. A., & Cioè-Peña, M. (2016). Declaring freedom: Translanguaging in the social studies class-room to understand complex texts. In O. García & T. Kleyn (Eds.), *Translanguaging with multilingual students: Learning from classroom moments* (pp. 37–51). New York, NY: Routledge.

Conchas, G. Q. (2001). Structuring failure and success: Understanding the variability in Latino school engagement. *Harvard Educational Review, 71*(3), 475–504.

Freeman, Y. S., Freeman, D. E., Soto, M., & Ebe, A. (2016). *ESL teaching: Principles for success.* Portsmouth, NH: Heinemann.

Friend, M., & Cook, L. (1992). *Interactions: Collaboration skills for school professionals.* White Plains, NY: Longman Publishing Group.

García, O., & Wei, L. (2013). *Translanguaging: Language, bilingualism and education.* London, England: Palgrave Macmillan.

Gibbons, P. (2015). Scaffolding language, scaffolding learning: teaching English language learning in the mainstream classroom.Portsmouth, NH: Heinemann

Harris, A. (2008). *Distributed school leadership: Developing tomorrow's leaders.* New York, NY: Routledge.

Jones, S. M., & Doolittle, E. J. (2017). Social and emotional learning: Introducing the issue. *The Future of Children, 27*(1), 3–11.

Lave, J., & Wenger, E. (1991) *Situated learning: Legitimate peripheral participation* (12th ed.). Cambridge, England: Cambridge University Press.

NYC DOE Graduation Results, Cohorts 2001–2012. Retrieved from schools.nyc.gov/Accountability/resources/testing/default.htm#CT%20Regents

Salazar, M. D. (2013). A humanizing pedagogy: Reinventing the principles and practice of education as a journey toward liberation. *Review of Research in Education, 37,* 121–148.

Sánchez, M. T., García, O., & Solorza, C. (2017). Reframing language allocation policy in dual language bilingual education. *Bilingual Research Journal,* 1–15. doi: 10.1080/15235882.2017.1405098

Seltzer, K., & Collins, B. A. (2016). Building bridges & navigating turbulent waters: Translanguaging for academic and social-emotional well-being. In O. García & T. Kleyn (Eds.), *Translanguaging with multilingual students: Learning from classroom moments.* New York, NY: Routledge.

Walqui, A., & Van Lier, L. (2010). *Scaffolding the academic success of adolescent English language learners: A pedagogy of promise.* San Francisco, CA: WestEd.

Wenger-Trayner, E., & Wenger-Trayner, B. (2015). *Learning in landscapes of practice: Boundaries, identity, and knowledgeability in practice-based learning.* New York, NY: Routledge.

CHAPTER 9

Language and Literacy Learning Beyond Elementary School

Douglas Fisher and Nancy Frey

Alexis graduated from army boot camp and is now serving his country. Of course, thousands of young people decide to do this every year. But Alexis was not on that path when he entered Health Sciences High several years ago. In 9th grade, Alexis self-identified as a gang member and readily acknowledged his involvement in crime. At the beginning of the year, he regularly told his teachers "F*** you" and walked out of class. One day, when he was very angry about something, he punched three holes in the wall of a classroom. Alexis had been previously expelled from his middle school and did not attend 8th grade. His probation officer required that he attend 9th grade. Alexis attributes his change in heart to the humanizing aspects of his high school.

Alexis identifies as Latino and speaks Spanish with his friends and family. In 9th grade, his performance on the initial reading assessment indicated that he was in the lowest quartile of achievement. His writing assessment also indicated significant need for growth. His English language proficiency, as measured by the state assessment, indicated that he was at intermediate levels of proficiency, even though he had entered U.S. schools in 1st grade. A review of his records revealed that he had been at the intermediate level of proficiency for years. In California, this earns the student a designation of "long-term English learner" and correlational data suggest that this is an indicator that the student is likely to drop out, fail out, or graduate with very low levels of language proficiency.

Alexis needed to know a few things right away. First, he needed to know that his teachers cared about him. Second, he needed to know that his lack of proficiency would not be a source of shame or public humiliation. And third, he needed to know that his teachers had the skills to facilitate his learning such that he could achieve his aspirations. At the time, he did not want to enter the military. But he did say that he wanted to make "legal money to support my family."

Talking with Alexis now that he is an adult reveals some of the challenges that students face, especially when they are seen as having a deficit in language. As he said, "In middle school, they would make us read out loud in front of everyone else. I acted up so I wouldn't have to do that because it was so embarrassing. And

I felt like the teachers were frustrated that I didn't read and write very good. I thought it was my fault. I never got any extra help. They just seemed mad at me all the time. I didn't like any of them." His eyes welled up as he spoke. "It was easier to be the bad kid. That got me a better reputation."

Middle and high school teachers of all subject areas have the responsibility to continue to foster students' literate lives. Unfortunately, some students arrive in secondary schools without sufficient literacy skills to be successful. In those cases, teachers need to integrate effective interventions into their classrooms to ensure that all students progress along the literacy continuum. But literacy in secondary schools is not limited to students who are reading below grade level. English learners need to develop linguistic proficiency. Literacy progress should be an expectation of all students across their schooling experience, including immigrant students. Camangian (2015), in his research on a humanizing pedagogy in south Los Angeles, reminds us to "teach as if lives depend on it" (p. 424). Because they do. School should be a place where young people build their sense of identity and agency (Salazar, 2013). In this chapter, we explore the instructional aspects that have, for more than a decade, ensured that students who live in poverty make remarkable progress.

COMMUNITY AND SCHOOL CONTEXT

Health Sciences High and Middle College (HSHMC), a public charter school in San Diego, educates more than 700 students in grades 6–12. HSHMC is located in City Heights, one of San Diego's most densely populated, inner-city, economically distressed, urban neighborhoods. The City Heights community has a 38% poverty rate and more than 99% of children in the community are eligible for federal free lunch programs. City Heights was once a thriving residential neighborhood that has now transformed as recent immigrants take the place of long-term residents who have moved to the suburbs. A culturally rich area, the local press has labeled City Heights the "Ellis Island of San Diego." The residents of City Heights speak more than 30 different languages and almost half were born in another country and have immigrated to the United States. In addition, juvenile crime is far greater in City Heights than in other areas of San Diego. The population in the neighborhood is relatively young, with a median age of 26. Students in City Heights are more likely than those in any other area to have parents who have not graduated from high school. According to county publicized health statistics, teenage pregnancy and childhood asthma rates are higher in City Heights than in other parts of the city. There is little doubt that the families represented in the neighborhood experience life far differently from their counterparts in more affluent neighborhoods. The poverty and family support systems all contribute to placing students at risk for school failure.

Nearly 72% of students qualify for free lunch and 18% qualify for special education services. As well, 25% of the student body has been or is currently involved in foster care and/or adoptive homes. Demographically, 18% are African or African American, 65% are Latinx, 6% are Asian/Pacific Islander, 8% are White. There are upwards of 150 students who are at extreme risk for academic failure. They enrolled at HSHMC with insufficient credits needed to graduate and perform below grade level academically.

SCHOOL ELEMENTS THAT SUPPORT STUDENTS' LEARNING

We have reflected on 11 years' worth of school leadership, and specifically considered the impact that the school staff has had on multilingual learners. There are three major areas we believe have allowed students to learn language and to become increasingly literate: strong student–teacher relationships, amazing instructional experiences in which language learning has been embedded, and a sophisticated response to instruction and intervention approach that allows staff to notice students who need supplemental and intensive interventions. We believe that these three factors allowed the school to achieve success, as we will discuss in the outcomes section of this chapter, and that these are transportable to other secondary schools.

Strong Student–Teacher Relationships

Simply said, young people do not learn from old people they do not like. Sadly, there are some teachers in the profession who believe that their role in society is to humble and humiliate young people, controlling their every move and demanding respect from them. Our experience, and a strong research base, suggests that this is not the way to ensure that students learn at high levels. Instead, teachers need to develop, nurture, and maintain healthy, growth-producing relationships with their students.

In his extensive review of what works to improve learning, Hattie (2012) noted that student–teacher relationships have an effect size of 0.72. Effect sizes indicate the magnitude of change, or how much impact can be expected from a specific action. Hattie's results, extracted from a database of more than 300 million students worldwide, suggests that a 0.40 effect size is equivalent to a year's worth of growth for a year in school. Think of this as a benchmark for interpreting results. Thus, student–teacher relationships are one of the tools educators have for ensuring that students learn at the levels expected of them each year.

This was certainly the case with Alexis. He learned from adults he valued and who cared about him. The teachers at HSHMC work hard on the relationships they develop with students. They commit to knowing every student's name within the first week of school, and they commit to knowing how to pronounce students' names and at least one interest each student has. To our thinking, this is the start of a healthy relationship. And students notice it. Quaglia and his colleagues (2014) developed the Student Voice survey to assess student beliefs and the ways in which their school fosters aspirations. The national results suggest that 64% of students feel their school is "a welcoming and friendly place." At HSHMC, that number is 84%. There is room for growth, but it's still a positive indicator. In the national data, only 58% of students believe that their teachers respect students. At HSHMC, the figure is 82%. Again, room for growth, but an indicator that the work teachers have done is noticed by students.

Teachers shake hands with students (or high-five or fist-bump). They speak directly to students. They talk about things that students care about—things happening in their lives and in the news. And teachers attend a variety of extracurricular events to show support for students. We have agreed as faculty to each attend two activities per month, and to share successes we see with others on the staff. There is a concerted effort to get to know students and to develop relationships with them.

It was hard to get to know Alexis. He was often rebellious, distant, and declined handshakes. In some schools, rather than seeing such behavior as an attempt to communicate and to control the environment around him, this behavior would be seen as defiant and the student would be suspended or expelled. But Alexis's teachers knew better and were relentless in their efforts. They made home visits, asked about his life, offered him books to read that they thought might interest him, and asked him to share his ideas on a regular basis. In other words, they didn't give up. It was a slow process, but Alexis finally started shaking hands with some of his teachers in November of his freshman year, which we took as a small victory. Relationships are worth the effort because they contribute to students' sense of safety and belonging, which is an important factor in creating classroom communities that allow students to thrive.

But sometimes relationships are strained. It's easy to say that we have good relationships with students, and we do. Until we don't. Sometimes, blame for the breakdown in a relationship sits squarely on the shoulders of the student. Other times, it's the fault of the teacher. Either way, schools and teachers need procedures to repair relationships that are inevitably, and often unintentionally, damaged in the course of human interaction. Restorative practices (RP) are an approach that educators can use to ensure that healthy relationships are maintained (Costello, Wachtel, & Wachtel, 2009; Smith, Fisher, & Frey, 2015). In essence, restorative practices comprise a philosophy that harm must be repaired for the victim and the offender to move forward. Rather than seeing problematic behavior through the lens of broken rules, advocates of RP understand that it is relationships that are damaged.

The procedures involved with RP include impromptu conversations, circles, and restorative conferences. When students or staff are in conflict, these techniques provide a system for addressing the issue and moving forward. Sometimes, that requires an impromptu conversation, which is usually brief and allows one person to describe how a specific behavior impacted him or her. For example, when Alexis refused to do any classwork in his 10th-grade science class one day, his teacher had a private conversation with him, saying, "I worked really hard to plan a lesson that I thought would be interesting and would help you learn this important content. But you don't seem to be yourself today. Is everything okay? Is there something that I could be doing to engage you?" Alexis apologized, saying, "I didn't mean to disrespect you. I have a lot going on with my family. Can I have a few minutes? I promise to be back on my game when I come back."

Sometimes the harm is more extensive. Restorative conferences are conducted when significant harm has been done. Victims and perpetrators meet separately with a trained facilitator, and if both parties agree, then a restorative conference is held. Depending on the circumstances, family members or friends may also be invited. The facilitator uses a questioning protocol developed by Costello, Wachtel, and Wachtel (2009). These are posed to the person exhibiting the challenging behavior:

- What happened?
- What were you thinking of at the time?
- What have you thought about since?
- Who has been affected by what you have done? In what way have they been affected?
- What do you think you might need to do to make things right? (p. 16)

For the person affected by the challenging behavior, we ask:

- What did you think when you realized what had happened?
- What impact has this incident had on you and others?
- What has been the hardest thing for you?
- What do you think needs to happen to make things right? (p. 16)

The facilitator engages those present and asks the victim to state what he or she would like to see as an outcome of the conference. The perpetrator is also asked how he or she might make amends, and when agreement is reached, a contract between the two parties is created. Alexis participated in several of these meetings, often as a perpetrator and sometimes as the victim. What he learned over time was the value of making amends.

Restorative practices do not supplant other disciplinary measures. Disciplinary procedures remain in place and are sometimes used in conjunction with a restorative conference. Participation is voluntary, and occasionally we find that such a conference is not possible. But in the years since we have instituted these practices, we have not expelled any students, and our suspension rate has decreased more than 60%. As one teacher said after a conference, "Rules don't change behavior. People do."

Instructional Experiences with Embedded Language Learning

Relationships alone are not sufficient to ensure that students learn at high levels. The instruction also has to be strong. And it has to provide students with multiple opportunities to practice and develop academic language. This starts with clarity about learning expectations. Students should not have to guess what they are supposed to learn. They should hear directly from their teachers, every day in every lesson, what they will learn. Lessons do not need to start with the learning expectations, but sometime during the lesson students should know what they are learning. Call it an objective, purpose, learning intention, target, or goal (e.g., Hattie, 2012; Marzano, 2009). The name is less important than the components that ensure multilingual students continue to learn. We'll use the term *learning intention* for convenience. The learning intention is not the task. Rather, it should reflect the understandings students will gain as a result of their engagement in the lesson components. When lessons are planned with the end in mind, learning intentions are easier to develop. The two parts of the learning intention that we find especially effective for multilingual students are content and language.

Content. Part of the learning intention comes from the content standards. This ensures that all students have access to instruction based on high expectations. Planning an amazing lesson for 9th-graders based on 7th-grade standards will not ensure that the students reach high levels of achievement. Nor should the learning intention *be* the standard. Standards take time to master. It takes weeks to understand the causes and impact of World War II, so lots of daily learning intentions are required. When standards are not analyzed for their component parts and instead are used as the purpose, students stop paying attention to them. The standards might be posted on the wall, but they're like wallpaper to students: a decoration.

Language. A second component of the learning intention is the way students demonstrate their understanding of the content. The linguistic demand is critical for this component of the learning intention, and valuable for English learners who are doing double the work in middle and high school, learning content and language simultaneously. Teachers consider vocabulary, language structure, and language function when developing lessons. For some lessons, the important linguistic component might be related to the vocabulary of the discipline. In a math class, for example, part of the purpose might be for students to use logic vocabulary in their proofs. For other lessons, students need to focus on grammar, syntax, or signal words. A third way to think about the language component is by determining the function of language necessary to understand the content. Do students need to justify, persuade, inform, debate, hypothesize? Part of the purpose might be to justify your answer in writing.

Consider the impact that two daily lessons could have on Alexis. When his art teacher taught students how to look at paintings, he projected a famous work of art and said, "We're going to consider the role that perspective plays in fine art, and to do that we'll use specific technical vocabulary." When his algebra teacher taught quadratic equations, she said, "We're going to identify the properties of a quadratic equation and explain how we know whether equations are quadratic or not." In both cases, Alexis knew what he was expected to learn and the language that would be expected of him. He said years later, "I can't ever remember in middle school knowing what I was supposed to learn. They told us what we had to do, but I wondered why I should do it. In high school, the teachers made it really clear. They always told us what we were learning and how we could show them."

The daily learning intention drives the use of the instructional minutes. There any number of ways to provide students with high-quality instruction. We'll focus on two general areas that are important in the learning lives of multilingual students: modeling and collaborative learning. At HSHMC, teachers model their thinking for students and then invite students to work collaboratively to solve complex problems. In doing so, they develop their linguistic prowess.

Modeling. Teachers model and demonstrate to show students how a skill, strategy, or concept is used. Modeling typically involves thinking aloud to expose novices to the decisions made by an expert as he or she processes information. For this reason, modeling consistently contains "I" statements to invite the learner into the mind of the teacher. This is a profound shift from what most teachers are accustomed to doing. Much of classroom instruction is in the second person and is interrogative in nature ("When you look at this eruption, what do you see?"). Teaching and quizzing become the order of the day, and students walk away from the class under the false assumption that somehow the teacher just "knows" the answer. They are not made privy to the speculative, and at times hesitant, thinking of the content expert. What's lost are the natural stutter-steps made by someone who is deeply knowledgeable of the complexities of the topic. Teacher modeling provides students with examples of how the teacher's mind worked. Some of the indicators we look for during teacher modeling include:

- naming a strategy, skill, or task;
- stating the purpose of the strategy, skill, or task;
- using "I" statements;
- demonstrating how the strategy, skill, or task is used;
- alerting learners about errors to avoid; and
- assessing the usefulness of the strategy or skill.

Consider a mathematics teacher's modeling for solving problems with exponents. In this case, the exponents had variables in them, as in $2^{x+3} = 4^{2x}$. While modeling, the teacher said, "I see that the bases aren't equal, so I can't yet set the exponents equal. If I can get the bases equal, then I know that the exponents are equal. The strategy I can try is factoring because it might help me get the bases to be equal. I can't factor the left side any further, but I can factor the right side of the equation. Using my factor tree, I see that 4 can be factored into 2^2. But I have to be careful about the distributive property. I know that if I don't put parentheses around the exponents, I might forget to distribute the exponents correctly. Now that I have the bases equal, I know that the exponents are equal. So, my next step is to rewrite the equation: x+3 = 4x. And now, I just crank it through. When I get down to it, I think that the answer is 1. But I know that I'm not done yet. I have to check my answer by plugging it back into the original equation."

Although one problem modeled in this way may not result in students' complete understanding, regular use of modeling builds students' understanding of the skills they can use to understand the content. Over time, students develop habits for problem-solving and critical thinking that are discipline specific. We know that historians think differently from mathematics, scientists, artists, and literary critics (Shanahan & Shanahan, 2008) and students need to be apprenticed into that thinking. And then they need time to practice with their peers.

Collaborative Learning. So far in our discussion of high-quality instruction, we have focused on the actions of the teacher. Importantly, these two aspects (learning intentions and modeling) do not take a significant number of instructional minutes to accomplish. The bulk of instructional time is focused on student-to-student interaction using academic language. We aim for 50% of the instructional minutes, averaged over a week, in collaborative learning. It's a hard goal to realize, but an important one if students are to develop academic language. We do not believe students get good at things they don't do. They get good at things they practice, making errors along the way that highlight for their teachers the learning that still needs to occur. Inevitably, they share part of themselves in the process, humanizing the classroom and building strong relationships between and among students. Alexis says, "I developed some pretty amazing friendships because we got to talk to each other during class. I used to get in trouble for talking. At HSHMC, they want you to talk. Yeah, you have to get the work done, but it's okay to share your own thinking. I remember telling a friend about my family when we were talking about immigration in history. I never thought I would do that, but I did."

In addition, collaborative learning honors students' language. At HSHMC, students often engage in collaborative learning in languages other than English. They produce work for the teacher in English, but the process they use to get there can involve other languages. Students, including Alexis, find this powerful and a sign of respect for their learning.

Of course, students do not just show up in our classrooms knowing how to collaborate with their peers; the staff has to teach them how to do this. Students may need sentence starters at first to begin using argumentation in their discussions. For example, Alexis's English teacher provided her students with the following frames when they wanted to offer a counterclaim:

- I disagree with _____ because _____.
- The reason I believe _____ is _____.
- The facts that support my idea are _____.
- In my opinion, _____.
- One difference between my idea and yours is _____.

One structure for facilitating student reading and discussion is reciprocal teaching (Palincsar & Brown, 1984). Students use four comprehension strategies: predicting, questioning, summarizing, and clarifying. They pause periodically to talk about what they are reading. In some cases, they change roles each time they talk. In other cases, they practice the same role throughout the reading. It's important to note that reciprocal teaching groups do not have to consist of four students; they can share roles. Reciprocal teaching fosters deep understanding of a text through conversations. Reciprocal teaching has an effect size of 0.75 (Hattie, 2012).

Sophisticated Response to Instruction and Intervention Procedures

When strong relationships are in place and when students have access to high-quality instruction, their teachers can monitor who is responding well to the instruction and who still needs additional support. At HSHMC, we have built a system to monitor students' progress and to provide supplemental and intensive interventions when students are not learning. The evidence for these types of systems, called Response to Intervention (RtI), is strong. Hattie (2012), discussed earlier in this chapter, noted that RtI has an effect size of 1.07, a powerful influence on student learning. An effective RtI system requires initial screening to identify students who need additional support at the outset of the year. And it requires progress monitoring so that the staff can respond when students do not learn as expected. We use the language of RtI, which articulates three levels, called tiers, of instruction and intervention. Tier 1 describes high-quality core instruction for all students, and as we have described in this chapter, is of the utmost importance in developing students academically and personally. Tier 2 is intended to serve as additional supplemental instruction for students who are not yet making expected progress. This level of intervention is primarily conducted during small-group instruction. Tier 3 is the most intensive level, as the student and teacher meet for one-to-one intervention. At HSHMC, when students do not achieve mastery, we provide supplemental and intensive interventions to close the gap. Alexis participated in all three tiers during his high school years.

An RtI program begins with screening students who may need further support. At HSHMC, the first week of every year is called Welcome Week, and we use it for several purposes, one of which is screening. We engage students in a number of culture-building and teamwork activities. Every teacher in the school has a mixed-age group. We purposefully group them so that all new students get to know older students. As part of Welcome Week, students read, write, and speak, but they are not in academic classes. They are engaged in activities designed to build trust among students. The staff observes for any indicators that students may need additional support. Our screening tools are not as sophisticated as those other schools may use, but they are respectful of students' experiences. The screening tools do the job and allow us to spotlight students who need supplemental interventions. Students nominated by teachers during the first week as being at possible risk get a thorough records review. This early warning system assists us as a school in marshaling academic and behavioral support before students fail.

In addition, we have structured our grading policy as a means to conduct ongoing monitoring of every student's progress. We consider this a vital part of our Tier 1 high-quality core instruction because it provides us with another tool for our early warning system. Every class at HSHMC is competency based, meaning that the focus is on how students demonstrate mastery of the standards. Students are required to pass every competency at 70% or higher. Those who do not reach this are given an incomplete, signaling that they have not yet demonstrated mastery and are therefore not done. We do not grade homework or classwork; those are just for practice. We grade for mastery. We don't award meaningless points for bringing materials to class or returning a signed fieldtrip form. And here's why— the points that a student accumulates for homework, in-class assignments, coming prepared, and for various measures of compliance obscure what it is that a student knows and doesn't know. Alexis failed middle school classes that weighted these points into his grade for the course—he was not the kind of student in those days who was going to bring his notebook or do his homework. So, by October of every year, he would have dug himself into a hole that couldn't mathematically be overcome.

Now, you might be saying, "Well, he wasn't toeing the line, so he deserves to fail." But let's consider another hypothetical classmate of Alexis's. She brings a pencil every day and outwardly looks engaged. She gets points for her citizenship, and her teacher says she's a pleasure to have in class. She turns in her homework, even though the truth is she doesn't really understand it and a classmate helps her complete it. She doesn't do well on any of the unit tests, but the other points mean that she gets a C. In the meantime, all those extra points have masked the fact that she doesn't really understand the content. Her teacher, her parents, and the student herself remain blissfully unaware that she isn't really learning much. The competency grading system we use at HSHMC is for performance measures only, without the clutter that obscures true mastery. We do have a separate citizenship grade to address the important self-regulatory behaviors essential for learning. But we don't allow arriving to class on time to be mistaken for mastering algebra.

Here's where the competency grading system helps us find the students who need Tier 2 supplemental instruction. Every Sunday, an administrator does an electronic sweep of the grade books to produce a spreadsheet listing the students who currently have an "I" (incomplete) on a competency. The list is formatted such that we can see who is carrying several incompletes. Every adult in the school, certificated and classified, receives this notice so that we can marshal the many positive relationships the staff has with students. In most secondary schools, progress-monitoring tools are difficult to find and are of questionable use. Our use of competency-based assessments has allowed us to tailor support for students who need it most (Fisher & Frey, 2013).

From the beginning, Alexis was a regular on the Sunday incomplete report. Because of the systems in place at the school, Alexis began participating in Tier

2 supplemental instruction to clear his incompletes. To clear, a student must (re) do all the homework assigned in the unit, as these are for practice, not compliance. Once assignments are completed, students take another form of the competency. But completing assignments requires more tutoring and instruction. There are at least four ways students can seek additional tutoring and instruction. First, two 30-minute lunchtime open tutoring sessions are provided and staffed each day. Second, there are several scheduled after-school tutoring and instructional classes offered each day. Third, each grade has a 90-minute period scheduled once a week to allow for individual or groupwork, tutoring, and instruction. Fourth, a full range of required coursework and academic recovery is offered in summer sessions.

The Tier 2 tutoring helped Alexis keep his head above water, grade-wise, but as a frequent flier on this list, his constant presence signaled that he needed more intensive supports. Keep in mind that with the compliance measures removed, we could see more clearly that his struggle was with content. His teachers reported that although he often had a good grasp of the material, he struggled with putting his ideas on the page. In addition, we discovered that he had not formed any study habits whatsoever. He thought you just kept all that information in your head. Alexis needed some Tier 3 intensive intervention. At HSHMC, every adult who does not have direct classroom responsibilities is a potential Tier 3 interventionist within his or her area of expertise. The school's social worker meets individually with some students who need social and emotional support to get their work done. The mathematics instructional coach sees some students who need specialized feedback. A member of the restorative practices team who is a wiz at chemistry sees those students. In Alexis's case, he met regularly with an English teacher on the staff whom we employed for additional pay to work on developing his study skills. The English learner coordinator met with Alexis throughout his high school career to further develop his technical writing skills. He was enrolled in an English language development class, but the additional one-to-one supports made a difference. When Alexis decided in his 11th-grade year that he wanted to enlist in the U.S. Army, both of these staff members helped him study for the Armed Services Vocational Aptitude Battery (ASVAB). We should note as well that Alexis was able to be reclassified as proficient in English that same year. "I owe them my career," he said.

OUTCOMES

In addition to our students appreciating their school, as we have noted earlier in this chapter, we are very proud of the outcomes our students' experience. The average graduation rate for the past 10 years is 98.5%. We only offer classes that are approved by the University of California system for admission into college. And nearly every student who enrolls graduates. Of our graduates, 87% meet the admissions requirements for a 4-year university. This compares with 40% in neighboring schools and 50% statewide.

Figure 9.1. CELDT Criterion (Reported by Percentage)

	2013–2014	2014–2015	2015–2016	2016–2017
Health Sciences High	44	49	55	58
San Diego Unified School District	35	37	35	32
California	44	45	42	41

In California, high schools are accountable for ensuring that students are college and career ready. The state board of education developed the College and Career Indicator (CCI) to determine the percentage of students who were ready for their post–high school life. The CCI has many facets, including performance on the state accountability test, scores on advanced placement exams, dual enrollment in college classes, and completion of a career pathway. At HSHMC, 84% of our students were identified as "ready" on the CCI, a number that demonstrates our students beat the odds when it comes to preparation.

In terms of English learners, HSHMC students outperform the district average and the state average. Figure 9.1 shows the percentage of students who gained a year of English proficiency over a 4-year period. We have outperformed the district and state every year of operation. However, it is important to note that there is still a significant number of students who did not attain a year of language development. This is a source of concern for us and the focus of a significant amount of professional development and student intervention.

CONCLUSIONS AND RECOMMENDATIONS

We are struck by Freire's call to a humanizing pedagogy, summarized by Salazar (2013) as "humans are motivated by a need to reason and engage in the process of becoming" (p. 125). Although we have spent this chapter discussing the practices of education at the school where we work, Alexis is at the heart of this story. School is not a place young people go to watch adults work. It is a place in which we can make the choice each day whether to enact the same cycles of failure or walk with young people on their journey of becoming. Relationships permeate every aspect of the school, including instruction and intervention. The relationships and connections that we cultivate with students are too often relegated to some "getting to know you" classroom activities, which are soon forgotten as the academic tide rushes in. But in order for relationships to go beyond the superficial niceties of a well-oiled conventional classroom, we must be there for students when things aren't going well. When they are challenged by internal and external pressures they can't articulate, we must provide them with the language to understand and act. We are not speaking only of language as a corpus of words, but also the emotional language that comes from experience, reflection, failure, and success. And here's an important reminder: It's not *our* experiences that matter so much; it is trying over and over to understand theirs that is critical. It's dialogue, not monologue. They don't need to hear about how we had it rough, or overcame a challenge, or how we succeeded. We must look carefully, again and again. We must listen, especially when our urge is to lecture them.

Alexis's journey into becoming was facilitated by those inside and outside of school. In no way do we position our school as the force in his life that shaped him. His family, especially his mother, taught him love and empathy. His community taught him about identity. But an institution that is in conflict with family and community causes a young person to fracture. Our role as educators is to help students consolidate who they are and who they want to be. We have described systems our school has put into place to be a humanizing space, and the good news is that they are completely consistent with what we know about language development, academic learning and achievement, and social–emotional learning. Schools are replete with caring educators who give their very best each day. Many adults speak about a person who changed the trajectory of their lives, often beginning with the words, "There was this teacher. . . ." But without institutional systems in place to support these educators, their efforts are left to happenstance. Our recommendations for creating this humanizing space are as follows:

1. Create an institutional culture that is first and foremost about establishing, repairing, and cultivating positive relationships with students. We need a social–emotional press to match the academic press of consistently high expectations for each student.
2. Pair rigorous curriculum with stellar instruction and grading policies that support both. School shouldn't be a compliance game, where some are more adept than others. School is about learning experienced by all of humanity and within the individual. When oppressive grading policies reinforce "playing school" and give students no hope of ever changing their trajectory, they quit on us and on themselves.
3. Create supports and interventions that humanize learning. In too many schools, especially secondary schools, the very notion that you might get help is scattershot at best. Interventions need to be just in time, meaning that they are available when a student needs it. It shouldn't require moving heaven and earth (not to mention a whole lot of paperwork) to get help. Systematizing interventions mean that we can be responsive, flexible, and agile.

REFERENCES

Camangian, P. (2015). Teach like lives depend on it: Agitate, arouse, and inspire. *Urban Education*, *50*(4), 424–453.

Costello, B., Wachtel, J., & Wachtel, T. (2009). *Restorative practices handbook for teachers, disciplinarians and administrators*. Bethlehem, PA: International Institute for Restorative Practices.

Fisher, D., & Frey, N. (2013). Implementing RTI in a high school: A case study. *Journal of Learning Disabilities, 46*, 99–114.

Hattie, J. (2012). *Visible learning for teachers: Maximizing impact on learning.* New York, NY: Routledge.

Marzano, R. J. (2009). *Designing & teaching learning goals & objectives.* Bloomington, IN: Solution Tree.

Palincsar, A. S., & Brown, A. L. (1984). Reciprocal teaching of comprehension-fostering and comprehension-monitoring activities. *Cognition and Instruction, 1*(2), 117–175.

Quaglia, R., & Corso, M. (2014). *Student voice: The instrument of change.* Thousand Oaks, CA: Corwin Press.

Salazar, M. (2013). A humanizing pedagogy: Reinventing the principles and practice of education as a journey of liberation. *Review of Research in Education, 37,* 121–148.

Shanahan, T., & Shanahan, C. (2008). Teaching disciplinary literacy to adolescents: Rethinking content-area literacy. *Harvard Educational Review, 78,* 40–59.

Smith, D., Fisher, D., & Frey, N. (2015). *Better than carrots or sticks: Restorative practices for positive classroom management.* Alexandria, VA: ASCD.

CHAPTER 10

Learning and Practicing a Humanizing Pedagogy

One Teacher's Journey

Shelley Hong Xu and Jamie Schnablegger

This chapter will focus on the journey of how Jamie Schnablegger, a first-year teacher who identifies as Latinx, learns and practices a humanizing pedagogy in her class at a school with predominantly Latinx emergent bilinguals from mainly working-class families. The account of Jamie's journey is contextualized within the community of Hillside Elementary School, where Jamie completed a field-based teacher preparation program and her student teaching and is now a 4th-grade teacher during her first year of teaching (at the writing of this book chapter). The other context is the field-based Urban Dual Credential Program (UDCP) at California State University, Long Beach (CSULB). Both contexts nurture Jamie's growth from a teacher candidate to a student teacher and to a first-year teacher.

Beginning with a description of the context of Hillside Elementary and its professional development opportunities, the UDCP, Jamie's background, and Jamie's 4th-grade class, we then focus on the connections of pedagogical content knowledge, humanizing pedagogy, and field-based practices in teacher preparation. We describe how Jamie implements pedagogical content knowledge and humanizing pedagogy in her literacy instruction for emergent bilinguals. We conclude this chapter with some recommendations for teacher educators, classroom teachers, and school administrators, who all play a crucial role in educating children with varied linguistic and academic backgrounds.

SCHOOL AND COMMUNITY CONTEXT

Hillside, located in Los Angeles County, California, was a public school with more than 550 K–5th-grade students. About 90% of its students identified as Latinx, and the remaining students identified as White (5.7%), Black or African American (1.7%), and Asian (1.6%); less than 1% of students identified as either American

Indian, Alaska Native, Filipino, or two or more ethnic backgrounds. About 63% of students were considered socioeconomically disadvantaged and received free or reduced-price school lunches. Approximately 13% of students were emergent bilinguals, and 12.2% were students with special needs (such as learning or speech).

Jamie's 4th-grade class consisted of 33 students (25 Latinx, 6 Whites, 1 African American, and 1 Filipino). Two emergent bilinguals received ELD (English Language Development) services: Isabella was at the bridging (advanced) level, while Adam was at the expanding (intermediate) level (California State Board of Education, 2012). Students' home languages included Spanish, Tagalog, and Russian. Twenty-seven students were bilinguals, speaking Spanish and English. One student spoke some Tagalog, and another spoke some Russian. Five students received special education services. Academically, students ranged from proficient to below grade level standards in various content areas. Their reading levels ranged from 3rd-grade to early 5th-grade reading levels. Students were heterogeneously grouped based on literacy performance. Each group included four to five students with a range of proficiency levels.

SCHOOL ELEMENTS THAT SUPPORT STUDENTS' ACHIEVEMENT

School-Family Communication

Overall, Hillside was a close-knit school. Most parents were students here themselves. The school strived to include parents and the community in the school culture. Even though Hillsdale was not a designated bilingual school, school staff and teachers communicated with students and families in Spanish, if needed. The school hosted several parent education events, such as Family Literacy Night and Science Night. During these events, school staff or teachers were on-site to explain in Spanish, if needed. On Family Literacy Night for the primary grades, classrooms featured literacy activities that families and students could re-create at home to further develop the students' fluency and comprehension.

Instructional Support

Even though Hillside had only 13% emergent bilinguals, Hillside was committed to integrating California ELD standards in tandem with the Common Core State Standards (CCSS) in all content areas. During the designated ELD time (1 hour, 3 days per week), emergent bilinguals received targeted literacy instruction during which teachers used Spanish to help explain and clarify for students, who were always encouraged to demonstrate their understanding in Spanish.

Hillside also had Targeted Reading Instruction (TRI) and Targeted Math Instruction (TMI). TRI and TMI each took place 2 days per week for 1 hour. Students were grouped based on their individual needs: enrichment, pre-enrichment, benchmark, strategic, and intensive. Enrichment and pre-enrichment students, typically performing above average, received instruction that challenged them. The TRI and TMI for benchmark students, performing at grade level, reinforced concepts learned in class. Students in the strategic group, performing below grade level, received reteaching of concepts taught in the classroom. For intensive students who were far below grade level, instruction focused on the skills needed to access grade-level curriculum (for example, decoding or comprehension skills). Although students were grouped according to their individual needs, teachers practiced fluid grouping. Biweekly, teachers discussed student progress and the appropriateness of the current groupings, and made necessary changes so that students could benefit most from targeted instruction.

Professional Development

Hillside and the school district provided teachers with multiple opportunities to attend curricular workshops. At Hillside, every teacher was encouraged to welcome a literacy coach into his or her classroom to receive feedback or advice on anything ranging from literacy instruction to library setup. At grade-level meetings, teachers shared and reflected on teaching and discussed changes in content and pedagogy in subsequent teaching.

TEACHER PREPARATION AND TEACHER GROWTH

CSULB's field-based, 2-year UDCP prepared teacher candidates for both general education and special education teaching credentials. School leaders and teachers at Hillside considered having the UDCP at their school as a way to nurture future teachers through providing opportunities for them to observe effective teaching in action and through mentoring teacher candidates. During their first year, teacher candidates took two literacy methods courses and had 4 hours per week of field experiences, observing, helping with instructional activities, and teaching lessons in general education and special education (Tier 3 intervention) classrooms. They received feedback from their mentor teachers and their professors, and also reflected on their own teaching experiences.

During their second year, teacher candidates completed their student teaching in a general education classroom and a special education classroom. During student teaching, teacher candidates co-planned, reflected, and modified instruction with their master teachers and gradually took over the daily instruction. Jamie student taught in a 5th-grade classroom with 31 students (27 Latinx, 1 African American, 3 White).

At Hillside, the principal, literacy coaches, and teachers invited Jamie and her peers to attend district-sponsored workshops. Teacher candidates participated in a weekly debriefing with their mentor teachers on Fridays, discussing assessment data and making decisions on modified instruction.

Growing up as a native Spanish speaker, Jamie did not learn to read until 4th grade and her Spanish was not considered a strength. As a first-year teacher, she created an environment where her emergent bilinguals' cultural and linguistic assets were celebrated. In the beginning of the school year, Jamie learned from several Spanish-speaking parents about their hope for their children to become literate only in English because they did not want their children to repeat their own negative schooling experiences. She shared with families the values of bilingualism and found ways in her teaching to value and support students' native language.

Hillside offered continuing professional development. Jamie took a workshop on targeted instruction for emergent bilinguals, and applied instructional strategies, including reciprocal teaching. A workshop on balanced literacy instruction prompted Jamie to integrate reading, writing, language, speaking, and listening across content areas. After Jamie shadowed a colleague and observed the amount of student talk in comparison to the amount of teacher talk, she realized that her students did not have sufficient opportunity to talk in an academic setting. Jamie practiced what Souto-Manning and Martell (2016) called "teach by invitation" (p. 4). She invited students to have a conversation about what they were learning, and placed a heavier emphasis on academic discourse.

PROFESSIONAL LITERATURE

Becoming a teacher is a complex process in which a teacher candidate learns about multiple facets of teaching: knowledge about students and their backgrounds, knowledge about content areas and pedagogy, and teaching skills. Multiple bodies of literature collectively provide valuable insights into how teacher candidates learn to teach and continues fine-tuning the crafts of teaching (e.g., Darling-Hammond, Hyler, & Gardner, 2017; Desimone, Hochberg, & McMaken, 2016; Lucas & Villegas, 2013; Villegas & Lucas, 2007). For this chapter, three bodies of literature are relevant: pedagogical content knowledge, humanizing pedagogy, and field experiences in teacher education.

Pedagogical Content Knowledge (PCK)

Shulman's (1986) pedagogical content knowledge (PCK) framework bridges content knowledge and pedagogical knowledge. *Content knowledge* is what teacher candidates know about a subject area, such as knowledge about children's reading and writing development. *Pedagogical knowledge* refers to the ways of teaching content. For example, a teacher candidate reads aloud a children's book to teach concepts about print (e.g., reading from left to right; paying attention to punctuation marks). *Pedagogical content knowledge* is "the ways of representing and formulating the subject that make it comprehensible to others" (Shulman, 1986, p. 7). It "also includes an understanding of what makes the learning of specific topics easy or difficult" (Shulman, 1986, p. 7). For example, a teacher candidate equipped with pedagogical content knowledge varies his or her way of reading aloud a book to different groups of students. When reading aloud a book written in English to Spanish-speaking English learners, he or she draws students' attention to a question mark at the end of a sentence, pointing out that there is no question mark at the beginning of the sentence. Such a read-aloud experience helps English learners understand, in a relatively easy and comprehensible way, the difference in the use of a question mark in English and in Spanish.

Humanizing Pedagogy

Educators who practice humanizing pedagogy (e.g., Freire, 2000; Giroux, 2010; Huerta, 2011; Salazar, 2008, 2013) support the development of a humane world. Guided by the work of Freire and other scholars, Salazar (2013) reflected on her own schooling as a Mexican immigrant who experienced "a deep sense of isolation that resulted from systematic practices in the U.S. educational system that suppressed vital elements of my humanity, both at home and at school" (p. 121). She suggested 10 principles and practices of humanizing pedagogy for educators:

> 1) The reality of the learner is crucial; 2) Critical consciousness is imperative for students and educators; 3) Students' sociocultural resources are valued and extended; 4) Content is meaningful and relevant to students' lives; 5) Students' prior knowledge is linked to new learning; 6) Trusting and caring relationships advance the pursuit of humanization; 7) Mainstream knowledge and discourse styles matter; 8) Students will achieve through their academic, intellectual, social abilities; 9) Student empowerment requires the use of learning strategies; 10) Challenging inequity in the educational system can promote transformation. (p. 138)

Field Experiences in Teacher Preparation

Both pedagogical content knowledge and humanizing pedagogy are what teacher candidates must learn, practice, and reflect on during their field experiences. Mead, Aldeman, Chuong, and Obbard (2015) suggested having "real, robust local partnerships between districts or charter schools and the programs that prepare their teachers" and "providing effective teacher-mentors" (p. 4). Additionally, the American Association of Colleges for Teacher Education (AACTE) (2010, 2018) and National Research Council (NRC) (2010) both stressed the pivotal role of practical experiences in teacher preparation, and AACTE (2010) specifically pointed out that "high-quality preparation programs are *school-embedded*" (p. 5, emphasis in original). Similarly, Hammerness and Darling-Hammond (2005) regarded teacher preparation as "learning about practice *in* practice" (p. 401). Additionally, Darling-Hammond (2014) emphasized "how teachers come to integrate theory and practice in a way that allows them to become expert in making and enacting decisions to meet the very different needs of the children they serve" (p. 547). Similarly, McDonald et al. (2014) identified several benefits of practical experiences. One benefit is that teacher candidates learn to invite students to define learning targets, helping them take ownership of their learning.

Figure 10.1. A Dream Poster

LEARNING AND APPLYING A HUMANIZING PEDAGOGY

In this section, we share Jamie's first-year journey of advancing the literacies and languages of emergent bilinguals within the supportive context of Hillside, which provides teacher professional development and enables teacher decision-making (Darling-Hammond, Hyler, & Gardner, 2017).

Welcoming and Appreciating Students and Families

In the beginning of the school year, Jamie welcomed her students, saying, "Our class is just like a home. And it is your home, and you get to decorate it. Our class is also like a family. And it is your family, and we treat each other with respect and with love. We help each other in our learning." Then, Jamie asked students to share their aspirations. Figure 10.1 shows an example of a student's dream. Jamie's class also created a poster to which each class member contributed his or her notion of being wonderful (for example, caring, helpful, kind, cheerful, funny). When the poster was completed, Jamie and her students reflected on "Why we are wonderful and how although each of us is unique, together we are stronger." These welcome activities, largely student-led, prompted students to take charge of their own class.

Jamie's welcoming space also extended beyond her classroom walls. Asking and knowing about students' home environment helped bridge a connection between home and school life (Lazar & Weisberg, 1996; Schmidt, 2006; Schmidt & Lazar, 2011). Such a connection allowed her to see the whole child, not just the student. Jamie used opportunities to speak to students in Spanish. In passing, she often asked, "¿*Cómo estás?*" (How are you?) and the students responded in Spanish as well. If a student spoke Spanish in class, Jamie responded in Spanish. It seemed that the more Jamie encouraged Spanish, the more her students were comfortable using Spanish.

Figure 10.2. Bilingual and Multicultural Books

Jamie's welcoming classroom was also evident in the inclusion of bilingual and multicultural children's books (Figure 10.2) for her students to explore during independent reading and during various projects. Jamie used bilingual books to encourage Spanish-speaking students to develop their Spanish literacy and to expose non-Spanish-speaking students to a different language. Additionally, it was Jamie's top priority to provide students with mirrors of their own culture and windows into others' cultures (Bishop, 1990). For example, for a unit on descriptive language, she used the book *See the Ocean* (Condra, 1994) about a blind child who used her other senses to describe the ocean. In a unit on legends, Jamie included a bilingual book, *La Llorona/The Weeping Woman* (Hayes, 2014), about a well-known Hispanic legend.

Jamie's welcoming classroom was also accessible to students' families. By the classroom door, the Family Matters corner communicated class activities and posted information ranging from parent workshops to parent–child activities (Figure 10.3). Jamie's open-door policy welcomed parents to visit her classroom and volunteer to help. Besides holding regularly scheduled parent–teacher conferences, Jamie met with parents for a conference whenever a parent requested one. One time she conferenced, in both Spanish and English, with a student's grandmother and great-grandmother. The student's mother, who suffered from a mental illness, had moved back into the family's home and it had affected this student academically. Jamie offered to tutor the student in math every Friday after school without compensation. Throughout the school year, Jamie communicated with parents via Class DOJO (a classroom communication app) in English and Spanish. For example, before the school award ceremony, Jamie explained in

Figure 10.3. The Family Matters Bulletin Board

Spanish to a student's mother her reasons for presenting an award to the child. She wanted the mother to take part in the joy of understanding and celebrating her own child's accomplishments. And the mother did!

Engaging Students in Conversations and Learning

Jamie's classroom was often full of conversations. In her regular structured discussions, students were asked to draw inferences from text pictures. They were free to talk, in complete sentences or in phrases, about what they saw, without being concerned about their struggle to meet school expectations and without worrying about being judged as correct or incorrect. Students demonstrated skills that might not have otherwise become known to Jamie, such as paying attention to details (for example, the artistic aspect of the image), a skill vital to comprehending literature and informational texts. Such a conversation reflected an aspect of humanizing pedagogy, which "not only builds on students' lived experiences and background knowledge but also teaches mainstream or dominant knowledge and discourse styles" (Bartolomé, 1994, p. 14).

Word Analysis Conversations. When conducting a word analysis for academic vocabulary, Jamie's students had conversations about words. Jamie asked students to look at a word and its parts, think about what the word could potentially mean, and locate similar words in their heritage language. Then, students shared their thinking with members of their table group. After each group shared with the whole class the possible ideas about the word, Jamie wrote down the ideas on a word map. In the end, the class generated a student-friendly definition for the word. Some examples of English/Spanish cognates discussed were (1) *division/división* (for math), (2) *explore/explorar* (during an exploration unit), and (3) *segregate/separado* (during a close reading on an article by Ruby Bridges).

Wonder. To continue building a supportive class community where students respected and appreciated differences, Jamie guided her students in reading and discussing the book *Wonder* (Palacio, 2012), which depicted the experience of a boy with Treacher Collins syndrome in a 5th-grade classroom. Along with this book, Jamie included other bilingual and multicultural books (Figure 10.2), such as *The Stranger and the Red Rooster/El forastero y el gallo rojo* (Villasenor, 2005), about seeing beyond a stranger's imperfect face; *The Name Jar* (Choi, 2001), about the cultural meaning reflected in a Korean name; and *Dare, Tough,* and *Weird* (Frankel, 2013a, 2013b, 2013c), a series about dealing with bullies.

Even though none of Jamie's students had facial abnormalities, as depicted in *Wonder*, they could relate to the themes and messages in this and other books. In one class, students discussed several issues that related to them (such as being different, bullying, and empathizing with others) (Dale & Hyslop-Margison, 2010). Some students brought up their insecurities and confronted others in class who had made them feel uncomfortable. One student said he was made fun of for wearing his glasses. Jamie told him that she also wore glasses. Now the class had a glasses club! In the end, students learned that although the books reflected different cultures, people, and places, people from different backgrounds all shared common struggles and appreciated empathy, trust, and friendship. Finally, the books were sent home so that students could read to or with their parents. On a Saturday, Jamie, her students, and their parents went to see the *Wonder* movie.

Opinion Writing. Another aspect of Jamie's humanizing pedagogy reflected the concept of reading the word and the world by Freire and Macedo (1987). While addressing CCSS about opinion writing, Jamie provided her students with a unique space where they learned how to use a language to effectively express an opinion on something important to them. In the first lesson, Jamie began by familiarizing students with the key elements of opinion writing. Together, Jamie and her students analyzed an opinion mentor text by a former 4th-grader, identifying the main components of opinion writing: introduction (a statement of an opinion); body (reasons, pros and cons, and supporting evidence); conclusion; and the use of transitional words.

During the second lesson, Jamie used a text of high student interest on *Pokémon Go* that students had previously read. After she modeled how to construct an opinion statement, students wrote opinion statements about *Pokémon Go*.

In the third lesson, which was less structured than the previous two, Jamie and her students discussed which important topics they would like to write about. First, Jamie shared an example of immigration as something important to her, which prompted her students to share about issues that mattered to them:

Jamie: Immigration policies and laws are important to me, because my sister is an undocumented immigrant. I would not like to be apart from her. What is important to you?

Diego: Immigration is also important to me.

Jamie: Do you feel okay sharing why? (Jamie already knew that Diego's dad had been deported and that Diego has had an extremely hard time with this. He had been very depressed, expressed that he wanted to kill himself, and pushed his friends away. Jamie spoke to his mother, in Spanish, almost daily. She also referred him to counseling and worked closely with Diego. Jamie celebrated all of his triumphs, no matter how small they were, and supported him in all areas. He did not like to talk about his father, and Jamie was surprised by his response).

Diego: My dad was deported.

Ella: I am scared of that. My mom doesn't have her immigration papers and can be deported at any time. I want to write about immigration, too.

Other students also shared their personal connections to the topics (Figure 10.4).

During the fourth lesson, Jamie went back to the *Pokémon Go* article and showed students how to identify pros and cons of playing Pokémon Go. Next, students identified a dilemma about their chosen topic, discussed the pros and cons about it, and shared their final decision on the topic.

In the fifth lesson, continuing with the Pokémon Go article, Jamie modeled how to support her opinion with reasons and how to use pros and cons as evidence to support each reason. Then, students provided evidence for each reason to support an opinion on the chosen topic.

For this lesson, Jamie worked closely with Tom, an emergent bilingual. Even with the support of a word bank and a graphic organizer that Jamie provided the class, the writing task as a whole still overwhelmed Tom. Hence, Jamie chunked the activity for him. First, she had a conversation with him about his topic. Next, she wrote a sentence starter to get his writing going with the statement, and then he supported his statement with reasons.

The next lesson involved Jaime modeling how to write an effective conclusion and students' writing their own conclusions. For the next two lessons, students completed their drafts and revised them. Jamie first conducted a mini-lesson on hooks for engaging the reader and then students revised their lead sentences. During the final lesson, students engaged in peer- and self-editing.

During this opinion-writing unit, Jamie created a space for her students to connect school learning to their home life and to participate in a meaningful civic activity. An extension of this unit occurred on March 14, 2018, when Jamie led her students to walk around the campus for 17 minutes to honor 17 students whose lives were lost in the mass shooting at Marjory Stoneman Douglas High School in Florida a month earlier. They then continued discussing the issue of gun control. At the conclusion of this unit, students' opinion pieces were sent to their local district representative for the state senate. Students wanted politicians to hear their voices about issues that mattered to them. This opinion-writing unit reflected what Dale and Hyslop-Margison (2010) described: "they [teachers and students] employ the uniquely human capacity to be contemplative and

Figure 10.4. Student-Generated Topics for Opinion Writing

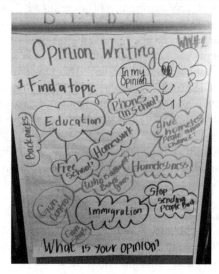

have in-depth discussion to encourage reflection and eventual transformation"
(p. 99).

Promoting Student Growth

Jamie asked her students to complete a weekly survey to help them become conscious of their own learning and so she could better understand her students' responses to her teaching and act upon any areas that she needed to improve (see, e.g., Lee & Hannafin, 2016). For example, toward the end of the opinion-writing unit, Jamie surveyed her students. One student, whose topic was gun control, wrote how he felt about choosing and writing about a topic meaningful to him: "I like it because I always wanted stricter laws for gun control because everybody over the age 18 can get guns and that's not good." Another student, who wrote about the same topic, shared her appreciation and value for making a connection between the topic and her home life: "This topic is related to me because some of my family lives in Florida and they might have gotten injured." A third student, who wrote about immigration, alluded to the importance of the home–school connection: "Because I love my dad and he got taken away from me. That is why it is important to me."

The space for reflection, as another aspect of student growth, was also evident in a goal and action plan that each student completed, which specified the individual student's learning goals, strengths and needs, and action plans (Figure 10.5). Hence, students were given an opportunity to become conscious of their own learning and learn to self-monitor to reach their academic goals (Bartolomé, 1994; McDonald et al., 2014). In planning literacy instruction, Jamie factored additional individual needs as shown in students' goal and action plans. These "personalized

Figure 10.5. Adam's Goal and Action Plan

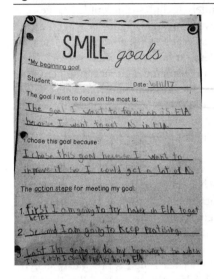
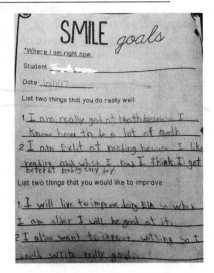

educational approaches" are an important aspect of humanizing pedagogy (Salazar, 2013, p. 127).

OUTCOMES

At the school level, Hillside provided students with a safe and welcoming environment for them to succeed. During the 2017 School's Healthy Family Survey, 99% of parents reported that they were satisfied with their child's school. Hillside had supportive school administrators and dedicated teachers who strived for teaching excellence. Over the years, Hillside has earned several prestigious awards, including the California Department of Education's California Distinguished School, California Gold Ribbon School, Title 1 Academic Achievement Award, and California Business for Educational Excellence School Award.

At the classroom level, Jamie made all of her 4th-graders feel appreciated in her classroom and helped them become active participants in the learning community. She conducted weekly student surveys to adjust her teaching and to gain insight into students' perspectives on topics ranging from classroom engagement to school safety. For example, when she asked students if they felt important in her classroom, one student responded, "I do feel like an important part of the class because if you were to raise your hand and you forgot what you were going to say she'll (Mrs. Schnablegger) say she will come back to you." Although students gave different reasons for why they felt important, student responses shared a common theme of security and feeling respected in the classroom.

Treating and seeing themselves as more than just students helped Jamie's students work harder and become more invested in their own education. Additionally, students felt like their personal assets were used as collateral in the classroom. A student wrote, "Mrs. Schnablegger definitely includes different languages. . . . She sometimes tries to get us to think of a word in Spanish and see what it means in English. She tries to represent our cultures because sometimes she'll relate what life is like at home, or when we have problems at home she'll take it easy." These comments show that Jamie understood and considered student home life in her teaching. Knowing that something was going on at home (such as Diego's dad's recent deportation), Jamie did not stress little things (like a due date). Instead, Jamie appreciated and celebrated with her students any small moments, such as a student's simple smile, active participation in an activity, or positive communication with students.

At the individual student level, Jamie tried to work closely with those who needed special support. For example, at the beginning of the year, Adam was very reserved and unengaged. He felt it would be almost impossible to exit from ELD. He seemed angry at his culture and language, saying, "I hate that I speak Spanish. I don't understand why I have to pay and suffer because I speak Spanish." In developing Adam's (and others') love for his culture and language, Jamie incorporated multicultural and bilingual activities into her teaching (as previously shared). Every opportunity she got, Jamie celebrated Adam's language by telling him how special it was that he was able to speak a second language and reassuring him that he was not being punished but supported. Adam was beginning to develop an appreciation for his language. Additionally, Jamie worked hard to develop a positive relationship with Adam's mother. Now Adam was happy to come to school, excited to participate, and seemed like a completely different student. He wrote in one weekly survey, "I do like coming to class because I want to learn and move on so I can get a good job. I also like to be with the teacher because she is funny, nice, and trustworthy." In late March, Adam passed the required tests and exited from ELD!

CONCLUSIONS AND RECOMMENDATIONS

The supportive community at Hillside and the strong component of field experiences in the UDCP program facilitated Jamie's growth in becoming a teacher who tried to implement a humanizing pedagogy. As a teacher candidate, she observed how classroom teachers practiced principles of humanizing pedagogy. She also had multiple opportunities to practice her pedagogical content knowledge during her field experiences and student teaching. The autonomy provided by her mentor teacher during her student teaching allowed Jamie to learn, try out, and reflect on her ability to meet the needs of her students. Her mentor teacher's constructive feedback and her opportunities to participate in school and district professional development helped her apply her pedagogical content knowledge and humanizing approaches to teaching.

As a first-year 4th-grade teacher, it is not easy for Jamie to meet the needs of students with a variety of learning and language profiles. However, with a humanizing pedagogy, Jamie creates a space that invites each student to participate in learning activities and to demonstrate language and literacy knowledge and skills in his or her own way. Additionally, Jamie uses scaffolding to create a learning space for all students through tapping into students' cultural and linguistic assets and connecting school learning to students' home lives. Thus, Jamie is able to make all class activities accessible to all students. Opening space for student reflection is another example of Jamie's humanizing approach to teaching. She considers reflection to be a tool for students to become conscious of their own learning as well as a way for her to gain insight about her own teaching and adjust it to meet students' needs. Working closely with students' families is an additional support for Jamie's emergent bilingual students.

Insights gained from Jamie's journey of becoming a teacher within the context of the UDCP and the Hillside community provide some valuable implications for teacher educators, classroom teachers, and school administrators.

Teacher Preparation: A teacher education program must partner with a local school (AACTE, 2018; Darling-Hammond, 2010, 2014) so that teacher candidates can witness effective instruction in action with students from various cultural, linguistic, academic, and family backgrounds. The Hillside school welcomes teacher candidates as part of its community, and teachers are willing to mentor teacher candidates, showing them ways of teaching, and providing constructive feedback.

Professional Development: There is a strong need to help teachers appreciate appropriate asset-based views of students and learn about the knowledge, traditions, literacies, and languages that students bring to school. School and district administrators need to continue acknowledging the value of teachers' ongoing professional development and provide support for all teachers to participate in such professional development. Such support also needs to extend to teacher candidates in a field-based teacher preparation program.

Teacher Autonomy: Teacher autonomy is a very basic condition for teachers to try out humanizing pedagogy that values and capitalizes on each student's cultural and linguistic heritage, experiences, and perspectives. With teacher autonomy, teachers can collaborate to customize teaching for maximizing individualized learning while addressing a common set of curricular standards. Additionally, teacher autonomy allows teachers to adjust teaching on the spot to assist students in need in a timely manner.

Conversations and "Teach by Invitation": Conversations among students during instructional activities enable them to draw from their prior knowledge and experience and think aloud in supportive, low-risk engagements (Barone & Barone, 2016; Souto-Manning & Martell, 2016). Such a process can help students try different learning strategies, make connections, and reflect on their use of strategies, among other things. Additionally, this process becomes an informational assessment, providing a teacher with data about the level of mastery of certain concepts and skills (for example, a student focuses on minor details in a text while overlooking key details), which might be otherwise absent from traditional worksheets or tests. Finally, providing a space for a conversation about anything under study makes it possible for all students to participate in instructional activities.

Collectively, these educational practices reflect various aspects of humanizing pedagogy: robust, field-based teacher preparation programs; continuous professional development for teachers and teacher candidates; precious teacher autonomy; and constant instructional conversations and "teach by invitation." As Salazar (2013) put it, "schools should be spaces where all students feel supported as their multiple identities evolve within a meaningful sense of achievement, purpose, power, and hope" (p. 141). Jamie's students enjoyed such spaces in their classroom. We hope that humanizing spaces are soon present in all classrooms.

REFERENCES

American Association of Colleges for Teacher Education. (2010). *The clinical preparation of teachers.* Washington, DC: Author.

American Association of Colleges for Teacher Education. (2018). *A pivot toward clinical practice, its lexicon, and the renewal of educator preparation.* Washington, DC: Author

Barone, D. M., & Barone, R. (2016). *Literary conversations in the classroom.* New York, NY: Teachers College Press.

Bartolomé, L. (1994). Beyond the methods fetish: Toward a humanizing pedagogy. *Harvard Educational Review, 64,* 173–195.

Bishop, R. S. (1990). Mirrors, windows, and sliding glass doors. *Perspectives: Choosing and using books for the classroom, 6*(3), ix–xi.

California State Board of Education. (2012). California English language development standards. Retrieved from www.cde.ca.gov/sp/el/er/documents/eldstndspublication14.pdf

Choi, Y. (2001). *The name jar.* New York, NY: Knopf.

Condra, E. (1994). *See the ocean.* Nashville, TN: Inclusive Books, LLC.

Dale, J., & Hyslop-Margison, E. J. (2010). *Pedagogy of humanism (Exploration of Educational Purpose,* Vol. 12, pp. 71–104). New York, NY: Springer.

Darling-Hammond, L. (2010). *Policy brief: Recognizing and developing effective teaching.* Washington, DC: AACTE.

Darling-Hammond, L. (2014). Strengthening clinical preparation. *Peabody Journal of Education, 89,* 547–561.

Darling-Hammond, L., Hyler, M. E., & Gardner, M. (2017). *Effective teacher professional development.* Palo Alto, CA: Learning Policy Institute.

Desimone, L. M., Hochberg, E. D., & McMaken, J. (2016). Teacher knowledge and instructional quality of beginning teachers. *Teachers College Record, 118*(5), 1–54.

Frankel, E. (2013a). *Dare! A story about standing up to bullying in schools* (The Weird Series). Minneapolis, MN: Free Spirit Publishing.

Frankel, E. (2013b). *Tough!: A story about how to stop bullying in schools.* (The Weird Series). Minneapolis, MN: Free Spirit Publishing.

Frankel, E. (2013c). *Weird! A story about dealing with bullying in schools* (The Weird Series). Minneapolis, MN: Free Spirit Publishing.

Freire, P. (2000). *Pedagogy of the oppressed.* New York, NY: Continuum.

Freire, P., & Macedo, D. (1987). *Literacy: Reading the word and the world.* Westport, CT: Bergin & Garvey.

Giroux, H. A. (2010, November 23). *Lessons to be learned from Paulo Freire as education is being taken over by the mega rich.* Retrieved from archive.truthout.org/lessons-to-be learned-from-paulo-freire-as-education-is-being-taken-over-by-the-mega-rich

Hammerness, K., & Darling-Hammond, L., with Grossman, P., Rust, F., & Shulman, L. (2005). The design of teacher education programs. In L. Darling-Hammond & J. Bransford (Eds.), *Preparing teachers for a changing world* (pp. 390–441). San Francisco, CA: Jossey-Bass.

Hayes, J. (2014). *La Llorona/The Weeping Woman.* El Paso, TX: Cinco Puntos Press.

Huerta, T. M. (2011). Humanizing pedagogy: Beliefs and practices on the teaching of Latino children. *Bilingual Research Journal, 34*(1), 38–57.

Lazar, A. M., & Weisberg, R. (1996). Inviting parents' perspectives: Building home–school partnerships to support children who struggle with literacy. *The Reading Teacher, 50,* 228–237.

Lee, E., & Hannafin, M. J. (2016). A design framework for enhancing engagement in student-centered learning. *Educational Technology Research & Development, 64,* 707–734.

Lucas, T., & Villegas, A. M. (2013). Preparing linguistically responsive teachers. *Theory Into Practice, 52*(2), 98–109.

McDonald, M., Kazemi, E., Kelley-Petersen, M., Mikolasy, K., Thompson, J., Valencia, A. W., & Windschitl, M. (2014). Practice makes practice: Learning to teach in teacher education. *Peabody Journal of Education, 89,* 500–515.

Mead, S., Aldeman, C., Chuong, C., & Obbard, J. (2015). *Rethinking teacher preparation.* Washington, DC: Bellwether Education Partners.

National Research Council. (2010). *Preparing teachers: Building evidence for sound policy.* Washington, DC: The National Academies Press.

Palacio, R. J. (2012). *Wonder.* New York, NY: Alfred A. Knopf.

Salazar, M. (2008). English or nothing: The impact of rigid language policies on the inclusion of humanizing practices in a high school ESL program. *Equity & Excellence in Education, 41,* 341–356.

Salazar, M. (2013). A humanizing pedagogy: Reinventing the principles and practice of education as a journey toward liberation. *Review of Research in Education, 37,* 121–148.

Schmidt, P. R. (2006). *Preparing educators to communicate and connect with families and communities.* Charlotte, NC: Information Age Publishing.

Schmidt, P. R., & Lazar, A. M. (2011). *Practicing what we teach: How culturally responsive literacy classrooms make a difference.* New York, NY: Teachers College Press.

Shulman, L. S. (1986) Those who understand: Knowledge growth in teaching. *Educational Researcher, 15*(2), 4–14.

Souto-Manning, M., & Martell, J. (2016). *Reading, writing, and talk: Inclusive teaching strategies for diverse learners, K–2.* New York, NY: Teachers College Press.

Villasenor, V. (2005). *The stranger and the red rooster/El forastero y el gallo rojo.* Houston, TX: Piñata Books.

Villegas, A. M., & Lucas, T. (2007). The culturally responsive teacher. *Educational Leadership, 64*(6), 28–33.

PART IV

FINAL WORDS FROM A GLOBAL PERSPECTIVE

CHAPTER 11

Building Equity, Literacy, and Resilience Within Educational Systems

Mark Conley

The chapters in this text have illustrated the many ways that individuals—researchers, educators, families, and policymakers—can join to promote equity for all students, and particularly for multilingual students in underserved communities. From the Bronx to San Diego, from Georgia to South Texas, the schools profiled in this book are working to support the literacies, languages, and lives of multilingual students. Each book chapter highlights a distinct set of initiatives, such as preserving and developing students' home languages (Chapters 2 and 8), working with caregivers and communities to instill culturally affirming schools (Chapters 3, 4, 5, and 6), providing programs that combine cultural relevance and academic rigor (Chapters 2, 5, 7, 8, and 9), and linking a university with a school to prepare a new educator for a diverse language community (Chapter 10).

These schools are united in providing a humanizing pedagogy that recognizes students' knowledge traditions and linguistic assets. The authors describe strong school leaders and teachers who combine culturally responsive/sustaining teaching with academic rigor. They observe school climates of authentic and critical caring, where educators know and advocate for students and link with caregivers and community members to enhance students' learning opportunities. They describe trusting relationships between school leaders and teachers, exemplified through systems of distributive leadership and structures that invite teacher decision-making in curriculum and lesson design. Some authors identified meaningful literacy instruction combined with a focus on strengthening specific skills and strategies. Many of these schools employ educators who are multilingual and share their students' heritage and language traditions. Some enhance educators' cultural competence through hosting community events, conducting caregiver surveys, and visiting caregivers at home. Several schools employ staff to maximize support for multilingual learners through the presence of teacher aides, co-teachers, and language specialists. They embed additional supportive school structures through the presence of student mentors/buddies, orientation programs, cultural affiliation clubs, and after-school programs.

These schools seek to make students resilient against poverty and racism, or any of the other ways that systematically conspire to limit students' possible futures. By taking into account the range and richness of what these schools offer multilingual students, I am tempted to ask: What might happen if educators assessed their schools in relation to the goals, structures, and systems presented in this book? Such a self-study would help guide educators toward creating the kinds of schools that all students deserve.

For the United States, the question persists about how to make these school-based efforts systemic, so that equity and resilience are embedded within and throughout educational systems and not just individual schools. We can look to these chapters as a guide for how to bring more systemic change across district, state, and federal levels. What would it take for an entire educational system—a nation, for instance—to achieve equity in opportunity and educational outcomes? How would we know when we arrived?

EQUITY IN TOP-PERFORMING EDUCATIONAL SYSTEMS

Results from the Programme for International Student Assessment (PISA) provide some clues (OECD, 2016). Across the 65 countries that participate in PISA, 31% of students from disadvantaged backgrounds (personal or family circumstances, ethnic origin, low socioeconomic or social circumstances) are considered resilient, meaning that unlike students in the United States, they are among the best performers of all students of similar background internationally. Specifically, the majority of students from economically stressed backgrounds in Korea, Hong Kong, and Shanghai were ranked among the top quarter of students internationally. Over 35% of students from underserved backgrounds in Canada, Finland, Japan, New Zealand, Poland, Portugal, Spain, and Singapore were also resilient, outperforming their peers in many other countries. What accounts for the difference?

Quite simply, students fare better in countries with enacted commitments to reducing school failure and increasing educational opportunity, commitments that include supports for families as well as students. Policies in these countries are grounded in the view that every individual serves an important role in building healthy and productive societies, cultures, economies, and nations. In countries that perform at the top of the PISA performance rankings in literacy, resilient students spend more time studying in class with the resources they need and with greater access to well-prepared teachers in comparison with their U.S. counterparts. Given opportunities to learn, combined with nurturing and pastoral care from expert teachers, students can and do succeed in school and beyond.

Educational systems that produce these results share a set of nine principles or building blocks (National Center on Education and the Economy, 2016). These include providing:

- strong supports for children and families;
- more resources for students with the greatest needs;
- world-class, highly coherent instructional standards and systems;
- clear gateways for students through the system with no dead-ends;
- an abundant supply of highly qualified teachers;
- schools where teachers can interact as professionals who continuously improve their professional practice;
- an effective system of career and technical education;
- a leadership development system for all educators; and
- a governance system responsible for coherent, powerful policies, including sustained funding.

THE UNITED STATES AS AN EDUCATIONAL SYSTEM

The chapters in this book are examples of what can happen with literacy and learning overall in a variety of educational settings with programs that reflect principles for equity and student success found in many other countries. But what about the United States as an educational system? To what extent are these principles embedded in our educational system?

Other countries have been working over the past several decades and more to ensure that no child is forgotten. There is tangible evidence that they translated their policies into action. Finland is the most famous example of a nation dissatisfied with the status quo over 20 years ago. Finland's government designed and implemented some of the most far-reaching reforms imaginable to improve the country's educational system. This included eliminating funding disparities among schools and communities, dramatically improving working conditions for teachers, and establishing clear pathways for students through the system while supporting students with the greatest needs.

Meanwhile, the United States, enamored with the slogan No Child Left Behind (NCLB), was increasing pressure on the system while reducing resources. Teachers became solely responsible for their students' test performance, without recognizing or addressing other factors that affect performance. In top-performing countries, however, student performance is considered the responsibility of the entire school, in concert with government supports to alleviate undermining family stresses related to health and housing. If one teacher's students are not doing well, everyone pitches in to figure out what to do about it. At the time NCLB was enacted, U.S. teachers' salaries and benefits were battered by a severe recession. Salary increases for years on the job or for advanced degrees were dramatically reduced or eliminated. In top-performing countries, teacher expertise is both supported and rewarded. A deficit view of U.S. teachers regularly filtered into the media, unfavorably comparing U.S. teachers to their international counterparts. This media view is never accompanied by a description of the multiple supports that teachers in other countries receive both to gain expertise and improve their students' performance.

NCLB was followed by Race to the Top (RTTT) in what some have referred to as the stick and then the carrot of policy implementation. RTTT held out funding incentives for innovative practice. However, the emphasis on the individual teacher's responsibility for student performance was unaccompanied by much, if any, systemic support. RTTT encouraged increased data gathering to measure teacher performance, including multiple measures of educator effectiveness, adoption of Common Core Standards, and relaxed rules for charter schools and turning around failing schools—often by closing rather than improving them, putting additional stresses on teachers, students, families, and communities.

A review of the nine building blocks underlying the performance of top-performing countries reveals just how piecemeal and fragmented these U.S. policies were. U.S. policies zeroed in on measuring teachers, ignored children and families, strived for coherence with the Common Core, neglected the children most at need of assistance, reduced resources, added charter schools without considering the entire system, and vacillated from one powerful yet ineffective policy after another.

The great irony is that U.S. school performance did not get better during the 15 or so years that spanned NCLB and RTTT. In some cases, literacy scores actually got worse. Performance on the National Assessment of Educational Progress in reading remained flat. Twelfth-graders scored lower in reading during the last assessment in 2015 than 12th-graders did in 1992 (Kena et al., 2016). As for PISA, the story is about declining scores and rankings. At the outset of NCLB in 2000, the United States was ranked 15th out of 32 tested countries. In 2003, we dropped to 18th out of 41 tested countries. In 2012, after 4 years of Race to the Top, the United States slipped to 24th out of 65 tested countries. More recently, in 2015, the United States remained flat in reading, ranking number 24 out of 72 countries tested (Center for International Educational Benchmarking, 2016).

An unintended outcome from this period concerns rapidly growing teacher shortages. The U.S. national percentage for teachers leaving the profession each year is 8%. This compares with reductions of 3 to 4% each year in Finland, Ontario, and Singapore, all of which are at the top of the PISA performance ladder. Reductions in enrollment in teacher preparation in the United States are as high as 35%. Prospective teachers are not coming into the system and many experienced teachers are not staying because of negative perceptions and dissatisfaction with the job (Sutcher, Darling-Hammond, & Carver-Thomas, 2016).

Clearly, the U.S. educational system is in trouble on so many levels. The Every Student Succeeds Act (ESSA) accounts for little more than a restatement of the past policies—increased pressure on teacher performance and failing school turnaround strategies. ESSA amounts to another deficit view of the U.S. educational system accompanied by federal divestiture of responsibility or support. Though there are many policy pressure points, particularly around testing and school failure, the U.S. system hardly operates in a systemic way, with one component building on another. Given this picture, it is difficult to imagine how the U.S. educational system would ever get to the principles of equity, access to educational opportunity, and, ultimately, literacy at multiple levels enjoyed by many other countries, and by the determined schools and systems described in this book and found elsewhere in the country but not systemically adopted as models across the United States.

BUILDING SYSTEMS TOWARD EQUITY AND LITERACY

Asking how the U.S. education system can move toward greater equity and literacy ignores some important aspects of the U.S. system. First, one could argue that the United States is really not a single system, as previous federal policy would have us believe. It is a confederation of thousands upon thousands of smaller systems, at the state, district, and community school levels. We have in our policy DNA a deep respect for local control that is often in conflict with other levels of the "system." So, it would be great to take the chapters in this book and say, "Let's do that for the entire educational system!" Yet we would be immediately stymied by the complexity of the thousands of competing systems.

That said, there are notable examples of states and provinces that have attempted a systemic approach to building equity and literacy. By "systemic," I mean they have tried to address each of the nine building blocks of the top-performing countries in their respective jurisdictions. Maryland recently completed a self-study that resulted in a plan for reshaping the state's education system with "world-class" principles (Commission on Innovation and Excellence in Education, 2018). Highlighted in the report was the need for greater emphasis on early childhood education, increasing the supply of high-quality, diverse teachers and school leaders, specifying clear pathways for college- and career-readiness education with no dead-ends, increasing resources for the neediest students, and creating a more powerful system of governance to ensure sustained support for schools.

Iowa is increasing access to diverse, highly qualified teachers with its teacher leadership and compensation system (see www.educateiowa.gov/teacher-leadership-and-compensation-system). The system is the first comprehensive educator career ladder in the United States. While it focuses on compensation and support for increased teacher expertise as in top-performing countries, it is uniquely adapted to the U.S. context of local control. The system is held together by the following organizing principles: increasing recruiting and compensation for new teachers, supporting and rewarding advanced teacher expertise, retaining teachers through opportunities for advanced roles, and improving student achievement through improved instruction. Yet the 330 participating school districts propose their own versions for how the system functions within their settings.

It is likely that any systemic build toward equity and literacy in the United States will need to proceed along these lines—strong, visionary leadership at the state or national level, with freedom and encouragement to act and adapt at the local level. Though this multilayered approach is not new to the United States, these are the first attempts to apply principles of world-class educational systems to the U.S. context. Canadian provinces, including Ontario and British Columbia, have also experienced success in improving their systems with principles of world-class educational reform. Where before U.S. policymakers emphasized sole teacher accountability and retribution for a school's low performance, the emerging possibility is that we can incorporate principles of successful international educational systems to build up our own system toward greater equity and literacy.

Against the backdrop of research and vignettes about systemic change, I will now turn to each of the chapters to discuss what might be gained by building on the work with more of a systemic view. My goal in this analysis is to consider what it would take to make the initiatives in each chapter more systemic while improving literacy in our educational systems.

In Chapter 2, "Nurturing Lifelong and Life-Wide Literacies Through Humanizing Pedagogies," the authors examine the positive impact of K–5 dual-language immersion school experiences. They discuss reasons for the program's success, including teacher autonomy, strong linkages to community, and the promotion of bilingualism and multicompetencies among students. The school demonstrated that drawing on students' critical theorizing and funds of knowledge developed an atmosphere for learning that had lasting positive effects on the student population. Additionally, teachers were trusted to know what was important for the education of children. Many top-performing countries have similar dedication to teacher autonomy and linkages to the community. To sustain teacher autonomy, however, there is almost always a concomitant commitment to building and supporting teacher expertise in ongoing ways. I frequently encounter teachers who have developed expertise in a variety of areas, from helping students learn to read by grade 3 to code-switching from one linguistic context to another. These specific successful local efforts need to be made more visible to a wider audience.

The other issue raised in this chapter has to do with trust in the system. Our legislators and policymakers do not trust teacher autonomy, especially when there may be little knowledge or expertise behind it. One might start with this chapter as a prompt to define the human expertise underlying the program's success and then figure out ways to build and expand that expertise to other schools in the country.

Chapter 3, "A School That ROARS," begins with findings about the features of schools that are considered successful across an ESL assessment consortium. Although analyzing large banks of data is not unprecedented—notable examples include the National Assessment of Educational Progress and the National Center for Educational Statistics—there are few places that gather data and create generalizations about best practices and schooling for bilingual and multicultural students. As it happens, this research is situated in British Columbia, one of the Canadian provinces that has taken on systemic educational reform based on PISA research. The chapter centers on a school that has adopted a code of conduct that permeates the hallways and classrooms and positively sets a stage for learning. In the spirit of systems improvement, this chapter could be a foundation for considering how this information can be used to improve early childhood education; add to our understanding of high expectations within coherent curricular systems; produce more diverse, high-quality teachers; and improve leadership and resource allocation throughout our educational systems. It is clear that this work consists of an admirable consortium of educators, families, and policymakers. The work ahead will be to ensure that all aspects of the system are impacted and so sustained.

Chapter 4, "Humanizing Education: Teachers and Caregivers Collaborate for Culturally Responsive Literacy Learning," describes teachers, administrators, and parents who share knowledge about students' language, cultures, and countries to create culturally sustaining literacy lessons. The multilingual, multiethnic community is engaged on multiple levels, both with one another and in studying culturally responsive teaching practices. Similarly, research on classrooms in top-performing countries and schools finds that classroom structures and routines are often reorganized to facilitate these kinds of engagements. Qualitative differences in background, experiences, and expertise are made available to everyone. In this elementary school, the system provides two certified teachers in every classroom of 25 students. This structure promotes co-thinking, co–lesson creation, and co-teaching and learning. Additionally, parents and caregivers are included in the processes and presentations, drawing upon family backgrounds and experiences and connecting these understandings with the required curriculum. Teachers and parents across grade levels are encouraged to share their work through a variety of grade-level and cross-curricular meetings. Similarly, successful PISA schools are deliberately restructured so that teachers teach half as many hours as in the United States. Class sizes might be larger, with greater attention to engaging content, freeing up teachers to collaborate with one another. The payoff is that everyone in the system has the opportunity to grow in their understandings of children and teaching practices that help them succeed. The risk is that without thoughtful restructuring of the school, innovations can come and go with school leadership, consultants, school and community personnel, and even funding. Because of this risk, the Syracuse Academy of Science Charter Schools might plan and implement a structure that would not depend on individuals coming and going. Teacher leadership teams could be given release time schedules to prepare and promote culturally responsive teaching and learning for individual classroom and schoolwide activities. This would be a promising step toward sustaining support for CRTL for the entire school system.

Chapter 5 is "Framing Literacy as 'Revolutionary': Creating Transformative Learning Opportunities in a Predominantly Latinx-Serving High School." The authors describe school conditions and priorities that shape learning with the goal of presenting a much more complex picture from previous research. What stands out here is an unquestioned commitment to forming partnerships with expert community members to enhance learning possibilities in and after school. Often referred to internationally as "co-curricular" learning, the learning experiences are not relegated to just "after school." They exist simultaneously with the curriculum. In a recent overseas visit, I observed a school where every teacher was assigned or signed up for a co-curricular activity. Every teacher had a mentor teacher who had previously and successfully led that co-curricular activity. The range of activities extended through sports, music, art, dancing, and even marching. An important question raised by this chapter is: How can we build into our system the recognition that we are dealing with whole human beings with complex and diverse aspirations? After-school or co-curricular activities might be some of the best ways for students to explore who they are and where they are going in life.

This chapter has also captured elements of community engagement. Their humanizing efforts appear in a curriculum that embraces the diverse communities in their location and searches for connections with meaningful leadership. Curriculum orientation is aimed toward literacy that promotes individual change and purposeful reform, and multilingualism is considered a significant aspect of innovative and motivational teaching and learning.

Chapter 6, "Creating Welcoming Environments for Latinx Families in New Latino Diaspora Schools," describes initiatives that produced a more welcoming school environment for Latinx parents and students at a high school. The author observes that educators in New Diaspora communities may not be familiar with multilingual students and communicating with their families. The school mounted a sizeable and admirable effort to identify the needs of Latinx families, particularly to remove barriers inhibiting parents from being more involved in their children's schooling. This chapter illustrates the importance of establishing systems of communication with families and continually monitoring these systems. Also, some aspects of culture and schooling can remain hidden, often over several generations. In a recent conversation with a bilingual director at a large city school system, the author of the chapter reported an experience with her own son. Her husband is from Mexico and she grew up in a predominantly White community in the United States. She found herself constantly advocating for her son's needs as he became angry with the system ignoring him. She assumed that her son understood his blended heritage until one day in 10th grade when he asked: "Am I Latino?" She was shocked by the question because Spanish was always spoken in the home and she always talked with him about his heritage. The experience also caused her to reflect for the first time on how the system rarely, if ever, understood her son. Creating mechanisms for ongoing responsiveness to changing and even hidden cultural and linguistic insights might be the key to sustaining this important work.

Chapter 7, "The Effects of a Humanizing School Culture on the Literacy Engagement of Bilingual Students: Portrait of a High School in South Texas," describes the impact of efforts focused on affect and creating a school based on principles of authentic care, high academic standards, and culturally responsive teaching. A key component to this school's success is a dynamic principal who works closely with teachers and parents to establish a school climate that is both nurturing and rigorous. This is similar to a policy in top-performing Singapore, a country that recently revamped its curricular focus to include new outcomes aimed at the whole child, especially concerning character development, love, nurturing, and pastoral care. A reason for the change was the observation that focusing solely on academic achievement was increasingly stressful for students, while ignoring a personal view of who they are and where they want to go in life. There was also a recognition that this policy change represented a fundamental shift in the system. The chapter authors describe work that also recognizes that personalized learning and caring deeply matter. This could be expanded nationally into broader conversations, recognizing that our current starting point is far from seeing the whole child.

Chapter 8 is "'I'm Multilingual': Leveraging Students' Translanguaging Practices to Strengthen the School Community." This chapter describes a multifaceted program that invites multilingualism, educates teachers about translanguaging, values academic rigor through the open enrollment of the International Baccalaureate Program, recognizes the expertise of students, and utilizes a system of distributed leadership where teachers take charge of planning and designing programs that support students' literacy and language learning. Teachers carefully monitor how students use language, which determines how they will scaffold instruction to advance students' development in both Spanish and English. This successful program model might be expanded in other school communities by building in sustaining mechanisms like pairing teachers and students experienced in the program with new teachers and students entering the school for the first time. Many top-performing educational systems develop "cascading" systems of mentoring for more advanced roles. In some systems, there are accomplished teachers, senior teachers, and master teachers. Each role has a mentor, a person already accomplished in a role. A mentoring system like this builds and supports expertise throughout the system. When such a system is grounded by a goal of multilingualism, it can provide a transformative space for learning.

Chapter 9, "Language and Literacy Learning Beyond Elementary School," reviews instructional interventions in a middle and high school that have shown remarkable results for emergent bilinguals. The chapter explores a constellation of initiatives from high expectations, strong teacher relationships with students, teacher modeling, collaborative conversations, and well-constructed response to instruction and intervention procedures. This chapter follows the U.S. tradition in research where interventions are often developed in collaboration with practitioners. This approach is also seen in top-performing countries, but in those countries, it is often accompanied by an expectation that expertise grows and needs support and ongoing development. In some countries, there is a division of labor where researchers set the stage for innovation and teachers develop and evolve what is called "craft" knowledge. A synergy often emerges from this relationship where there is continuous research, learning, and adaptation with constant improvement of professional practice. This chapter demonstrates a similar research to learning to application to improvement loop that enables sustained contribution by exploring and leveraging the expertise among researchers and practitioners.

Finally, in Chapter 10, "Learning and Practicing a Humanizing Pedagogy: One Teacher's Journey," the story of Jamie is familiar to me as a veteran teacher educator. Beginning teachers are perennially passionate about entering the profession. I am astonished whenever the system forgets that. I was taken by the statement that Jamie was awarded teacher autonomy. However, that autonomy takes place within a local context of ongoing professional development and mentoring. Similarly, in leading international settings, teacher autonomy is almost always part of the discussion about emerging, developing, and supporting teacher expertise. Although we have thick descriptions of Jamie's teaching, this only adds to the vast narrative of lessons unless we consider what makes what she is doing responsive, deep in subject matter knowledge and skill, and ultimately, effective. No teacher does his or her best work in their first year, but this is a picture of a good start in an exemplary supportive teaching environment that offers ongoing professional development and feedback. Questions that go along with this journey for Jamie and any new teacher include: How is the teacher's work contributing to students' growing cultural and self-awareness? Their sense of belonging? Their possible futures? Answers to these questions begin to enrich the teaching narrative, bridging from the personal to the possibly systemic.

IMPROVING WHILE HUMANIZING OUR EDUCATIONAL SYSTEMS

In sum, the chapters in this book bring much-needed and often neglected insights to our work with many diverse students. The chapters also highlight that, although national and state policies may be in significant disarray, the good work goes on to improve education for students, including helping them become better human beings. This text will deliver on its promise if policymakers, educators, and parents can gather these insights and learn to apply them in the context of the best practices of top-performing educational systems all over the world.

REFERENCES

Center for International Educational Benchmarking. (2016). Comparative data for top performing countries. Retrieved from ncee.org/what-we-do/center-on-international-education-benchmarking/comparative-data-for-top-performing-countries/

Commission on Innovation and Excellence in Education. (2018). *A call to action.* Annapolis, MD: Author.

Kena, G., Hussar, W., McFarland, J., deBrey, C., Musu-Gillette, L., Zhang, J., . . . Dunlop Velez, E. (2016). *The condition of education 2016.* Washington, DC: U.S. Department of Education, National Center for Education Statistics.

National Center on Education and the Economy. (2016). *9 building blocks for a world-class education system.* Washington, DC: National Center on Education and the Economy, Center on International Education Benchmarking.

OECD. (2016). *PISA 2015 results (Volume II): Policies and practices for successful schools.* Paris, France: PISA OECD Publishing.

Sutcher, L., Darling-Hammond, L., & Carver-Thomas, D. (2016, September). *A coming crisis in teaching? Teacher supply, demand, and shortages in the U.S.* Washington, DC: Learning Policy Institute.

About the Contributors

Steven Z. Athanases is professor and the Dolly and David Fiddyment Chair in Teacher Education, School of Education, University of California, Davis. His recent publications appear in the *Bilingual Research Journal, Journal of Teacher Education, Educational Forum, Journal of Adolescent and Adult Literacy,* and *The International Multilingual Research Journal.* He is coeditor of Mentors in the Making with B. Achinstein (Teachers College Press, 2006). Athanases is project manager (2018) for a James S. McDonnell Foundation Teachers as Learners grant focused on new teachers learning disciplined improvisation for meaningful talk in diverse classrooms.

Mark Conley, PhD, is professor of instruction and curriculum leadership at the University of Memphis. Among the recent national and international committees and boards on which he has served are the Committee to Evaluate the PISA Assessments, the Committee Evaluating the ACT, and Cambridge Curricula and Assessments using the Common Core State Standards and the National Center on Education and the Economy. In 2015, he coedited, with Dr. Seglem, *Taking Ownership Over Teacher Performance Assessment in Language Arts: Special Edition of the Language Arts Journal, Language Arts.* He also authored *Content Area Literacy: Learners in Context* (2nd ed.).

Brian Collins is an associate professor in the Department of Curriculum and Teaching at Hunter College, CUNY. Dr. Collins is a coinvestigator on the Harvard Project on Child Language and Developmental Psychiatry (CLDP), which follows more than 200 bilingual Latinx children from kindergarten to 12th grade. He is also an associate investigator on New York State Initiative for Emergent Bilinguals (CUNY-NYSIEB) and is committed to connecting his research to educators, clinicians, and specialists who work with bilingual immigrant children.

Marnie W. Curry is a researcher at the Center for Educational Research in the Interest of Underserved Students at the University of California, Santa Cruz. A former middle school and high school teacher, she is committed to bridging the worlds of academia and K–12 schools in order to advance educational equity for youth who have been historically underserved by their schools and districts. Her research has been featured in *Teachers College Record, Phi Delta Kappan, American Educational*

Research Journal, and *Urban Education*. She is currently writing a book, provisionally titled *Authentic Cariño: Transformative Schooling for Latinx Youth*.

Reginald D'Silva, PhD, has a multidisciplinary background in engineering, computer science, and the social sciences. He is a senior instructor in the Department of Language and Literacy Education at the University of British Columbia (UBC) and the academic director of the UBC Ritsumeikan Academic Exchange Programs. He is currently involved in the scholarship of teaching and learning of language and content courses and is interested in understanding English language learners' development of academic literacies during their university years.

Ann Ebe began her work in schools as a bilingual elementary school teacher, reading specialist, and administrator. Her primary research interests include exploring translanguaging and the ways in which teachers can support emergent bilinguals' literacy development. Dr. Ebe serves as a consultant for teachers and administrators in the United States, Mexico, Ecuador, Norway, China, Singapore, Malaysia, and has worked in Hong Kong. Her latest coauthored book is *ESL Teaching: Principles for Success*.

Ivana Espinet is the current project director for CUNY-NYSIEB. She has taught courses in the Childhood/Bilingual and Special Education Department at Brooklyn College and in the School of Education at Long Island University. Her research interest focuses on emergent bilinguals in a variety of settings in school and in after-school programs.

Douglas Fisher is professor of educational leadership at San Diego State University and a teacher leader at Health Sciences High in San Diego, California. He is the coauthor of *Visible Learning for Literacy* and the president of the International Literacy Association.

Nancy Frey is professor in educational leadership at San Diego State University and the recipient of the 2008 Early Career Achievement Award from the Literacy Research Association. Nancy is a widely published researcher and coauthored *Visible Learning for Literacy* with Doug Fisher and *Visible Learning for Mathematics* with John Hattie. Nancy is a credentialed special educator, reading specialist, and administrator in California, and is a cofounder and administrator at Health Sciences High and Middle College.

Norma González is professor emerita in the Department of Teaching, Learning, and Sociocultural Studies at the University of Arizona. She is an anthropologist of education whose work has focused on language practices and ideologies, language socialization, community–school linkages, bilingual education and Funds of Knowledge. She is past president of the Council of Anthropology and Education and author of *I Am My Language: Discourses of Women and Children in the Borderlands* and coeditor, with Luis Moll and Cathy Amanti, of *Funds of Knowledge: Theorizing Practices in Households, Communities and Classrooms*.

Nadia Granados earned her doctoral degree from the Language, Reading & Culture program in the department of Teaching, Learning & Sociocultural Studies at the University of Arizona. She is now a postdoctoral research associate at the University of Utah. Her research has appeared the *Bilingual Research Journal* and the *Journal of Literacy Research.*

Lee Gunderson, PhD, is a professor in the Department of Language and Literacy Education at the University of British Columbia, where he teaches undergraduate and graduate courses in the theory and practice of ESL (EAL) and reading instruction. He has conducted school-based research in British Columbia since the early 1980s.

Usha Gurumurthy teaches English literature in the International Baccalaureate Diploma Program and Advanced Placement in English Language and Composition in the Corpus Christi Independent School District. She is multilingual, speaking several of the Indian languages, and earned a doctoral degree in curriculum and instruction from Texas A & M University, Corpus Christi. She was awarded Teacher of the Year by the school district in 2014.

Althier M. Lazar is a professor in the Department of Teacher Education at Saint Joseph's University in Philadelphia. Her research focuses on preparing teachers to advance the literacies and languages of students in underserved schools. Her edited books include *Rethinking 21st Century Diversity in K–12 Education: Promises, Perils, and Provocations* (2018), with coeditor Suniti Sharma; *Reconceptualizing Literacy in the New Age of Multiculturalism and Pluralism* (2nd ed.) (2015), with coeditor Patricia Ruggiano Schmidt; and *Bridging Literacy and Equity: The Essential Guide to Social Equity Teaching* (2012), with coauthors Patricia Edwards and Gwendolyn McMillon.

Guofang Li is a professor and Tier 1 Canada research chair in Transnational/Global Perspectives of Language and Literacy Education of Children and Youth in the Department of Language and Literacy Education, University of British Columbia, Canada. Li has published 12 books and more than 100 journal articles and book chapters in English and Chinese, and presented more 100 papers worldwide. Her work and contribution has been recognized by numerous national and international awards.

Melissa Pérez Rhym, PhD, has been an educator in various counties in Georgia for the last fifteen years. She currently serves as the Parent and Community Director at Cedar Shoals High School in Athens, GA. Her research interests focus on the parental engagement practices of Latinx families. She is also committed to working towards eradicating the barriers Latinx students face while continuing their postsecondary education.

Patricia Ruggiano Schmidt is professor emerita of education at Le Moyne College in Syracuse, New York. Her 20 years of teaching in elementary and secondary schools became the foundation for pursuing a doctorate in literacy and language learning. Since 1991, her research, teaching, and publications have centered around culturally responsive literacy. *Practicing What We Teach: How Culturally Responsive Classrooms Make a Difference* (coedited with Althier Lazar) serves as a helpful addition for teacher preparation. After retiring in 2013, Dr. Ruggiano Schmidt returned to consulting for culturally responsive teaching at a public charter school system in an economically stressed city. Her coauthored book, with Dr. Wen Ma, *50 Literacy Strategies for Culturally Responsive Teaching (K–8)* acts as a guide for parents, teachers, and administrators.

Jamie Schnablegger is a teacher at Markham Middle School at Los Angeles Unified School District, where she strives to create a safe and supportive learning community in which all students have access to instructional activities, take pride in their cultural and linguistic heritage, and actively engage in learning. She earned a BA in Liberal Studies and her Multiple Subject Teaching Credential and Education Specialist Teaching Credential from California State University, Long Beach (CSULB). In 2018, she was awarded the College of Education Outstanding Initial Credential Student Award. Currently, Jamie is pursuing a master's degree in the Education Specialist and Clear Credential Program at CSULB.

Suniti Sharma is an associate professor in the Department of Teacher Education at Saint Joseph's University, Philadelphia. Her research focuses on preparing critical multicultural teachers, education of at-risk youth, and the intersection of diversity, culture, and curriculum. She has been published in *Girls Behind Bars: Reclaiming Education in Transformative Spaces*; a coedited collection called *Internationalizing Teacher Education for Social Justice: Theory, Research and Practice*; and in education and curriculum journals such as *Race, Ethnicity and Education, Teachers College Record, Issues in Teacher Education*, and *Journal of Curriculum Theorizing*.

Shelley Hong Xu is a professor in the Department of Teacher Education at California State University, Long Beach. She is literate in English and Chinese. Her research focuses on literacy instruction for English learners and bilingual English–Mandarin students, preparing teacher candidates for teaching literacy to diverse students, and integrating technology into teacher education. She has published and/or served on the editorial review boards of *Reading Research Quarterly, Journal of Literacy Research, The Reading Teacher*, and *Action in Teacher Education*; authored *Teaching English Language Learners*; and coauthored *Literacy Instruction for English Language Learners, PreK–2*.

Index